Starting a
Home Business

FOR

DUMMIES®

A Wiley Brand

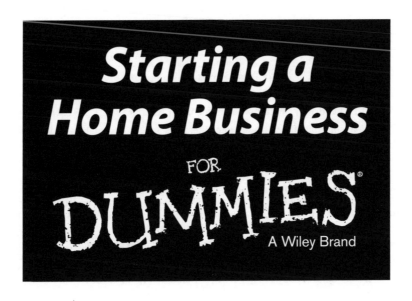

by Rachel Bridge, Paul Edwards, Sarah Edwards and Peter Economy

Starting a Home Business For Dummies®

Published by: **John Wiley & Sons, Ltd.,** The Atrium, Southern Gate, Chichester, www.wiley.com

This edition first published 2014

© 2014 John Wiley & Sons, Ltd, Chichester, West Sussex.

Registered office

John Wiley & Sons Ltd, The Atrium, Southern Gate, Chichester, West Sussex, PO19 8SQ, United Kingdom

For details of our global editorial offices, for customer services and for information about how to apply for permission to reuse the copyright material in this book please see our website at www.wiley.com.

Wiley publishes in a variety of print and electronic formats and by print-on-demand. Some material included with standard print versions of this book may not be included in e-books or in print-on-demand. If this book refers to media such as a CD or DVD that is not included in the version you purchased, you may download this material at http://booksupport.wiley.com. For more information about Wiley products, visit www.wiley.com.

Designations used by companies to distinguish their products are often claimed as trademarks. All brand names and product names used in this book are trade names, service marks, trademarks or registered trademarks of their respective owners. The publisher is not associated with any product or vendor mentioned in this book.

For general information on our other products and services, please contact our Customer Care Department within the U.S. at 877-762-2974, outside the U.S. at (001) 317-572-3993, or fax 317-572-4002. For technical support, please visit www.wiley.com/techsupport.

For technical support, please visit www.wiley.com/techsupport.

A catalogue record for this book is available from the British Library.

ISBN 978-1-118-73757-6 (pbk), ISBN 978-1-118-73754-5 (ebk), ISBN 978-1-118-73755-2 (ebk)

Printed in Great Britain by TJ International Ltd, Padstow, Cornwall

10 9 8 7 6 5 4 3 2 1

Contents at a Glance

Table of Contents

Part III: Avoiding Problems 173

Part IV: Making It Work: Moving Ahead 207

Introduction

W ho doesn't dream of starting their own business and being their own boss? Increasingly, this dream is becoming more relevant to the challenges of today's economy. And it's not just a pie-in-the-sky dream anymore; starting a home-based business is a reality that has created opportunity and satisfaction for many people who decided to take the plunge – just as it can for you.

Starting a Home Business For Dummies presents and explains an incredibly wide variety of information – aimed at ensuring your home-business success. Whether you need information on choosing the right business opportunity, avoiding scams, marketing your business, pricing your products and services, keeping accounts, understanding legal do's and don'ts, or growing your business, you can find the help you need here.

This book provides you with the very best ideas, concepts and tools for starting and successfully operating your home business. Apply this information and we're convinced that you can create exactly the kind of business you've always dreamed of and find exactly the level of success you've always wanted.

About This Book

Starting a Home Business For Dummies is full of useful information, tips, and checklists for everyone who aspires to start a successful home-based business. Your current level of business experience (or lack thereof) doesn't matter. Don't worry about not having years of it under your belt or about not knowing the difference between *direct selling* and *franchising*. For a fraction of the amount you'd pay to get an MBA, this book provides you with an easily understandable road map to today's most innovative and effective home-based business techniques and strategies.

The information you find here is firmly grounded in the real world. This book isn't an abstract collection of theoretical mumbo-jumbo that sounds good but doesn't work when you put it to the test. Instead, we've included only the best information, the best strategies and the best techniques – the exact same ones that top business schools teach today. This book is a toolbox full of solutions to your every question and problem.

This book is also fun – it reflects our strong belief and experience that running a business doesn't have to be a bore. We even help you maintain a sense of humour in the face of the challenges that all home-based businesspeople face from time to time – after all, we've been there and done that!

And one more thing: the Internet has forever changed the world of business, which includes home-based businesses. This book contains the latest information on using e-commerce, starting and operating a successful business on the Internet, and using websites to your advantage. It's also full of our own personal Internet bookmarks for the best home-business resources the web has to offer.

Foolish Assumptions

While we were writing this book, we made a few assumptions about you. For example, we assume that you have at least a passing interest in starting your own business! Maybe you've already started a home-based business, or perhaps it's something you want to try. We also assume that you can produce and deliver products or services that people will be willing to pay you for. These products and services can be anything – you're limited only by your imagination (and your bank account). Finally, we assume that you don't already know everything there is to know about starting your own home-based business and that you're eager to acquire some new perspectives on the topic.

Icons Used in This Book

Icons are handy little graphic images that point out particularly important information about starting your own home-based business. Throughout this book, you find the following icons, conveniently located along the left margins:

This icon directs you to tips and shortcuts you can follow to make your home-based business a success.

We've seen some pretty interesting things while working with home-based businesses. This icon points out some inspirational stories.

Remember the important points of information that follow this icon, and your home-based business will be all the better for it.

Danger! Ignore the advice next to this icon at your own risk!

We provide insightful (we hope!) answers to a variety of home-business questions. This icon points out these tough questions and their answers.

Beyond the Book

In addition to the material in the print or ebook you're reading right now, this product also comes with some access-anywhere extras on the web.

Go to www.dummies.com/extras/homebasedbusiness for free online bonus content about starting a business from home and www.dummies.com/how-to/content/ten-steps-to-a-great-small-business-marketing-plan.html for a helpful article about creating a marketing plan for your business. And for a great article which debunks the myths about working from home, check out www.dummies.com/how-to/content/busting-myths-about-working-from-home.html

Where to Go from Here

If you're new to business, you may want to start at the beginning of this book and work your way through to the end. A wealth of information and practical advice awaits you. Simply turn the page and you're on your way! If you already own and operate a home-based business and are short of time (and who isn't short of time?), turn to a particular topic to address a specific need or question you have. Use the table of contents and index to help you navigate. Regardless of how you find your way around this book, we're sure you'll enjoy the journey.

Part I
Getting Started with Your Home Business

In this part...

- ✔ Find out what's involved in starting and running a home business.

- ✔ Decide whether to start from scratch or buy an existing business or franchise.

- ✔ Write business and marketing plans.

- ✔ Get funding from different sources.

- ✔ Choose a legal structure for your business.

- ✔ Start to understand your customers and what they want.

Chapter 1

Where the Heart Is: Welcome to the World of Home-Based Businesses

. . . .

In This Chapter

▶ Understanding the basics of home-based businesses

▶ Taking a look at the pros and cons of running a home-based business

. . . .

Congratulations! You've decided to start a home-based business. You are joining many others who have already made the decision to start a home-based business. According to the home business network Enterprise Nation, more than 2.1 million home-based businesses operate in the UK, and between them these businesses have a combined turnover of over £364 billion. Over 60 per cent of all new businesses are begun at home, with 1,400 home-based businesses starting up every week in the UK. Take it from us: owning your own home-based business may be the most rewarding experience of your entire life – and not just in a financial sense (although many home-based businesspeople find the financial rewards to be significant). Having your own home-based business is also rewarding in terms of doing the work you love and having control over your own life.

Of course, every great journey begins with the first step. In this chapter, we provide you with an overview of this book and look at the basics of home-based business – including getting started, managing your money, avoiding problems and moving ahead. Finally, we reveal some of the good news – and the bad – about starting your own home-based business and explain how to know when it's time to make the move.

Fitting work into your lifestyle

When Deborah Duddle was made redundant from her job with a workwear clothing company in 2009, she used her savings to start her own home-based business selling handmade personalised baby gifts. She turned the garage of the family home in Ruthin, Denbighshire, into a home office and sewing room, and named the business Izzy and Floyd after her daughter and the family dog. She has continued to run her business from home ever since, even relocating the business along with her family when they moved house to another part of Wales.

For Deborah, the real advantage of running a business from home has been being able to fit it around the needs of her family. She takes her two young children to and from school and nursery every day, and can take time off to spend with them during school holidays.

She says: 'The benefits are being with the children. I don't have to rely on anyone else to look after them, and I don't have to worry about them. I really missed out when I worked for someone else, but now I can watch my children growing up.'

Being based at home has other advantages too: 'It's really nice being at home during the day because whenever I get a spare moment I can do the shopping or put the washing on. It's much less stressful than having to go away and work elsewhere.'

She sells her products, which include baby clothes, toys and skincare products, online via her website, www.izzyandfloyd.com, and also on www.notonthehighstreet.com, an online marketplace for creative small firms.

Looking at the Basics of Running a Home-Based Business

Not surprisingly, a *home-based business* is a business based in your home. Whether you do all the work in your home or you do some of it on customers' or third-party premises, whether you run a franchise, a direct-sales operation or a business opportunity, if the centre of your operations is based in your home, it's a home-based business.

Each part of this book is dedicated to a specific aspect of starting and running your home-based business. In the following sections, we take a closer look at the topics we cover in the rest of this book.

Determining the kind of business you want to have

After you decide you're going to start your own home-based business, you have to answer two questions: exactly what kind of home-based business do you want to start and what's the best way to market your products or services?

You basically have two types of home-based business to choose from: businesses you start from scratch and businesses you buy. The latter category is further split into three types: franchises, direct-selling opportunities and business opportunities. Whether you prefer to march to the beat of your own drum and start your business from the ground up or get a business-in-a-box depends on your personal preferences.

The advantage of a business you start from scratch is that you can mould it to fit your lifestyle and existing and emerging markets, which provides you with a boundless variety of possibilities. Businesses started from scratch account for the majority of viable, full-time businesses – in other words, they tend to be more successful over the long run than businesses you can buy.

Each type of home business that you can buy, on the other hand, has its own unique characteristics. The following sections illustrate how the three types are different from one another. We go into more detail on these three types in Chapter 2.

Franchise

A *franchise* is an agreement in which one business grants another business the right to distribute its products or services. Some common home-based franchises include the following:

- ✔ Green Thumb (lawn-treatment service)
- ✔ Molly Maid (domestic cleaning service)
- ✔ Little Kickers (football classes for pre-school children)
- ✔ ProKill (pest prevention)
- ✔ Snap-On Tools (professional tools and equipment)

Direct selling

Direct selling involves selling consumer products or services in a person-to-person manner, away from a fixed retail location. The two main types of direct-selling opportunities are:

- ✔ **Single-level marketing:** Making money by buying products from a parent company and then selling those products directly to customers.

- ✔ **Multi-level marketing:** Making money through single-level marketing and by sponsoring new direct sellers.

Some common home-based direct-selling opportunities include the following:

- ✔ Captain Tortue (children's clothes)

- ✔ The Pampered Chef (kitchen tools)

- ✔ Herbalife (nutrition products)

- ✔ Kleeneze (household products)

- ✔ Cambridge Weight Plan (weight management programme)

Business opportunity

A *business opportunity* is an idea, product, system or service that someone develops and offers to sell to others to help them start their own similar businesses. With a business opportunity, your customers and clients pay you directly when you deliver a product or service to them. (Another way to think of a business opportunity is that it's any business concept you can buy from someone else that isn't direct selling or franchising.) Business opportunities that aren't categorised as either franchises or direct selling are less common in the UK than in the US, but one example of a business opportunity that you can easily run from your home is ClosetMaid (storage and organisational products).

Interested in how to find more companies and how to get in touch with them? You can find a database of home-based franchise opportunities at www. whichfranchise.com and a list of home-based direct-selling opportunities on the Direct Selling Association website (www.dsa.org.uk). To find business opportunities, search the Internet using the keywords *business opportunity*.

After you decide on a business, you have to find the money to get it started. Then you have to market your products or services and persuade people to buy them. You can choose conventional methods of promotion, such as advertising and public relations, as well as newer selling opportunities, such as the Internet and social media. Check out the rest of Part I for more information on choosing and marketing your business and on creating a sustainable income in challenging times.

Managing your money

Money makes the world go round, and because we're talking about your financial well-being here, it's very important that you're in control of your business finances. To get the control you need, do the following:

- ✔ **Find the money you need to start your business.** The good news is that many home-based businesses require little or no money to start up. If you decide to buy a franchise or business opportunity from someone else, however, you definitely need some amount of start-up funding. To find this funding, consider all your options, including help from friends and family, savings, credit cards and bank loans.

- ✔ **Keep track of your money.** In most cases, keeping track of your money means using a simple accounting or bookkeeping software package, such as Sage or QuickBooks, to organise and monitor your business finances.

- ✔ **Set the right price for your products and services.** If you set your prices too high, you'll scare customers away; if you set them too low, you'll be swamped with customers, but you won't make enough money to stay afloat. Make sure that you charge enough to cover your costs while generating a healthy profit.

- ✔ **Plan for your retirement.** When you have your own business, you're the one who needs to arrange a retirement plan for the day when you're ready to wind up your business and ride into the sunset.

- ✔ **Pay taxes.** As Benjamin Franklin once said, 'Nothing can be said to be certain except death and taxes.' Well, taxes are definite, so make sure that you pay all the taxes you owe for your home-based business.

Check out Part II of this book for more information on managing your money.

Avoiding problems

Eventually, every business – home-based or not – runs into problems. Whether the problem is being late on a delivery or hitting a snag with HM Revenue and Customs, as the owner of your own business, you need to avoid problems whenever possible and deal with them quickly and decisively when you can't. Some problems you may have to deal with include the following:

- ✔ **Legal issues.** Keep a lawyer handy to help you deal with legal issues when they inevitably arise. After a good accountant, the next best friend of any business owner is a good lawyer.

✔ **Issues with support services.** Find skilled and reliable outside support services – bankers, business consultants and insurance brokers. This task isn't necessarily easy, especially if your business is in a small town where you're pretty much stuck with what's down the road.

✔ **Scams and rip-offs.** Beware home-based business scams and don't rush into just any business opportunity. Take your time and fully explore every opportunity before you sign on the dotted line. And remember, if it looks too good to be true, it probably is.

Part III has heaps more on how to avoid problems in your home-based business.

Moving ahead

One of the best things about owning your own business is watching it develop. After all, a growing business is the gift that keeps on giving – all year round, year after year. To keep your business moving ahead, consider doing the following:

✔ **Make the Internet work for you.** Doing business and generating sales and interest in your business via the Internet is practically a given for any home-based business today. You can make the Internet work for you in any number of ways, from starting a website to networking with others through online forums or social networking sites, such as Twitter, Facebook and LinkedIn.

✔ **Maintain a serious business attitude.** Just because your business is located at home instead of in a big office building doesn't mean you shouldn't treat it like the business it is. While you can have fun and work all kinds of creative schedules, don't forget that the business part of your business is important, too; you have to treat your business like a business if you hope to be successful.

✔ **Look for ways to grow.** For many businesses, growth can turn an operation that's doing well financially into an operation that's booming. Growth allows you to take advantage of economies of scale that may be available only to larger businesses, to serve more customers and to increase profits. For these reasons and more, growing your business should always be on your agenda.

To discover in-depth information on these particular topics and more, check out Part IV.

Working from home means s(h)aving money . . .

When Will King started his own business selling shaving oil in 1993 at the age of 28, running it from home was the obvious choice. With hardly any start-up funds, he couldn't afford to rent a separate office, and the house he shared with his girlfriend in Ruislip, Middlesex, had a spare bedroom that he could turn into a home office.

The kitchen was also important in his endeavours – he filled his first 10,000 bottles of shaving oil by hand using a pump in the kitchen.

As well as low overheads, Will soon discovered the other advantages to running his business from home: 'I had two dogs, so being at home meant I could take them for a walk every day at lunchtime. It was good because it got me out of the house and gave me time to think. I loved it.'

While still running the business from home, Will managed to secure an order for his bottles of shaving oil from Harrods, and then from Boots. He only moved the business into dedicated offices when he took on a business partner and needed more space.

His business, King of Shaves, now sells a range of shaving products and has an annual turnover of £10.2 million.

Leaving your full-time job for your part-time business

Some people run a home business as well as holding down a conventional full- or part-time job. An important consideration many home-based business owners face is whether or not to leave a full-time job in favour of a home-based business. Before you give up your full-time job, ask yourself these questions:

- ✔ Has your home-based business experienced a steadily growing flow of new customers?

- ✔ Has your business, even though it's only been part-time, produced a steady flow of income through seasonal or other cycles typical of the business?

- ✔ Are you turning away business because of limits on your time? If not, do you think business would increase if you had the time to market or take on more customers?

If you can answer at least two of these questions in the affirmative, consider it a good sign that you could safely leave your full-time job. Of course, you should also be aware of any developments that could worsen the outlook for your business to grow, such as pending legislation, new technology, the movement of the kind of work you do outside the UK or the decline of an industry your business depends on.

If your day job has been providing you with the contacts you've needed to build your part-time business, you need to find ways to replace them before you leave your job.

Breaking the umbilical cord of a regular salary is an uncomfortable step for most people. So the closer the current income from your business is to the amount of money you need to pay your basic business and living expenses, the more confident you can be.

Examining the Good News and the Bad

Anyone can start a home-based business. You can be 10 years old or 100, male or female, rich or poor or somewhere in between, experienced in business or not.

So how do you know if starting a home-based business is right for you? Like most things in life, starting your own home-based business has both advantages and disadvantages, but the good news is that the advantages probably outweigh the disadvantages for most prospective home-business owners. So in the spirit of putting your best foot forward, we start with the good news.

Good reasons to start a home-based business

When you start a home-based business, you may be leaving behind the relative comfort and security of a regular career or nine-to-five job and venturing out on your own. Or you may be entering the world of work again after devoting many years of your life to raising a family. How far out you venture on your own depends on the kind of home-based business you get involved in. For example, many franchises provide extensive support and training, and *franchisees* (the people buying the franchise opportunities – you, for example) are able to seek advice from experienced franchisees or from the *franchisor* (the party selling a franchise opportunity) when they need it. This support can be invaluable if you're new to the world of home-based business.

At the other end of the spectrum, some business opportunities offer little or no support whatsoever. If you're a dealer in organic hair oil, for example, you may have trouble getting the huge, multinational conglomerate that manufactures the oil to return your calls, let alone send you some product brochures. And you won't find any training or extensive hands-on support when you run into the inevitable snags, either.

This wide variety of home-based opportunities brings us to the good news about starting and running your own home-based business:

- ✔ **You're the boss.** For many owners of home-based businesses, just being their own boss is reason enough to justify making the move out of the nine-to-five work world.

- ✔ **You get all the benefits of your hard work.** When you make a profit, it's all yours. No one else is going to try to take it away from you (except, perhaps, the tax man – see Chapter 8).

- ✔ **You have the flexibility to work when and where you want.** Are you a night owl? Perhaps your most productive times don't coincide with the standard nine-to-five work schedule that most regular businesses require their employees to adhere to. And you may find that – because interruptions from co-workers are no longer an issue and the days of endless meetings are left far behind – you're much more productive working in your own workshop or home office than in a regular office. With your own home-based business, you get to decide when and where you work.

- ✔ **You get to choose your clients and customers.** The customers may always be right, but that doesn't mean you have to put up with the ones who mistreat you or give you more headaches than they're worth. When you own your own business, you can fire the clients you don't want to work with. Sounds like fun, doesn't it? (Believe us, it is!)

- ✔ **You don't waste time travelling to and from work.** Money can buy lots of things but time isn't one of them. Depending on how close your current business premises are, you could spend a lot of time each day travelling to and from them.

- ✔ **You can put as much or as little time into your business as you want to.** Do you want to work for only a few hours a day or week? No problem. Ready for a full-time schedule or even more? Great! The more effort you put into your business, the more money you can make. As a home-based business owner, you get to decide how much money you want to make and then pick out the kind of schedule that helps you meet your goal.

These reasons to start your own home business are just the tip of the iceberg. But when you add up everything, you're left with one fundamental reason for owning your own home-based business: freedom.

Admittedly, starting a home-based business isn't for everyone. In fact, for some individuals, it can be a big mistake. If, however, you have an entrepreneurial spirit, and you thrive on being independent and in charge of your life, a home-based business may be just the thing for you.

You have only one life to live. If you're tired of working for someone else, being second-guessed by your boss or having your creativity stifled, if you're full of great ideas (ideas you know will lead you to success if you have the opportunity to put them into practice), or if you long for something better, running a home-based business could be the answer you're looking for. When you find the business that's right for you, it can change your life and the lives of those around you.

Knowing the pitfalls of owning your own home-based business

Starting a home-based business isn't the solution to every problem for every person. Although many home-based businesses are successful and the people who started them are happy with the results, more than a few home-based businesses end up causing far more headaches than their owners anticipated. Some home-based business owners even go bankrupt as a direct result of the failure of their businesses. Starting your own business is hard work and success isn't guaranteed.

So the next time you're lying on your sofa, dreaming of starting your own home-based business, don't forget to consider some of the potential pitfalls:

- **The business is in your home.** Depending on your domestic situation, working in your own home – a home filled with any number of distractions, including busy children, stressed spouses or significant others, televisions, fridges full of tempting food, and more – can be a difficult proposition at best.

- **You're the boss.** Yes, being the boss has its drawbacks, too. When you're the boss, you're the one who has to motivate yourself to work hard every day – no one's standing over your shoulder watching your every move. For some people, focusing on work is very difficult when *they* are put in the position of being the boss.

✔ **A home-based business is (usually) a very small business.** As a small business, you're likely to be more exposed to the ups and downs of fickle customers than larger businesses are. And a customer's decision not to pay could be devastating to you and your business.

✔ **You may fail or not like it.** No one can guarantee that your business is going to be a success or that you're going to like the business you start. Failure may cost you dearly, including financial ruin (no small number of business owners have had to declare bankruptcy when their businesses failed), breakdown of personal relationships and worse.

Regardless of these potential pitfalls, starting a home-based business remains the avenue of choice for an increasing number of people. Are you ready to join them?

Taking the Home-Based Business Quiz

Many people talk about starting home-based businesses and many dream about becoming their own bosses. Making the transition from a full-time career to self-employment, however, is a big change in anyone's life. Are you really ready to make the move, or should you put the idea of having your own home-based business on the back burner for a while longer?

To help you decide, take the following quiz. Circle your answer to each of these questions, add up the results and find out if you're ready to take the plunge.

1. How strong is your drive to succeed in your own home-based business?

    A. I can and will be a success.

    B. I'm fairly confident that if I put my mind to it, I will succeed.

    C. I'm not sure. Let me think about it for a while.

    D. Did I say that I wanted to start my own business? Are you sure that was me?

2. Are you ready to work as hard as or harder than you have ever worked before?

    A. You bet – I'm ready to do whatever it takes to succeed.

    B. Yes, I don't mind working hard as long as I get something out of it.

    C. Okay, as long as I still get weekends and evenings off.

    D. What? You mean I'll still have to work after I start my own business?

3. Do you like the idea of controlling your own work instead of having someone else control it for you?

  A. I don't want anyone controlling my work but me.

  B. That's certainly my first choice.

  C. It sounds like an interesting idea – can I?

  D. Do I have to control my own work? Can't someone control it for me?

4. Have you developed a strong network of potential customers?

  A. Yes, here are their names and numbers.

  B. Yes, I have some pretty strong leads.

  C. Not yet, but I've started kicking around some ideas with potential customers.

  D. I'm sure that as soon as I let people know that I'm starting my own business, customers will line up.

5. Do you have a plan for making the transition into your home-based business?

  A. Here it is – would you like to read the executive summary or the full plan?

  B. Yes, I've spent a lot of time considering my options and making plans.

  C. I'm just getting started.

  D. I don't believe in plans – they cramp my style.

6. Do you have enough money saved to tide you over while you get your business off the ground?

  A. Will the year's salary that I have saved be enough?

  B. I have six months' expenses hidden away for a rainy day.

  C. I have three months' worth.

  D. I'm still trying to pay off my student loan.

7. How strong is your self-image?

  A. I have huge self-esteem!

  B. I strongly believe in my own self-worth and in my ability to create my own opportunities.

  C. I feel fairly secure with myself; just don't push too hard.

  D. I don't know – what do you think?

8. Do you have the support of your significant other and/or family?

    A. They're all on board, are an integral part of my plan and have been assigned responsibilities.

    B. They're in favour of whatever makes me happy.

    C. I'm pretty sure that they'll support me.

    D. I'm going to tell them about it later.

9. If it's a necessary part of your plan, will you be able to start up your home-based business while you remain in your current job?

    A. Yes – in fact, my boss wants to invest in it.

    B. If I make a few adjustments in my routine, I can't see any other reason why I can't.

    C. Maybe I'll be able to work on it for a few hours a month.

    D. Would you please repeat the question?

10. What will you tell friends when they ask why you left that great job?

    A. I'm free at last!

    B. That the benefits clearly outweigh the potential costs.

    C. I don't know; maybe they won't ask.

    D. I'll pretend that I'm still working for my old employer.

11. Do you have enough room to run a business from home?

    A. I've already turned the spare bedroom into a home office.

    B. I'm thinking about turning the garden shed into a dedicated workspace.

    C. Sure – how much space does a computer take up anyway?

    D. I haven't really thought about that yet.

12. Is there any reason why your neighbours might object to you starting a business from home?

    A. I've already applied for all the necessary permits and licences from the local council and they've raised no objections.

    B. I've deliberately chosen a type of business that won't generate any noise or disturbance.

    C. I'm hoping the neighbours won't notice.

    D. I'm really hoping the neighbours like the smell of roasted garlic.

Give yourself 5 points for every A answer, 3 points for every B, –3 for every C and –5 for every D. Now add up your points and find out whether you're ready to jump into your own home-based business:

35 to 60 points: Assuming you were honest with yourself as you answered the questions (you were, weren't you?), you're ready! What are you waiting for? There's no time like the present to take the first step on your journey to success with your own home-based business. Whether you decide to leave your day job or ease into your new business gradually, you're ready to give it your all. Read the rest of this book for tips on making your endeavour a raging success.

1 to 34 points: You're definitely warming up to the idea of starting your own home-based business. Consider starting your own business in the near future, but keep your regular job until you have your venture well under way. Read this book to get a better idea of how to make a relatively painless and successful transition from your present career to your own home-based business.

0 points: You can go either way on this one. Why don't you try taking this test again in another month or two? Read this book before you begin your own home-based business.

–1 to –34 points: Unfortunately, you don't appear to be quite ready to make the move from career to home-based business. I strongly recommend that you read this book and then take this test again in a few months. Maybe working for someone else isn't the worst thing that can happen to you.

–35 to –60: Forget it. You were clearly born to work for someone else. Take this book and sell it to a friend.

Are you ready to make the move to starting a home-based business? If the quiz indicates otherwise, don't worry – you'll have plenty of opportunities in the future. When you're ready for them, they'll be ready for you. If you're ready now, congratulations! The rest of this book shows you what you need to do to make owning a successful home-based business a reality.

ASK THE EXPERTS

Keeping up with the office gossip

Q: I've never regretted starting my own business, but the one thing I do miss is being in the middle of the corporate buzz. How can I stay connected with what's going on in the corporate world?

A: You can get connected without leaving your home by joining and participating in groups on social networking sites like LinkedIn, Facebook and Twitter. If social networking isn't for you, the first step is to figure out just what you miss from corporate life. Being part of the daily routine of an organisation provides people with a whole array of experiences. Some, like office politics and dreadfully dull meetings, are a joy to get away from. But others, like the following, leave a void that you need to find ways to fill:

✔ **Feeling like you're part of the business community:** Even when you're working from home, getting out of the house and participating in the business world is important. Join your local chamber of commerce and go to lunches, after-work networking events or evening meetings. Get active in various civic and charitable activities in your local area. After all, you can develop valuable business relationships while keeping up with current local business news.

✔ **Getting the inside information and latest gossip in your field:** Become active in a local chapter of your professional or trade association or participate in its online forum. To find professional and trade associations in your field, search the Internet using the keyword *association* and the name of your industry.

Though the Internet isn't a substitute for face-to-face contact, beyond the social networking sites, you can use it to locate other individuals, networks and organisations in your own local area through, for example, the message board operated by a trade or professional group you belong to.

✔ **Being part of a group that's working together towards a common goal:** If you crave group experiences, affiliate with others and work on joint projects instead of working strictly solo.

✔ **Finding moral support and positive peer pressure to stay focused – someone with whom to bounce ideas around, celebrate victories and commiserate over disappointments:** To fulfil this need, form a group of colleagues with whom you can meet weekly over lunch and call regularly to spur one another on towards your goals.

✔ **Seeking out the expertise of superiors you can turn to for advice, getting honest feedback or talking over strategies and crucial decisions:** If you're missing this type of interaction, seek out a mentor, form an advisory board for your business or hire a consultant whose experience you respect. Some professional associations have formal mentoring programmes that offer this kind of contact. If yours doesn't, suggest that it considers adding such a service – or even volunteer to help organise one.

Chapter 2

Mirror, Mirror on the Wall, What's the Best Business of All?

....

In This Chapter

▶ Starting a new business from scratch

▶ Buying an established business

▶ Considering your options

▶ Specialising to find where you fit best

....

So what do you do after you decide that starting a home-based business is right for you? First, you have to choose which kind of home-based business to run. Although on the surface making this decision may seem like a fairly easy proposition, for many people it isn't. With thousands and thousands of businesses to choose from, each with its own set of pros and cons, you may feel a bit like a child in a sweet shop. Not to mention that an opportunity that's hot today can be as cold as ice tomorrow.

Before picking your business, research your options thoroughly. And above all, listen to your heart. Make sure that the opportunity is right for *you* – that it's first and foremost something you will truly love doing – but at the same time that it's going to provide the potential for long-term success. After all, we're talking about your future here (and, perhaps, the well-being of you and your family), and what you do today to prepare for it will pay off in a big way down the road.

In this chapter, we take a closer look at the many different home-based business options available to you. Make sure that you turn to Chapter 15 as well for a look at ten enduring home-business opportunities.

Starting Something from Scratch

Perhaps the quickest and least expensive way to start your own home-based business is to do so from scratch. No need to fill out a load of application forms, save up money to buy into a franchise or take weeks or months to learn some complex, structured way of doing business. If you really want to, you can start your own business from scratch right now.

The satisfaction you get from making something with your own two hands is hard to beat. It's the same pleasure a sculptor gets from creating a beautiful piece of art or a musician gets from mastering a difficult score. You may not get it right the first time – after all, it took Thomas Edison thousands of tries before he hit on the right material for a successful light bulb filament – but when you find the right formula for success, the feeling of satisfaction you experience is priceless.

If you decide to start a home business from scratch, you're in good company. Some of today's largest and most successful companies were originally home-based businesses. Here are a few notable examples:

- ✔ **Virgin Group.** Richard Branson started his global empire at the age of 17 in 1968 by selling *Student*, a youth-culture magazine he created, from his rented basement flat in Lancaster Gate, west London. He started the business with £4 borrowed from his mother to pay for phone calls. He then ran a mail-order record business from his home on a barge in Little Venice, near Notting Hill. Branson has actually continued to run Virgin Group from home ever since – home now being Necker Island, his private island in the British Virgin Islands. The Virgin brand now encompasses more than 100 businesses, operates in 40 countries and has an annual turnover of £13 billion.

- ✔ **Apple Computer.** In 1976 Steve Jobs and Stephen Wozniak started Apple Computer building computers in the garage at the home of Jobs' parents in California, raising US$1,300 to get the business off the ground by selling Jobs' Volkswagen van and Wozniak's Hewlett-Packard programmable calculator. Today the company has annual revenues of more than US$32 billion.

- ✔ **Amazon.com.** Jeff Bezos started Amazon.com, selling books online from his rented two-bedroom home in Washington State in the US. He converted the garage into a workspace by making desks out of three wooden doors, using pieces of wood and metal brackets to fix them together. Amazon.com now has annual revenues of more than US$61.1 billion.

Sweet, sweet success

In 2002 Michael Parker started up an online business selling traditional sweets such as flying saucers and sherbet fountains from his home in Buckinghamshire, inspired by memories of buying sweets as a child from the sweetshop at the corner of his road. Having very little money to start the business, he designed the website using a free demo disk from a magazine and spent £85 buying sweets from his local cash and carry shop. Every time he got an order he weighed out the sweets, packaged them up and sent them out. His business, A Quarter Of (www.aquarterof.co.uk) now stocks more than 700 different varieties of sweets and has a turnover of more than £3 million annually.

Of course, these home-based business success stories are exceptional, but many home-based business owners find exactly the level of success they're seeking – paying the bills, doing exactly the work they want to do, spending more time with loved ones and serving the customers they want to serve. The real beauty of owning your own home-based business is that it's first and foremost *your* business. When you start a business from scratch, you write the rules and you decide what's important. You may grow your business into the next Virgin, or you may simply enjoy more satisfaction in your work.

Here are a couple of examples of people who found exactly the level of success they were looking for by starting their own home-based businesses:

- ✔ Full-time mother Anna Gibson started selling children's micro scooters from her home in Clapham, south-west London, after buying one for her son and being constantly stopped by other parents on Clapham Common asking where they could buy one too. Soon she was ordering them in bulk and selling them locally, storing them behind the sofa and under beds at home. Gibson and her friend Philippa Gogarty became the official UK distributors for the micro scooters and now their business, Micro Scooters Ltd, is worth £4.3 million.

- ✔ Julie Deane founded The Cambridge Satchel Company from her kitchen table in Cambridge (of course) in order to be able to send her children to private school. Her colourful handmade satchels, which are based on a traditional design, were initially aimed at school children but have gone on to become a sought-after fashion accessory. Deane went from making three satchels a week to 1,500 a week within the space of three years and the business now has a turnover of £12 million.

Ten home-based business opportunities

A recent survey by *Real Business* magazine (www.realbusiness.co.uk) found that ten of the best businesses to run from home in the UK included:

- ✔ Travel agency
- ✔ Data consultancy
- ✔ Luxury clothing brand
- ✔ Dancing school
- ✔ Specialist recruitment agency

- ✔ Estate agents
- ✔ Hotel reservation service
- ✔ Career break resource
- ✔ Marketing agency
- ✔ Online transcription service

As this list shows, you can successfully run an incredibly wide range of businesses from home.

When starting a business from scratch, you can use one of two main approaches: choose to do the same kind of work you've been doing in your regular job or career, or choose to do something totally different. In the following sections, I take a closer look at each approach and the advantages each one offers you.

Sticking with what you know

As you consider the different options available to you in starting your own business, you may be considering doing what you've already been doing in your usual job.

And why not? You know the job and you're already experienced in the business. You also know what your customers want and how to give it to them. You may even have a network of potential customers waiting to sign up for your products or services. Not surprisingly, doing what you've been doing has several advantages, including the following:

- ✔ You can start up your business more quickly (right *now!*) and easily than if you choose to do something you've never done before.

- ✔ You don't have to spend your time or money on training courses or workshops, and you don't have to worry much about a learning curve.

- ✔ You'll be much more efficient and effective because you've already discovered the best ways to do your job, along with time-saving tricks of the trade.

✔ You can capitalise on your good reputation, which may be your most important asset.

✔ You can tap into your network of business contacts, clients and customers (when ethically appropriate) and generate business more quickly than when you start something new and different (see Chapter 3 for more tips on turning your current business contacts into customers . . . ethically!).

For many people, doing something they've been doing is the best choice. So because doing what you've been doing is often the quickest and least expensive route to starting your own home-based business, make sure you take a close look at this option before you consider any others. And as you build your home-based business, check out www.peopleperhour.com or www.elance.com, both good sources of freelance work opportunities in a wide variety of categories, to help you get started.

Examples of home businesses that follow naturally from your former job might include cooking, selling holidays or houses, or providing consultancy advice about the industry you used to work in.

In with the new: Doing something different

Although doing what you've already been doing in a job offers many advantages, doing something new and different has its own benefits too. If you're weary of your current job and you dream of making radical changes in your career or lifestyle – for example, trading your high-pressure career as a lawyer for a much more relaxing home-based massage business – then doing something new and different may well be exactly what the doctor ordered.

Girl power: Facts about women-owned businesses

Here are some interesting facts from Prowess 2.0, formerly the National Association of the Promotion of Women's Enterprise, about the impact women-owned businesses are having in the UK today:

✔ Roughly 620,000 businesses in the UK are majority-owned by women and between them they generate £130 billion.

✔ Women run 15 per cent of the 4.8 million enterprises in the UK and account for 29 per cent of people who are self-employed.

✔ Around 48 per cent of female entrepreneurs own businesses in the service sector compared to 36 per cent of male entrepreneurs.

✔ About 10 per cent of women in the UK are thinking of starting up a business.

When you start your own business, you become the boss, and you decide how to run your own enterprise. So don't just dream about one day being the boss and running the show – go for it!

Here are some key advantages of doing something new and different:

- ✔ Getting a fresh start in your career can be an extremely energising experience with positive repercussions for every aspect of your life, opening up exciting new possibilities and opportunities for you along the way.

- ✔ Tapping into new career options allows you to find work that may not have even existed when you first started your career – for example, designing websites or mobile phone applications.

Many successful home-based business owners have created businesses that have nothing to do whatsoever with their former full-time jobs. If you're sufficiently motivated, nothing can stand between you and success, no matter which business you choose. If you're looking to shake up the status quo or to make a break from the past, doing something completely new may well be the best option for you.

When Sam Bompas (who worked in marketing) and Harry Parr (an architecture graduate) started doing something completely new and making traditional English jellies for parties and events, they had no idea whether the demand from caterers was enough to enable them to turn their venture into a profitable business. So they launched it from their kitchen table in their spare time, spending less than £50 each on equipment. In fact, their jellies – which they can make in the shape of famous buildings such as St Paul's Cathedral and the Taj Mahal – proved so popular that after eight months Bompas was able to give up his day job in marketing to work on the business full time, as did Harry when he finished his architecture degree. The pair now employ two people in their studio in Borough, south-east London, and have a turnover of £1 million a year.

Buying a Business

For many people, buying a ready-made home-based business is the way to go. Instead of figuring out how to run a business the hard way – through trial and error – when you buy a business, you buy a proven product, system and support organisation. Of course, you have to pay for these benefits upfront, but the financial rewards of your new business can easily outweigh the investment – if you make it wisely.

As you consider the different home-based business opportunities available to you, keep the following tips in mind:

- ✔ **Make sure you fit the business.** Some franchises and network marketing opportunities require that you adhere to strict company rules and procedures, including the clothes you wear and the way you present yourself and your business. If you're not comfortable with these kinds of restrictions, avoid such businesses.

- ✔ **Make sure a market exists for the product or service you plan to offer.** Talk to others who have bought the business you're interested in and ask them for their honest and candid feedback on the attractiveness of the opportunity. Don't just rely on a list of happy people provided by the company – do some research, contact or visit owners at their places of business and find people who may be more willing to tell you the real story.

✔ **Make sure the company you select is credible and viable.** This consideration may very well be the most important one you make. A large number of businesses that offer franchises, direct-selling opportunities and business opportunities (all three of which we describe in the following sections) go bust within five years, leaving their owners high and dry (and sometimes bankrupt and out of work). Make sure that any company you're considering has been in business for five years or more.

Four options for finding a new opportunity

The roots for new businesses usually come from the following four sources and successful home-based business owners invariably tap into one or more of them:

✔ **Talent.** Everyone has innate talents or skills at which he or she excels. When you tap in to such a talent or gift and when others value it and are willing to pay for it, developing a business around it can be rewarding, both financially and emotionally. About one in six home-based business owners become successful by taking advantage of their special talents or skills, such as teaching a language or musical instrument from home.

✔ **Mission.** Those who follow a higher purpose – to make a positive difference in the lives of the people and the world around them by providing healthcare solutions, for example – are following a mission. Although fewer than one in six people take this route in creating their home-based businesses, for those who do, the personal rewards of seeing the impact of their work on others can be profound.

✔ **Passion.** For some home-based business owners, the passion they feel to be their own bosses or to pursue the work they truly love is so strong that it creates success in and of itself. For the person with a fire in the belly, no obstacle stands between them and the successful achievement of their goals. About one in four home-based business owners has chosen this path to success by doing what they love, from making furniture to creating bespoke perfumes.

✔ **Assets.** Everyone brings assets when starting a home-based business. In some cases, these assets may take the form of previous work experiences; in other cases, they may take the form of a network of friends or business contacts. Although almost half of people who start home-based businesses tap in to their assets to do so – making it the most popular route by far – these businesses, such as PR and talent management, typically don't fare as well as those based on talent, mission or passion. Why? Assets by themselves don't create excitement, intensity of purpose or motivation, and without these kinds of emotions, the business owners don't feel as much drive to succeed.

As you review potential business opportunities, be aware of your own talents, mission or passion, and keep them foremost in your mind because your success will be directly proportional to the motivation you bring to your work.

The major categories of home-based businesses that you can buy are franchises, direct-selling opportunities and business opportunities, which we cover in the following three sections.

Home-based franchises

If you've ever eaten at a McDonald's restaurant, you know what a franchise is. No matter which McDonald's restaurant you visit, whether it's in London, Edinburgh or Bristol, you can be fairly certain that your cheeseburger and French fries are going to look, feel and taste the same. Franchising has taken the world of business by storm. According to the British Franchise Association (www.thebfa.org), franchises employ 594,000 people in the UK and produce an annual turnover of £13.4 billion.

Although popular franchises such as Subway, Bathstore and Pizza Hut are easy to recognise, you may not be able to think of a popular home-based franchise. However, many home-based franchises are out there, in an incredible array of sizes, shapes and styles. From cleaning services to babysitting to photography studios, home-based franchising opportunities cover a wide variety of businesses and can fit most needs.

Defining a franchise

A *franchise* is an agreement in which one business grants another business the right to distribute its products or services. Typically, the company that grants the franchise has developed a successful and proven business model that others can easily replicate. Three elements define a franchise company:

- ✔ Use of a trademark or a trade name
- ✔ Payment of fees or royalties
- ✔ Significant assistance provided by the franchisor

As the old saying goes, 'It takes two to tango.' Similarly, every franchise agreement involves the following two key parties:

- ✔ **Franchisor:** The company that owns the franchise trademarks, trade secrets and successful business model.
- ✔ **Franchisee:** The individual or other entity who pays the franchisor for use of the trademarks, trade secrets and successful business model.

Ten ways to do what you love

Can you honestly say that you love your job? If not, have you ever thought about what you'd do for a living if you had the opportunity to do anything? Guess what? You do have the opportunity to do what you love! Millions of home-based business owners are doing just that and creating incredible success for themselves in the process. Here are ten ways you can do what you love:

✔ Provide a service to others who do what you love

✔ Focus on doing just the things you love

✔ Teach others to do what you love

✔ Write about what you love

✔ Speak about what you love

✔ Create a product related to what you love

✔ Sell or broker what you love

✔ Promote what you love

✔ Organise what you love

✔ Set up, repair, restore, fix or maintain what you love

Of course, all the trademarks, successful business models and assistance come at a price. The franchisee pays fees to the franchisor in the form of one or more of the following:

✔ A one-off payment which you have to cough up when the franchise begins.

✔ An on-going flat-fee payment which you have to pay every year.

✔ On-going sliding-scale payments which vary from year to year.

✔ On-going royalties as a percentage of annual sales or profits.

✔ Advertising fees which may vary and you have to pay every year.

The fees that the franchisee pays to the franchisor vary considerably from opportunity to opportunity. For example, Molly Maid, a popular UK home-based business franchise that specialises in domestic cleaning services, has an upfront franchise fee of £16,975 plus up to £15,000 in *working capital* (this is the amount you need to run the business on a day-to-day basis to pay for things like equipment, cleaning products, uniforms and so on) and an on-going royalty rate of 8 per cent of sales.

For an extensive list of franchising opportunities, both home-based and not, check out the British Franchise Association website (www.thebfa.org) which provides full descriptions and contact details of all its accredited members. Also check out the Franchise Direct website (www.franchisedirect.co.uk/homebasedfranchises) for a directory of current home based franchises.

Tackling legal issues in franchising

As with many areas of business, franchising is framed by laws and regulations. Before you buy a franchise you need to closely examine two key documents – the franchise prospectus and the franchise agreement.

✔ The *franchise prospectus* is essentially a marketing brochure that has been prepared by the franchisor to outline the opportunity on offer. It typically starts off with a history of the business before going on to provide details of the franchise business and how it operates, and what the franchisee is expected to do. Check for information about the market it operates in and the prospects for the franchise within that market.

You can expect a prospectus to contain information about the following:

- Details about the franchisor's experience, background and financial position.

- Information about the qualifications and responsibilities of directors and senior executives.

- The franchise *proposition*. The proposition describes the franchise business, including information about what services and training the franchisor provides to the franchisee, the initial investment required and what other payments need to be made to the franchisor.

- The number and location of existing franchisees in the network.

- Financial projections showing the levels of profit you can attain if you reach certain turnover levels, or what franchisees have achieved in practice to date. The franchisor must clearly state the basis on which any quoted figures were obtained. The prospectus should inform you that financial projections aren't promises of performance and that the success of any franchise depends on the franchisee's own individual skill and commitment.

✔ Franchises depend on *franchise agreements* – contracts setting forth the rights and obligations of the franchisor and the franchisee – to define the legal relationship among all involved parties. A franchise agreement is negotiable. Make sure you read and understand it thoroughly before you sign it. Even better, get a competent solicitor who specialises in franchise law take a look at it. Believe us: a few hundred pounds invested in a legal review upfront may save you many thousands of pounds (and countless headaches) down the road.

Here are the most common elements of a franchising agreement:

- **Grant of franchise:** Defines the nature of the franchising agreement.

- **Use of trademarks, patents, and copyrights:** Spells out exactly how you can use the franchisor's trademarks, patents and copyrights.

- **Definition of the parties:** Lists the parties to the agreement and sets forth the independent relationship between the parties.

- **Payments:** Spells out the franchise fee and any other required royalties or payments.

- **Term of agreement:** Enumerates the length of time that the agreement will be in effect.

- **Renewal of franchise agreement:** Details the mechanism for renewing the agreement.

- **Development and opening:** Details the length of time you have to open your business after signing the agreement, usually 90 to 120 days.

- **Territory:** Spells out any restrictions on the areas in which you may operate (generally, the larger the territory, the larger the franchise fee payable).

- **Advertising:** Sets forth requirements for using the franchisor's logos, advertising designs, trademarks and so on in advertising.

- **Equipment and supplies:** Spells out what supplies and services the franchisee must purchase directly from the franchisor.

- **Franchisor-provided training and assistance:** Details the training that the franchisor offers, as well as any ongoing support and assistance.

- **Assignment of franchise:** Describes any special rules for transferring ownership to another person or entity if the franchisee decides to sell the business.

- **Termination of franchise agreement:** Sets forth the legal requirements for terminating the agreement

Franchise agreements are complex legal documents, so before signing anything, find a solicitor who specialises in dealing with franchising. The solicitor who advised you on the sale of your house or drawing up a will may not be the right person for this job. You need someone who's done this many times before, is familiar with the British Franchise Association Code of Ethics and who can provide you with a comprehensive report highlighting your rights and duties; anything that may be unusual or missing in the contract; and areas that you need to clarify with the franchisor. The cost depends on how much work is involved but expect to pay anywhere from £500 to £2,000 plus VAT. The British Franchise Association has a list of accredited solicitors who can provide specialist advice on their website.

Make absolutely sure that you understand every part of your franchising agreement – and agree with its terms and conditions – before you sign it. This doesn't just mean reading it over and being generally familiar with the opportunity; it means that you understand *exactly* what every sentence means and how it will affect the way you do business, as well as your rights and obligations now and in the future. You have your greatest leverage at the point where you're considering a variety of franchising opportunities – not after you sign your agreement.

If you aren't happy with anything in the contract you can try to negotiate but if it's non-negotiable and you strongly disagree with certain clauses, think hard about whether you still want you proceed. If in doubt, walk away. Other opportunities are around the corner!

Identifying he pros and cons of franchising

Buying a franchise brings potential positives and negatives. When deciding whether buying a franchise is the best way to start your own home-based business, weigh up the pros and cons below and work out the best path for you. Here are some of the elements that franchises often have in their favour:

- ✔ Buying into a franchise that has a proven track record and on-going training and support can translate into a quick start-up phase and almost immediate cash flow. And don't forget: happiness is a positive cash flow (see Chapter 6 for more about this).

- ✔ Established, successful franchises are proven systems that can meet your financial expectations if you work hard and play the game by the franchisor's rules.

- ✔ A good franchisor provides extensive training in how to operate and market the business, which is a definite plus for people who have never owned or run a business before.

- ✔ You have access to a network of other people who are in a business just like yours. Many franchisors sponsor special websites, conferences or conventions that get franchisees together to share their experiences.

- ✔ Many franchisors provide opportunities for regional and national coop-erative advertising – saving you money while giving your business more exposure than you'd probably get on your own.

Of course, you also need to think about the downsides to buying a franchise. Before you sign on the dotted line of that franchise agreement, make sure that you're comfortable with these potential negatives:

- ✔ You have to follow the franchise's policies and procedures whether you agree with them or not (which ultimately means the franchisor is the boss). If you don't, you may be in violation of your franchise agreement – potentially resulting in nasty legal action, loss of income and the termi-nation of your business. For some prospective home-based business owners, the whole point of starting a business is to get away from following someone else's rules.

- ✔ You work without a great deal of supervision and direction. No one's going to get on the phone to wake you up if you're late to work; no one's going to constantly urge you to work harder or sell more. If you're not a self-starter, or if you lack the confidence to sell yourself and your prod-ucts or services, you may jeopardise your prospects for success by fran-chising. Running a home-based business may not be right for you at all.

✔ You may be required to pay an on-going fee or royalty to the franchisor for the life of your business. Of course, if you're making lots of money, these fees won't be a problem. But if your business is marginal, franchise fees and royalties can quickly become an anchor that drags you and your business down with it.

✔ Franchises aren't guarantees. Your business may or may not be a success, despite all your hard work, all the money you invest and all the time you devote to it. Any business is a risk, and a home-based business that you own makes that risk a very personal one.

✔ The franchise agreement may not protect you against competition from other distributors, which means that you could end up making less money than you thought or were led to believe you would.

What kind of people do best with franchises? Research indicates that a number of personality traits come into play, including a person's influence with others, their willingness to comply with company rules and their ability to think on their feet. If you decide that franchising is something you'd like to explore further, thoroughly research all the possible opportunities to find the best fit for you. After you identify an opportunity that you want to pursue, talk to current owners of the franchise and get their candid opinions of the opportunity – both the good and the bad. And make sure you check the internet for more information about your prospective franchise. Disgruntled franchisees often aren't shy about telling others about their bad experiences, and some post their stories online. Some former franchisees have even set up their own websites specifically to warn others. Just be sure that you take such stories with a pinch of salt until you can verify that they're indeed true.

Buying and operating a franchise often requires a lot of money and a lot of your time and effort over a long period of time. Be absolutely sure *before* you sign the franchise agreement that it's the best option for you.

Direct-selling opportunities

Direct selling means selling a consumer product or service in a face-to-face manner away from a fixed retail location, for example, from your home. According to the Direct Selling Association (DSA; www.dsa.org.uk), more than 400,000 people in the UK are involved in direct selling, generating sales of more than £2 billion each year. The kinds of products sold include home and family care products, such as cleaning supplies, cookware and cutlery; personal care products, such as cosmetics, jewellery and skin care products; wellness products, such as weight-loss products and vitamins; and leisure and educational products, such as toys and games.

The companies that offer direct-selling opportunities are often household names, such as Avon, Betterware, Herbalife, Neal's Yard Organics and Kleeneze.

The two main types of direct-selling opportunities are single-level and multi-level marketing.

Single-level marketing

Single-level marketing is simple: a direct seller makes money by buying products from a parent organisation and selling them directly to customers. Home-based businesspeople have been pursuing single-level marketing for years, and it accounts for a sizeable proportion of direct-selling revenues.

Multi-level marketing

Multi-level marketing (also known as *network marketing* or *person-to-person marketing*) gives you two ways to make money – by buying products from the parent company and selling them to customers and by sponsoring new direct sellers and earning a commission from their efforts. Multi-level marketing has a unique system of selling, in which salespeople take on the following two key roles:

- ✔ **Distributor:** As a distributor of a product, your job is to buy a product from the parent company and sell it directly to the public – usually to friends, relatives and work associates. Every time you sell an item, you make a profit.

- ✔ **Recruiter:** As a recruiter, you sign up other distributors to work for you. Every time your distributor buys an item from the parent company, you receive a percentage of the profit.

As you sign up new distributors, you create a team of all the people you sponsor into the programme, as well as the people they sponsor, and so on. The most successful multi-level marketers make far more money through their teams than they do actually selling products themselves. For this reason, many multi-level marketers focus most of their efforts on recruiting new distributors to join their teams and motivating the individuals in their teams to recruit new distributors.

A multi-level marketing organisation *cannot* only recruit distributors – and collect fees from them – without also selling products. Such an arrangement is called a *pyramid scheme*, and it's against the law. A pyramid scheme is set up specifically to make its creators rich while relieving everyone else of their hard-earned money. Be particularly careful about so-called opportunities in which you sell something that has little or no intrinsic value, such as a 'special' report on how to make money on the internet. Such thinly veiled pyramid schemes could land you in very hot water if you get caught up in them.

Finding a home-based business that's compatible with bringing up children

Q: I'm a full-time mother and am looking for a business with low start-up costs and overheads that I can run from home on a part-time basis while looking after the children. I'd like to find a business that could then bloom into something full-time as they grow older.

A: Many full-time businesses can be started from home, initially as a part-time venture. In fact, part time is the preferable way to start out on your own. That way you can test the viability of your idea without committing all your resources to it. The best sideline businesses don't require a lot of marketing or administrative tasks, leaving you free to devote your limited time to income-producing work. In other words, you want to choose a service or product that's in high demand and easy to sell. Also, your business has to have flexible hours so that you can run it around looking after the children, working in the hours they're at school or in the evenings when they're asleep.

Whatever business you choose needs to be something you truly enjoy doing, something you know enough about to do well and something for which you can identify a specific market that you can easily reach.

Often the best solutions are quite unique to the business owner. For example:

- ✔ Full-time mothers Celina Ong and Deborah Fiddy started their business selling high-quality silk bedding from their respective homes in south-west London in 2003, with Ong setting up a home office in the corner of her kitchen. The arrangement not only saved on costs, it also meant the two of them could juggle running the venture with caring for five young children. Their business Gingerlily now has a turnover of £800,000 and their silk duvets and pillows are stocked in Harrods and Selfridges, and sold via mail order and online all over the world.

- ✔ Kamal Basran, a full-time mother of two, started making samosas in the kitchen of her home in Manchester, using a recipe she learnt from her mother, after finding some on sale in her local supermarket and deciding they tasted horrible. She started supplying small batches of her samosas to the delicatessen in her local village. As demand grew, she starting making other products such as onion bhajis and spring rolls and then expanded into chilled ready meals. Her business, the Authentic Food Company, now has a turnover of £42 million a year and employs 248 people.

These businesses certainly won't work for everyone, but they were ideal matches for their owners.

Identifying the pros and cons of direct selling

According to the enthusiastic sales pitches of recruiters for many direct-selling opportunities, signing up to sell their products will put you firmly on the road to riches. Although you may very well turn out to be highly successful (every direct-selling opportunity has its successes, often people who get into the business early and establish a large multi-level marketing team), you also may not, so you need to go into it with your eyes open. Here are some benefits of direct selling:

- ✔ Because start-up costs are generally low, you have little financial risk if the business fails – certainly lower than most franchises and business opportunities. (Beware of direct-selling opportunities with high start-up costs – they're often scams. Check out Chapter 10 for tips on how to elude these scams.)

- ✔ High earning potential is possible (although relatively few people actually make six-figure incomes). Mary Kay Inc, a global direct-selling business offering beauty products, really does give out pink Cadillacs to its top salespeople, for example.

- ✔ Most direct-selling programmes are designed specifically to be home-based businesses and are often geared to women (in the UK, around 76 per cent of all direct sellers are women).

- ✔ The direct-selling parent company generally provides you with sales and promotional materials, as well as bookkeeping, sales tracking and commission data.

- ✔ You can work as many or as few hours as you like. All kinds of work arrangements – part time and full time – abound in direct selling. In fact, the clear majority of people who've chosen direct-selling opportunities work part time, some while working other full-time jobs.

Because of the need to continuously recruit new distributors (a *downline*) in multi-level marketing – to replace those who fall by the wayside, as well as to grow organisations – competition for recruits can be quite lively. This intense competition tends to put a lot of pressure on the people being recruited. In addition to this, you may experience a number of other negatives with direct selling. Here are a few:

- ✔ Many direct-selling businesses are here today, gone tomorrow. Although a number of companies have been around for years (including Amway in the US, which celebrates its 55th anniversary in 2014, and Mary Kay Inc, which has been in business since 1963), far too many direct-selling firms have life spans you can measure in months.

- ✔ Direct selling has a poor reputation with many people, often making recruiting new distributors (and selling products) a difficult proposition.

- ✔ Motivating your team to sell more products and sign up new distributors can require more of your time and attention than you may anticipate. Plus, the more distributors you sign up, the bigger the job.

- ✔ Few people in direct selling make enough money to make it a full-time profession. According to industry figures, around 82 per cent of direct sellers work on a part-time basis. Direct salespeople rarely make enough money in their own businesses to support themselves and their families.

✔ **How much money you want to make.** Do you just want a little extra money for a rainy day, perhaps on a part-time basis? Or do you want to make enough money to pursue your business full time? Your answers to these questions will point you towards certain businesses and away from others (for example, many people in direct-selling opportunities only make a few hundred pounds a year).

✔ **How unique you want to be.** Do you want to stand out from the crowd or are you happier blending into a well-established corporate identity? Starting a business from scratch allows you to be as unique as you want to be. Franchises, direct-selling opportunities and business opportunities allow you to closely affiliate with an established corporate identity.

✔ **How much control you want.** Different business options have dramatically different levels of control. Starting a business from scratch may put you in full control, while buying a franchise may give you little control over how the business is marketed and run. Be sure that you're aware of the level of control you want and that the business you choose provides it.

✔ **What your long-term goals are.** Is your goal to make lots of money? Meet interesting people? Work as little as you possibly can? Retire early? Whatever your long-term goals are, make sure the opportunity you select is compatible with and helps you achieve them. Check with other people who have invested in your prospective opportunity and see where they are in their lives. Were they able to leave their careers behind? Are they now independent and able to have that holiday home in France that they always dreamed of? Were they able to retire early? Make sure you find out the reality behind the sizzling sales pitch for your particular opportunity before you jump head first into it.

Do your research and trust your instincts. You'll find the best home business for you.

Chapter 3

The ABC of Starting Your Own Business

*O*ne of the biggest obstacles facing many prospective home-based business owners is simply how to answer this important question: what are you going to live on while you get your new business off the ground? In order to ensure the long-term success of your business, you have to start with sufficient income – from whatever source – to pay your bills.

Three out of every ten people in the UK dream of starting a business of their own. Yet most of them don't. Why not? In many cases, it's because they're afraid they don't have enough money to do it. The fact is, although certain home businesses require a significant investment in equipment and products, many home-based businesses require little or no money to start. But aside from start-up costs, you have to put in a lot of work and careful planning to build a business that can pay the bills over the long run, which is why understanding the right ways (and the wrong ways) to make the move from working for someone else to running your own business is so important.

In this chapter, we review the steps you need to take to set up a home-based business – specifically, what you need to do before you leave your day job behind. We cover how to secure financing and where to find the money you need. We also show you how to develop an effective business plan.

Making the Move to Running Your Home-Based Business

Starting your own business is exciting. For those people who have spent all their working lives employed by someone else, it's often the culmination of a dream that's lasted for years, perhaps decades. Imagine the power and personal satisfaction you'll feel when you realise you're the boss and you call the shots – from setting your own work schedule, to deciding how to approach your work, to choosing your computer and office furniture. Believe us, it's a feeling you won't forget in a hurry.

But there's a right way and a wrong way to make the move. Your goal is to make sure you maintain a sufficient supply of cash to pay the start-up costs of your business while paying for the rest of your life – the mortgage or rent, the gas and electricity bills, school fees, your daughter's karate lessons . . . the list goes on and on.

The fact is, within the first six months of operation, few businesses – home-based or otherwise – bring in all the money necessary to get them off the ground and keep them going for a prolonged period of time. In other words, you may need *a lot of cash* – from your current job, your partner's job, your savings, or loans from friends, family or a bank – to keep both your business and your personal life going until the business generates enough revenue to take over.

Although you have to decide for yourself exactly what schedule to follow while making the move to running a home-based business, unless you're unemployed or retired, we generally recommend that you start your business on a part-time basis while you continue to hold down your regular full-time job. Why? For a number of reasons, including the following:

- ✔ You can develop and test your new business with virtually no risk – you still have your regular job to fall back on if your new business doesn't work out (and remember, no matter how great your business idea is, there's a chance it won't work).

- ✔ You aren't under the intense pressure to perform and produce enough money very quickly that you'd be under if your new business were your only source of income.

- ✔ You can keep your established holiday pay, pension contributions and other benefits.

- ✔ You have a steady source of income that you can use to pay your bills while you establish your new business.

✔ You may be able to take advantage of tax benefits, like the ability to write off business expenses against income (see Chapter 9 for more on taxes and deductions).

✔ You have a stronger basis for obtaining bank loans and other financing for your new business.

Indeed, so many people are choosing to start up their home-based business this way that they even have a name: the five-to-niners, describing people who do their regular nine-to-five day job and then come home to run their home-based business in their spare time at evenings and weekends.

However, bear in mind the downsides to starting a business while continuing to hold down a full-time day job:

✔ Doing both won't leave much time for doing anything else – your social life will definitely suffer and your family life may too as you find that all your spare time is taken up working.

✔ Your health may suffer if you're constantly working at 100 per cent capacity and have no time to yourself.

✔ Once your home-based business starts making money you may need to pay for an accountant to ensure that you're paying the right amount of tax.

✔ Your employer may not look too kindly on the idea of you starting up a business in your spare time. Indeed, many companies have a specific policy banning employees from taking up any other trade or occupation which interferes with the performance of their duties.

Of course, the decision is ultimately up to you. When starting a home-based business, make sure the transition fits into your schedule and your life.

In the following sections, we take a close look at six steps you need to take before you leave your regular job to devote all your time and energy to being your own boss. We also walk through the different steps involved in the process of establishing your home-based business.

Knowing what to do before leaving your day job

After you're consistently earning enough income from your part-time home-based business to cover your bare-minimum living and business expenses, you're ready to make the jump to a full-time commitment of your time and attention. Before you hand in your resignation, however, take the following six steps:

1. **If you're a member of the company pension scheme, find out how it operates, in particular whether it's a final salary or defined benefits scheme.** Make sure you know what will happen to the pension pot you've accumulated after you resign. If you're near retirement age it may make sense to time your resignation so that you maximise the benefits available to you. For example, if you're close to retirement it might be worth waiting, especially if you're on a final salary scheme. Ditto company share schemes – if you're a member of one, find out if you're able to sell your shares.

2. **Find out when you can expect to receive any bonus money or profit sharing.** You may, for example, be in line to receive an annual performance bonus or profit sharing a month after the end of the company fiscal year. This information can help with the financial planning for your home-based business because it lets you know when you'll have the money available to help you get your business off the ground.

3. **If you have medical insurance provided by your employer, have all the check-ups and routine procedures done while you're still covered.** If you want to continue having a medical insurance policy after you leave, check to see whether you can convert your group coverage to an individual policy at a favourable rate.

4. **If you own a house and you need some extra cash to help you through the transition from salaried job to running your own home-based business, consider extending the mortgage on your home or taking out a personal loan before leaving your current job.** Having a pot of cash to draw upon can be invaluable during the first two years of your new business, and your chances of getting a loan approved are much greater while you're employed in a regular job. Sadly, after you leave your job, you probably won't qualify for a mortgage extension or personal loan until your business has been successful for at least three years.

5. **Pay off as much as you can on your credit cards while you still have a steady job.** You help your credit rating (a measure of how safe you are for banks to lend to you; always a good thing) and provide yourself with another source of potential funds to help finance various start-up costs (and depending on the nature of your business, you may have plenty of those).

   Borrowing and always paying it down to the agreed schedule helps your credit rating more than having no credit card borrowings. Check out this website for ways to boost your credit score: `www.moneysaving expert.com/loans/credit-rating-credit-score#improve`.

6. **Take advantage of training and educational opportunities, conferences and meetings that can help your preparations or provide you with contacts who can help you in your own business.** You can then hit the ground running when you decide it's time to start your own business.

Time for a flutter: The odds of success

All kinds of alarming statistics abound about the likely success rates of home-based businesses and start-up businesses in general – it's estimated that 80 per cent of all new businesses in the UK fail within the first five years, for example. Scary stuff perhaps, but the good news is you have several ways of making sure that you and your business don't end up being one of the casualties.

The four key indicators of business success are:

✔ **Sound management practices:** Including an ability to manage projects, handle finances and communicate effectively with customers.

✔ **Industry experience:** Including the number of years you've worked in the same kind of business you intend to start and your familiarity with suppliers and potential customers.

✔ **Technical support:** Including your ability to seek and find help in the technical aspects of your business.

✔ **Planning ability:** Including setting appropriate business goals and targets, and then creating plans and strategies for achieving them.

If you, or the combination of you and a partner, possess all four traits, the probability of your business succeeding is much higher than if you're missing one or more of these traits. If you're missing any of these attributes, find people who can help you fill in the gaps.

Don't make your announcement or submit your resignation until you're really ready to go. Some companies are (sometimes justifiably) paranoid about soon-to-be former employees stealing ideas, proprietary data or clients and may try to speed up your exit!

After completing these steps, you're ready to take what may well be one of the most significant steps forward you'll ever take in your life: starting your own home-based business.

Understanding what you have to do to start your own home-based business

In the sections that follow, we go through exactly what you need to do to start up your own home-based business. We cover these topics in much greater detail in Chapters 4, 6, 10 and 11.

Develop a business plan

Despite what you may read on many small-business websites or blogs, many home-based business owners can get by without drafting a business plan. Indeed, just the thought of having to draft a 50-page tabbed and annotated business plan is enough to scare many potential home-based business owners away from their dreams. The truth is that most business owners today use their business plans to obtain financing from third parties, such as banks or investors, and many successful businesses – home-based or otherwise – have been started without one.

That said, the process of drafting a business plan can be very beneficial – both to you as a business owner and to your business. Taking the time to draft a plan helps you do the right things at the right time to get your business off the ground; plus, it forces you to think through potential challenges and what you can do about them before they overwhelm you.

In essence, a good business plan:

- ✔ Clearly establishes your goals for the business.
- ✔ Analyses the feasibility of a new business and its likelihood of being profitable over the long haul.
- ✔ Explores the expansion of an existing business.
- ✔ Defines your customers and competitors (very important people to know!) and points out your strengths and weaknesses.
- ✔ Details your plans for the future.

Even if you think your business is too small to have a business plan, the process of developing the plan for your business produces a clarity of thought that you can't find any other way and is more than worth your time. See the 'Putting Together a Business Plan' section later in this chapter for more details.

Consult outside professionals

As a new home-based businessperson, you need to consider establishing relationships with a number of *outside professionals* – trained and experienced people who can help you with the aspects of your business in which you may have little or no experience. If you run into questions that you can't easily answer yourself, don't hesitate to call on outside professionals for help as you go through the business start-up process (and be sure to check out Chapter 10 for detailed information on this topic).

Any professional advice you get at the beginning of your business may well save you heartache and potentially expensive extra work down the road.

Here are just some of the outside professionals you may choose to consult as you start your home-based business:

- ✔ **Solicitor.** A solicitor's services are an asset not only in the planning stages of your business, but also throughout its life. A solicitor can help you choose your legal structure, draw up incorporation or partnership paperwork, draft and review agreements and contracts, and provide information on your legal rights and obligations. Look for a solicitor who specialises in working with small businesses and start-ups.

✔ **Accountant.** Consult an accountant to set up a good bookkeeping system for your business. Inadequate record keeping is a principal contributor to the failure of small businesses. Regardless of how boring or intimidating it may seem, make sure you understand basic accounting and the bookkeeping system or software you're using, and don't forget to closely review all the regularly produced financial reports that the accountant compiles for your business using your software – such as tax returns and VAT returns (and make sure you actually receive them!).

✔ **Banker.** The capital requirements of a small business make establishing a good working relationship with a bank absolutely essential. They can provide you with a business account, loans and overdrafts; and a good business-focused bank can also help with more complex needs such as credit-checking services and invoice factoring. Choose a bank with a strong track record in supporting start-up businesses – bank websites give you a good idea of where their priorities lie.

We recommend establishing a relationship with your banker *before* applying for a loan, not after you decide to initiate the loan process. This relationship may make the difference between getting approval for the loan you need and being turned down.

Establishing a good relationship with your banker isn't difficult – arrange a meeting before you apply for a loan to talk through the prospects for your business, or even invite your banker to visit and see your business in action. Make sure you're fully prepared with any financial facts and figures to hand, and always act in a professional manner.

✔ **Business consultant.** Every person has talents in many areas, but no one can be a master of everything. Consultants are available to assist in the areas where you need expert help. You can use business, management and marketing consultants; promotion experts; financial planners; and a host of other specialists to help make your business more successful. Don't hesitate to draw on their expertise when you need it.

✔ **Insurance agent/broker:** Many kinds of insurance options are available for business owners, and some are more necessary than others. An insurance agent or broker can advise you about the type and amount of coverage that's best for you and your business. The agent may also be able to tailor a package that meets your specific needs at reasonable rates.

The relationships you establish with outside professionals during the start-up phase of your business can last for years and can be of tremendous benefit to your firm. Be sure to choose your relationships wisely. In the case of outside professionals, you often get what you pay for, so be penny-wise but don't suffer a poor-quality outside professional simply to save a pound or two.

Using the 'five Cs' to build a better banking relationship

Bankers consider the 'five Cs' of credit analysis, factors they look at when they evaluate a loan request. When applying to a bank for a loan, be prepared to address the following points:

- **Character.** Bankers lend money to borrowers who appear honest and who have a good credit history. Before you apply for a loan, obtain a copy of your credit report and clean up any problems.

- **Capacity.** This is a prediction of your ability to repay the loan. For a new business, bankers look at the business plan. For an existing business, bankers consider financial statements and industry trends.

- **Collateral.** Bankers generally want you to pledge an asset you can sell to pay off the loan if you lack funds.

- **Capital.** Bankers scrutinise your *net worth*, the amount by which your assets exceed your debts.

- **Conditions.** Bankers are influenced by the current economic climate as well as the amount you're asking to borrow.

Choose the best legal structure for your business

Most home-based businesses begin as sole traders or partnerships because they're the easiest business structures to run and the least expensive. But as these businesses grow, many explore the transition to another kind of legal entity. Before you decide what kind of business you want yours to be, consider the pros and cons of the following legal structures:

- **Sole trader.** A *sole trader* is the simplest and least regulated form of organisation. It also has minimal legal start-up costs, making it the most popular choice for new home-based businesses. As a sole trader, one person owns and operates the business and is responsible for seeking and obtaining financing. The sole proprietor (you) has total control and receives all profits, which are taxed as personal income. The major disadvantages include unlimited personal liability for the owner (if the business is sued for some reason, the owner is personally liable to pay) and the fact that it may be harder to sell a sole trader business than one set up as a limited liability company because buyers can be worried about possible undisclosed liabilities and future possible liabilities that the sole trader themselves may not be aware of at the time of selling.

- **Partnership.** A *partnership* is relatively easy to form and can provide additional financial resources. Profits are taxed as personal income, and the partners are still personally liable for debts and taxes, meaning that their personal assets may be at risk if the partnership can't satisfy creditors' claims. A special arrangement called a *limited partnership* allows partners to avoid unlimited personal liability. Limited partnerships must be registered and must also pay a tax to the appropriate authorities in their jurisdiction. On the plus side, partnerships allow people to combine their unique talents and assets to create a whole greater than the sum of its parts. On the other hand, though, a partnership can become a nightmare when partners fail to see eye to eye or when relationships turn sour.

When entering into any partnership, consult a solicitor and insist on a written agreement that clearly describes a process for dissolving the partnership as cleanly and fairly as possible if the time comes.

✔ **Limited liability company.** A *limited liability company* can be a good choice for new start-up businesses because it's a separate legal entity to its directors, which means although you're responsible for the business, you won't be liable for its debts or other liabilities if it runs into trouble. Setting up a limited company is costlier and requires more administration than registering as a sole trader, but it can be more tax-efficient because the profits belong to the company, rather than you, so you're paid as an employee. You may also opt to become a shareholder and take dividends from the company as well.

As you set up your new home-based business, take time to think through the ramifications of your business's legal structure carefully. Each option has many potential advantages and disadvantages for your firm, and each can make a big difference in how you run your business. If you have any questions about which kind of legal structure is right for your business, talk to an accountant or seek advice from a solicitor who specialises in small businesses. Chapters 9 and 10 can also help you sort through the options.

Decide on a name

Naming your business may well be one of the most enjoyable steps in the process of starting up your own home-based business. Everyone can get in on the action: your friends, your family; even your clients-to-be.

Consider your business name carefully – you have to live with it for a long time. The name should give people some idea of the nature of your business, project the image you want to have and be easy to visualise. Names can be simple, sophisticated or even silly. Try to pick one that can grow with your business and not limit you in the future. Think of Ocado, Opodo and Qjump and see what they conjure up in your mind.

Along with a name, many businesses develop a logo, which provides a graphic symbol for the business. As with your name, your logo needs to project the image you want, so develop it carefully. Spend a few extra pounds to have a professional graphic artist design your logo for you.

After you come up with a name, check the Companies House website (www.companieshouse.gov.uk) to make sure it isn't already in use and register the name with them (see Chapter 10 for more details). Check that you can get the domain of the same name for your website, ideally with both the .com and .co.uk endings (you need both to stop anyone buying the other one).

Take care of the red tape (and it will take care of you)

Too many budding home-based entrepreneurs put off or ignore taking care of all the legal requirements of starting up a business. Unfortunately, ignoring the many legal requirements of going into business may put you and your business at risk.

Getting through the maze of government regulations can certainly be one of the most confusing aspects of starting up and running a business. But even though this process can be intimidating, you have to do it – and do it correctly – because non-compliance can result in costly penalties and perhaps even the loss of your business. This step fortifies the professionalism of your business and at the same time helps you rest easy at night, knowing that you're following the rules.

Even very small or part-time businesses must meet certain legal requirements. For example, if you're going to be preparing food, you may need to get a licence from your local council and arrange for their health and safety officers to inspect your kitchen to ensure that it complies with their food preparation standards.

Adhering to regulations that apply to your business is your responsibility. Fortunately, finding out what you need to do, and when, is straightforward. The government website (www.gov.uk) covers all the legal requirements you need to adhere to, and the HM Revenue and Customs website (www.hmrc.gov.uk) spells out all the taxation requirements. Other business organisations such as the British Chambers of Commerce (www.britishchambers.org.uk) can also advise you on what you need to do. For your sake – and the sake of your business – don't hesitate to ask for help when you need it.

Get the insurance you need

In today's expensive, litigious world of business, insurance isn't really an option – it's essential.

So what kinds of insurance do you need for your business? We recommend that you talk to an insurance agent to discuss your business and its needs. Some of the most common kinds of business insurance – some compulsory, some optional – include the following:

- **Public liability insurance:** Provides cover against claims arising if a customer or member of the public is injured or even killed or if their property is damaged because of your business.

- **Employers' liability insurance:** Provides cover for claims made by an employee who's injured at work or who becomes ill as a result of working for you.

- **Product liability coverage:** Covers liability for products manufactured or sold.

- **Professional liability insurance:** Also known as professional indemnity insurance. Protects your business against claims for damages incurred by customers as a result of your professional advice or recommendations.

- ✔ **Building insurance:** Protects the building from damage caused by disasters such as fire or flood.
- ✔ **Contents insurance:** Protects the contents of your business from damage, destruction, loss or theft.
- ✔ **Vehicle insurance:** Covers collision, liability and property damage for vehicles used for business.
- ✔ **Business interruption insurance:** Covers payment of business earnings if the business is closed for an insurable cause, such as fire, flood or other natural disaster.

A homeowner's building and contents insurance policy isn't usually enough for a home-based business for a couple of reasons. First, your typical homeowner's policy provides only limited coverage for business equipment and doesn't insure you against risks of liability or lost income. Second, your homeowner's policy may not cover your business activities at all. If you're going to be working from home, talk to your current home and contents insurance provider to ensure you're adequately covered.

Insurance is the kind of thing you don't think about until you need it. And in the case of insurance, when you need it, chances are you *really* need it! Take time to set up proper coverage now.

Decide on an accounting system

Accounting is one of those topics that makes people nervous (with visions of HMRC tax investigations dancing in their heads), but keeping the books doesn't have to be complicated. In fact, simplicity is the key to a good system for home-based businesses. Keep in mind that your records need to be complete and up to date so that you have the information you need for business decisions and taxes.

When you establish an accounting system, we recommend you use one of the excellent computer software programs dedicated to this purpose. You can choose to buy a software program for a one-off fee to install or download on to your computer, or you can choose to access an accounting system via a website on the Internet for which you pay an ongoing monthly fee. Increasingly, big accounting software suppliers such as QuickBooks and Sage offer both options. The benefit of an Internet-based option is that it automatically updates to reflect changes in VAT, for example, but ultimately the best option is the one you instinctively feel most comfortable using.

The two basic bookkeeping methods are *single entry* and *double entry*. Single entry is simpler, with only one entry required per transaction. We prefer this method for most home-based businesses as the vast majority can operate very well with the single-entry system. Double entry requires two entries per transaction, and provides cross-checks and decreases errors. Consider going with a double-entry system if someone else manages your books, if you use your accounting system for inventory management or if you want more sophisticated reporting for analysing your business. The accounting methods you use depend on your business. You may want to talk to an accountant for help in setting up your system. Even with the support of a professional, however, you need to understand your own system thoroughly.

Many home-based businesses can get by without detailed financial reporting or analysis – after all, if you can keep up with your bills and perhaps have a little bit of money to put away in your savings account, you must be making money, right? If you really want to understand your business's financial situation, however, you need some basic financial reports.

The following financial statements are the minimum necessary to understand where your business stands financially. With them in hand, you can review your business's financial strengths and weaknesses and make accurate plans for the future.

- ✔ **Balance sheets** show the worth of your business – the difference between its assets and its liabilities. Your balance sheet can tell you whether you'd have any cash left over if you shut down your business today, paid off all your bills and loans and liquidated your assets.

- ✔ **Profit-and-loss (P&L) statements** show you the difference between how much money your business is bringing in (*revenue*) and how much money it's spending (*expenses*). If you're bringing in more money than you spend, you have a profit. If you're spending more money than you bring in, you have a loss.

- ✔ **Cash-flow projections** tell you where your money is going and whether you're likely to have sufficient money each month to pay your bills and operate the business. For many start-ups – especially those with employees, rent and other significant recurring expenses – a cash-flow projection is the most important financial statement of all.

Years after starting his home-based business, author Peter still keeps a detailed cash-flow projection that shows expected revenues – by client – on a monthly basis for an entire year. By doing so, Peter can see any shortfalls that may be dangerous to his business's financial health far in advance and he can address them before they become major problems.

For many more details about these and other financial matters, including the use of financial ratios to gauge the financial health of your business and a much more in-depth look at accounting software packages, check out Chapter 6 and take a look at *Bookkeeping For Dummies*, 3rd Edition, by Jane Kelly, Paul Barrow and Lita Epstein, and *Sage One For Dummies* by Jane Kelly (both Wiley).

Develop a marketing plan

If you want to be successful, you need to let potential customers know about your new business, get them in to have a look and encourage them to buy your product or service. Marketing is all of this and more. Your specific approach to marketing depends on your business, your finances, your potential client or customer base and your goals.

Marketing sells your products and services, which brings in the cash you need to run your business. Marketing is so important to the survival (and success) of your business that it deserves a plan of its own. A *marketing plan* helps evaluate where your business currently is, where you want it to go and how you can get there. Your marketing plan should also spell out the specific strategies and costs involved in reaching your goals. You can integrate it into your business plan (if you have one) as one comprehensive section, refer to it regularly and update it as necessary.

Successful marketing for a small or home-based business is a terrific opportunity to use your creativity and hone your business sense. For more information on marketing your home-based business check out Chapter 4.

Seek assistance when you need it

An almost unlimited number of organisations and agencies – private, public and not-for-profit – are ready, willing and able to help you work through the process of starting up your home-based business. Check out the websites of each of the following organisations for an incredible amount of free information and help, and remember that this list is only the beginning:

- ✔ **UK government advice and information:** www.gov.uk

- ✔ **British Chambers of Commerce:** www.britishchambers.org.uk

- ✔ **HM Revenue and Customs:** www.hmrc.gov.uk

- ✔ **Enterprise Nation:** www.enterprisenation.com

- ✔ **Intellectual Property Office:** www.ipo.gov.uk

- ✔ **Companies House:** www.companieshouse.gov.uk

Six Ways to Get the Cash Flowing

Every new business starts at the beginning. No matter how much experience you have in your current job or how many other businesses you may have started in the past, when you create a new home-based business, you're starting from scratch. In the beginning, every sale counts, and your primary goal quickly becomes building financial momentum. The faster you get the cash flowing into your new business, the sooner you can leave your nine-to-five job behind and dedicate yourself fully to your home-based business. Consider these six approaches to getting the cash flowing as you start your business:

- ✔ **Begin part time with your new business.** When you start your own business, you usually have a choice to make: keep your day job or quit. As we mention earlier in this chapter, we recommend that you keep your regular job for as long as you can while building your own business part time. That way you still have your regular job to fall back on if your own business fails for whatever reason in its early stages. At some point – after your own business has built up a sufficient clientele – you can leave your regular job and devote yourself fully to your home-based business.

✔ **Work part time at your old job.** If you have enough work in your home-based business to keep you fairly busy, but not enough to make it your full-time vocation, consider working part time in your regular job. Depending on your particular situation, your current employer may be willing to be flexible with your schedule. For many employers, keeping a good employee part time is better than losing them altogether.

✔ **Turn your employer into your first client.** If you're really good at what you do, what better way to get your business off the ground than to do work for your current employer on a contract basis? Not only do you give your employer the benefit of your expertise while contracting with a known entity, but you also develop your business while working with people you already know, using systems and procedures you're already familiar with.

Take care, however, to clearly separate yourself from your former employer as an independent contractor rather than continuing to work in the role of an employee. If you don't make this distinction clear, HMRC may decide that you're effectively still an employee and that income tax must be deducted at source by the employer under the PAYE scheme. See Chapter 9 for a discussion on how to ensure you're on the right side of this fine line.

✔ **Take business with you (ethically, of course!).** Although stealing clients away from a previous employer is unethical (and may very well land you in court), you may be able to get your employer's blessing if you let them know exactly what you want to do. When a company restructures they may need to divest themselves of customers or product ranges that don't fit with their new business methods, which is where you can take over. The advantage of taking clients with you to your new business is that you maintain the strong working relationship you already have in place – which greatly benefits both your new business and your new clients.

✔ **Finance your business with start-up funds.** You need money to start a business – any business. By lining up sources of start-up funds, you can ease the financial entry into owning your own home-based business. Although the list of potential sources of start-up funds is practically endless, we let you in on the best ones in the 'Working Out Where to Get Your Start-up Funds' section later in this chapter.

✔ **Look to your spouse or significant other for support.** If you have a significant other, he or she may be able to support you financially while you start your own home-based business. Although your overall income will be reduced until you're able to crank up your sales, you have the shelter of one secure job and benefits. Such a shelter can save you a lot of sleepless nights, allowing you to focus your attention where it's most needed – on building your business.

ASK THE EXPERTS

Bringing a partner into your business

Q: I'm looking for a business partner for my company. Do you have any suggestions on how to find one?

A: The best business partner is someone with whom you have a long track record of working well – someone with whom you share common goals and compatible work styles. The more experience you've had working together, the better. But don't despair if you can't find anyone from your existing pool of contacts to team up with. You can find partners by networking through professional and trade organisations, or by getting referrals from others whose judgement you value and respect. Here's what we suggest:

- Don't go directly from stranger to business partner. That's like getting married on the first date. Instead of telling people you're looking for a business partner, put the word out that you're looking for an associate to run a joint venture with. This initial joint venture should be a short-term or separate project that gives you a chance to get to know a prospective partner and see whether you have the chemistry to work well together.

- Ask for referrals from those in a position to know people who will meet your criteria: the officers of a trade association, the president of the chamber of commerce, the editor of the trade journal, or a valued supplier or client. You can network with such individuals online as well as in person. These days, you need not limit yourself to teaming up only with colleagues in your local area. Many people successfully use email, collaboration software, landlines and Skype to team up with associates anywhere in the country or even internationally.

As you talk with people about the possibility of collaborating on an initial venture, look for compatibility in the following areas:

- Strengths that complement yours
- Honesty
- Fairness
- Professional attitude and etiquette
- Personal integrity
- Positive attitudes about family/work priorities
- Good understanding of money and financial issues
- Timeliness and punctuality
- Strong work ethic
- Good manners and treatment of others
- Positive attitudes about your profession or business

Take note of any red flags. If anything like the following comes up in initial conversations, watch out!

- A history of financial problems
- A history of combative relationships or lawsuits
- Soap opera tales of woe about previous partners or joint ventures
- Unprofessional behaviour, such as being late to meetings or frequently putting down others
- Unwillingness to put plans and agreements in writing

When you find someone you click with, do several short-term projects or joint ventures together before committing to a formal, legal partnership. Make sure that your initial assessment is accurate and that you can, in fact, trust your partner and work well together.

Head to Chapter 13 for more about finding a business partner.

Working Out Where to Get Your Start-up Funds

The number-one concern for most people who plan to start their own home-based businesses isn't what kind of business to start, where to start it or how to market their products and services. It's not who their customers will be, who their competition is or whether they should involve a partner in the business. Their number-one concern is money. More specifically, it's where to get the money they need to start up their home-based businesses.

Although many home-based businesses don't need much money to get started, with cash, you can buy the things your business needs to operate, and stock up on the inventory of products you plan to sell to your customers and clients.

But where does this initial money come from, and what are the best ways to pull together the cash you need to start up your home-based business? Here are 18 of our best suggestions:

- **Bartering.** Although not strictly a source of cash, *bartering* with others – trading your products or services for theirs – can be a great way of getting the things you need to get your business off the ground. Need a computer? Well, if you're starting a massage business in your home, you may be able to find someone who'd love to trade some massages for a second-hand computer. Craigslist (craigslist.co.uk) or Gumtree (gumtree.com) are good places to give bartering a try.

- **Business idea competitions.** Some organisations run business idea competitions, with the prize for the winner being start-up funding to get their business off the ground. Shell Livewire (shell-livewire.org), for example, offers start-up awards of £1,000 in cash each month and £10,000 annually to young entrepreneurs aged 16–30 in the UK.

- **Charitable organisations.** The Prince's Trust (www.princes-trust.org.uk) offers small start-up grants and loans to unemployed young people between the ages of 18–30 as part of its Enterprise Programme.

- **Credit cards.** Home-based business owners often turn to credit cards as a source of cash for business start-ups. A word of caution: beware of high interest rates and extra fees for cash advances. If you do decide to use a credit card for your business, try to dedicate one solely to your business expenses. Doing so makes working out your taxes for the year a much easier task.

- **Credit union loan.** Because credit unions are owned by their members, they often offer better interest rates than regular banks or other financial institutions. If you belong to a credit union, try there for a loan first. Keep in mind, however, that credit unions are generally even more averse to risk than regular banks, so your credit has to be very strong for you to have a chance of getting the money you need.

✔ **Crowdfunding.** The Internet has made it possible to raise start-up funds by *equity crowdfunding*: asking lots of individuals to each invest a small amount of cash – as little as £10 – in return for an equity share in your fledgling business. They (hopefully) reap the rewards when you eventually sell your business for many millions. Social media such as Facebook and Twitter has made it easy to let people know what you're up to and how they can get involved.

Alex Kammerling managed to raise £180,000 from 85 investors, in return for a combined 23 per cent equity stake, to fund his start-up spirits business Kamm & Sons via Crowdcube (www.crowdcube.com).

Other popular crowdfunding options include Seedrs (www.seedrs.com) and Kickstarter (www.kickerstarter.com).

Individuals who own a tiny slice of equity may feel a sense of ownership towards the business and the entitlement to ask you questions about the way it is run.

See *Crowdsourcing For Dummies* by David Alan Grier (Wiley) for heaps more on crowdfunding.

✔ **Disability payment.** If you've been granted a disability payment or insurance payout because of an on-the-job injury that prevents you from pursuing your former vocation, the cash you receive may be useful as you begin a new career – running a business from home.

✔ **Funds from investors.** Many new companies rely on cash from investors to fund their start-up and initial operations. Be aware, however, that when you accept money from investors, you probably have to give them something in exchange. That something is usually equity in the company. And with equity comes the power to have a say in how the business is run. If you don't want anyone telling you how to run your business, you may not want to use investor funds to help you start your business.

✔ **Grants.** The days of government grants for start-ups are sadly long gone, but you may still find the occasional grant being offered by regional enterprise agencies and local development organisations. Check out the Business Finance and Support finder function on the government website www.gov.uk for details of any available financial assistance in your area.

✔ **Home equity line of credit.** If you have a home and have built up equity in it (the value of the home being over and above what you owe for it), you may be eligible for an equity line of credit. This is similar to an extension of your mortgage, except that you only pay interest on the additional amount borrowed when you actually draw on it (you may have to pay some sort of loan origination fee to set up the line of credit). Home equity loan terms are often much longer than standard loans – up to 15 years or more.

On the downside, you have to put your home up as security – which means that if you default on your loan, you may lose your house. You also need to secure the funding before you quit your job because the amount you can borrow is determined by your salary – and of course the assumption that you'll be using that salary to repay the loan, so you need to be absolutely confident that you can make the monthly repayment from your home-based business after you quit your job.

✔ **Inheritance.** Although an inheritance may be subject to taxation, depending on exactly how much you inherit and in what way (check with a tax adviser for all the details, and see `www.hmrc.gov.uk/rates/iht-thresholds.htm`), you may still be left with a substantial amount of funds that you can use to start your new business.

✔ **Incubator programmes.** Some businesses and organisations encourage start-ups within their industry by providing office space and funding for a limited period of time – typically six months to a year – in return for a stake in the fledgling business. This model is particularly likely in the new technology or bioscience sectors where the business sponsoring the entrepreneur might benefit from the innovations being developed. Telecoms firm O2 Telefonica, for example, runs the Wayra programme, in which tech start-ups are provided with free workspace, training and support at Wayra's headquarters in London for six months in return for O2 Telefonica taking a small stake in the business. Head to `www.wayra.org/en` for more details.

✔ **Life insurance policies.** No, we're not suggesting bumping off your spouse! Depending on the kind of life insurance policy you have (term, cash value and so on), you may be able to cash it in or take out a loan against it. Read the fine print of your policy or consult your insurance provider to see whether you have this option.

✔ **Loans from friends and family.** When aspiring home-based entrepreneurs don't personally have the resources to finance their new business, friends and family are often the first potential sources of funding they turn to. As long as your request for a loan doesn't cause your relationships to sour, loans from friends and family can be a great way to put together the financing you need. Be sure to treat relatives and friends as professionally as you would any business partner, using signed, written loan documents with clear terms and conditions.

✔ **Local seed-money funds.** Some regional enterprise agencies offer a small amount of initial funding (*seed money*) to help finance new businesses in their communities. Contact your local enterprise agency – details on the National Enterprise Network website `www.nationalenterprisenetwork.org` – to find out what's available in your area.

✔ **Microloan programmes.** The government provides loans to start-up businesses through its Start Up Loans programme (`www.startuploans.co.uk`). You must be between 18 and 30 and living in England or Northern Ireland to be eligible for a loan, which will typically be for around £2,500 depending on your business plan. The unsecured loan must be repaid within a five-year period at a fixed rate of interest, currently 6 per cent.

✔ **Personal assets.** You may be able to find some of the start-up funds you need by selling some of your superfluous personal assets such as furniture, games consoles, unwanted gifts, household items and so on. Think car-boot sales, eBay, Gumtree, or the classified ads in your local paper.

✔ **Personal savings.** Savings accounts are probably the first place most soon-to-be home-based business owners turn to when looking for cash to start up their new businesses. And why not? You get instant loan approval – no matter how good or bad your credit report may be – and you can't beat the interest rate of zero per cent!

ASK THE EXPERTS

How to patent your ideas

Q: I've invented a product and I want to take out a patent to protect it before I show it to anyone. How do I go about doing this?

A: A patent provides protection for a new invention or process for up to 20 years by giving the owner the right to take legal action to stop anyone else from making or selling it without their permission. Having a patent also enables an inventor to sell or license their invention to someone else.

Patents are awarded by the Intellectual Property Office (`www.ipo.gov.uk`). Your first step should be to check that nobody has thought of your idea already, by checking their database of awarded patents. If you still think your idea is unique you can apply to the IPO for a patent by submitting a full description of your invention, including any drawings. You can do this yourself but if your idea is in any way complicated, hire a patent attorney to do it on your behalf. Failure to use sufficiently precise wording can render a patent useless.

It can take two to three years for a patent to be granted but after your application has been filed you're free to discuss your invention with third parties, although you must ensure you stick to only what you have filed. You're also entitled to put the words 'patent pending' on your product while your application is granted, to deter would-be copycats.

The Intellectual Property Office produces two free booklets to help first timers called *Patents: Basic Facts* and *Patents: Essential Reading*, which you can download from its website. And check out *Patents, Registered Designs, Trade Marks & Copyright For Dummies* by John Grant, Charlie Ashworth and Henri Charmasson (Wiley).

Putting Together a Business Plan

Whether you write it on the back of a napkin or fill hundreds of pages with full-colour charts and photos of happy customers, your business plan can help you prioritise the actions you take to start up and run your business. Although today's businesses usually put together business plans for the benefit of bank managers and potential investors, even if you're lucky enough not to need external capital, the process of putting together a business plan for your home-based business is an education in itself – one you can't get anywhere else.

Even though you have some flexibility in determining the exact format of your business plan (especially when it's an informal one for your own use), if your intent is to use the plan for securing financing from a bank or investors, they expect to see certain information presented in specific ways. These expectations allow banks and investors to make informed judgements on the viability of your business and its potential for growth and profitability.

A formal business plan needs to contain, at the very least, the following elements:

- **Mission statement.** Your company's mission statement sets the tone for the business, relating it to its values and goals. Mission statements are inspiring and serve to galvanise you and any employees to work hard to attain the company's goals. For example, authors Paul and Sarah's mission statement is: 'We're authors, broadcasters and facilitators. Our mission is to explore new and better ways of living and working through the interface of nature and technology.'

- **Description of the company's products and services.** Here you provide a complete description of all the products and services your company presently offers and plans to offer in the future. If your home-based business specialises in producing the best wedding cakes in the UK, using the latest in confectionery technology, you'd explain that here. Be complete – leave nothing to the imagination.

- **Market analysis.** If you've already put together a marketing plan for your business (see the 'Develop a marketing plan' section earlier in this chapter for a description of a marketing plan), you already have the material you need to fill out this part of your business plan. The market analysis takes a close look at the markets in which you intend to sell your products and services, and details the number of potential customers, the potential growth rate of the market, information about your competition and the particulars of your marketing strategies.

✔ **Financial projections.** Do you plan to go from £100 a month in revenues to £100,000 a month? This part is where you present your financial projections, including revenues, expenses and profit or loss. Include the three basic financial statements – a balance sheet, a profit-and-loss (P&L) statement and a cash-flow projection – and be ready to back up your guesses and forecasts with hard data. (See the 'Decide on an accounting system' section earlier for more details about these financial statements.)

✔ **Management strategies for achieving company goals.** You have your products and services, your marketing strategies and your financial projections. Now, exactly how do you intend to achieve your goals? This section presents the details of the strategies for accomplishing your company's goals and lays out when and how you plan to achieve them. For example, what directors you plan to hire to help you grow the business and what their specific roles and responsibilities will be.

Check out *Business Plans For Dummies,* 2nd Edition, by Paul Tiffany, Steven Peterson and Colin Barrow (Wiley), for details on writing a successful business plan.

Outsourcing your business plan

Q: I want to start a business, but the bank needs a business plan before I can get a loan. I don't know how to write a business plan and am not good at writing. Can I hire someone to write a business plan for me?

A: You can certainly employ a professional business plan writer and you can find many advertising their services online. If you decide to go down this route, look for someone who has a general business background in the areas of accounting, bookkeeping and marketing, and familiarity with financial statements, business jargon and your local business community.

However, a business plan isn't just to impress a bank manager; it should also reflect you and your passion for what you do. Most importantly, you need to be able to explain and discuss your business plan in detail and bring it to life. This is far harder to do if you're reciting someone else's words and perceptions. Also, an overly polished glossy document can give the impression that your business is all style and no substance.

Our advice is to use a business plan template, perhaps provided by the bank itself, and ask a friend to help you get the wording and spelling right.

Chapter 4

Attracting Customers

. . . .

. . . .

*Y*ou're working hard to start your home-based business and get it going. But the most important thing you need to do is to convince someone to buy your products and services. You see, the greatest business ideas in the world – the greatest products and services – are essentially worthless if no one is willing to pay you for them. For your business to be successful, you have to become good at marketing your products and services so that prospective customers and clients hear about you and are encouraged to buy from you.

In this chapter, we help you identify your best customers and assess their needs. We take a look at different marketing methods – including *referrals,* one of the most effective marketing tools – and help you create a meaningful marketing plan. We also check in on the latest information about starting your own website for e-commerce.

Identifying Your Best Customers

Here's a secret that may make a very big difference in the amount of money you stand to earn from your home-based business: *some of your potential customers are better than others.* That is, some (the ones who are willing to pay full price for your products or services with little intervention on your part) earn you a lot of money, and some (the ones who try to squeeze out every last discount from you, complaining all the way) actually lose you money.

Because potential customers come in all sizes, shapes and spending profiles – and because customers don't come with their profiles stapled on their foreheads – your very difficult job is first to work out which ones are the most likely to become your best customers, and then to figure out how to attract and reach them. Because your time and marketing budget aren't unlimited, the best use of your money is to target specific people – the people who are most likely to buy your products and services. For example, instead of running expensive radio or newspaper advertisements day after day, hoping to get the attention of the customers you seek, you may find that targeted advertising via a specific magazine or website delivers a much greater payoff.

What does your ideal customer look like? Here are a few questions to ask as you create a picture. (Don't worry if you can't answer all the questions right now – just give it your best shot.)

- ✔ Who do you think your best customers are?
- ✔ Are they individuals or businesses?
- ✔ If they're individuals, what do they like and what don't they like?
- ✔ What are their needs and problems?
- ✔ How can you best address those needs and problems?
- ✔ Who do they buy from at the moment?
- ✔ What's most important to your best customers?
- ✔ What's least important to them?
- ✔ How can you deliver more of the former and less of the latter?

Based on these questions, develop a written description of your best customers and ask some of them to look it over to approve it or to make corrections. Invite your best customers or clients into your offices for an informal round table discussion over a buffet lunch (paid for by you). This gives them a chance to share their views and you a chance to learn more about them.

Here's a sample description of the ideal customer for a pet-sitting service:

> My ideal customer is a single working adult with one or more pets, including dogs, cats or birds, which require daily care and attention. My ideal customer often travels, has sufficient income ($35,000 or more per year) to afford to hire a pet sitter, and prefers to keep his or her pet in its home environment rather than in a kennel or other off-site care situation. My ideal customer loves his or her pets and wants them to have the best care possible. He or she wants to use a pet-sitting service for a week or more at a time several times a year, and may use it for up to two weeks at a time particularly in the Easter and summer holidays and over Christmas and New Year, as well as occasional weekends throughout the year. My ideal customer is willing to pay more than existing pet-sitting services in return for a superior level of care and service.

Promoting a new business

Q: I've started a home business creating websites for local businesses. At the moment my main way of marketing is to send out leaflets and then ring up businesses to try to arrange a meeting with the owner so I can explain the service I offer and show how it would benefit their business. Do you have any other suggestions on how to promote a new business without spending too much?

A: You are doing the right things – a leaflet is a good way of setting out what services you offer in an easy-to-read way, and ringing up business owners gives them a chance to speak to you in person to get a feel for what it would be like to work with you. Most start-ups begin by knocking on doors or making marketing phone calls. Here are a few more ideas that may help you:

✔ **Word of mouth is a very powerful marketing tool.** Encourage your existing customers to tell other businesses about your service by offering them an incentive – a free six-monthly review of their website for every new customer they refer, perhaps.

✔ **Start networking with local businesses in your area.** They are, after all, your potential customers – so attend as many local business networking events as you can find.

Even better, offer to speak at them, about how you started up your own business, perhaps, so that other attendees find out who you are and what you do.

✔ **Don't limit your marketing efforts just to local businesses.** Many other local organisations may need a website too, for example schools, doctors' surgeries, charities and even churches. Make sure they all know about your business and what it offers. Buy a list of business owners' email addresses so you can get in touch with them.

✔ **Find out if your area has a local online business directory and get your business listed on it.** Listings are usually free for basic information or cost a few pounds for a larger entry. Make sure yours looks as appealing as possible.

✔ **Establish a presence at local neighbourhood events to get your business noticed.** Take a stand at the village fete, provide a prize for a competition at the school fair or offer to provide T-shirts (bearing your business logo) for the local amateur football team.

The idea is to understand your best potential clients and customers inside out – to know what makes them tick and what motivates them. By doing so, you can work out which marketing approaches (website, blog, direct mail, radio ads, search engine listings, display advertisement, social networking on sites like Facebook, LinkedIn and Twitter, directory ads, such as electronic and print Yellow Pages, and so on) have the highest probability of not only reaching your best customers, but also inducing them to want to find out more about what you've got to offer. (Check out the 'Marketing: Taking Different Roads to Meet Your Goals' section later in this chapter for ideas on ways to market your products and services.)

Tapping into Your Customers' Needs

Which do you think is the better approach – creating a product or service that you're not sure anyone will want to buy and then trying to sell it, or first finding out what people want to buy and *then* creating a product or service that responds to that demand? Here's a hint: if you build a business around a product or service that you're not sure will sell, you're taking a very big risk.

Sir Clive Sinclair invented the C5 electric car in 1985, which was a complete failure – he only sold a few of them and after six months closed the venture down having lost £7 million. Milton Hershey started three unsuccessful candy companies in Philadelphia, Chicago and New York before founding the Hershey Company in 1894, which brought milk chocolate – previously a Swiss delicacy – to the masses. Walt Disney's first business, Laugh-O-Gram, was so unsuccessful that at one point he resorted to eating dog food to stay alive. Thomas Edison filed 1,093 patents, mostly for unsuccessful ventures, before striking gold with the light bulb in 1879. His statement 'I have not failed. I've just found 10,000 ways that won't work' is the stuff of legend.

Creating a product or service in a vacuum, without considering the input of your clients or customers, is a recipe for disaster because you're essentially designing a product or service that your prospects may neither need nor like. As a result, you have to market much harder – or offer a lot of incentives – to get your clients or customers to buy your products. Even then, they still may not buy.

Finding a need and filling it is one of the most basic marketing strategies. Your first step in marketing, therefore, begins before your product or service is available to the public, when you're designing and creating it. By tapping into your customers' needs early in the process, you not only build a product or service that your prospects truly want and need, but your marketing efforts also take far less personal energy, time and money to implement.

Understanding the WPWPF principle

Many home-based business owners are in love with the products and services they sell, as indeed they should be. After all, they are their own best cheer-leaders, creating infectious excitement whenever they have the opportunity to talk to someone about their business or their products or services. The problem is that some home-based business owners fall so deeply in love with their products and services that they fail to notice their prospective clients and customers aren't equally in love. And when this happens, a great idea remains only a great idea – not a great product or service.

The fact is that your products and services are only as good as what people are willing to pay for them. It's called the *WPWPF* (what people will pay for) *principle.* No matter how beautiful, clever or well thought out your products or services may be, if your clients and customers don't want them, they aren't worth even a fraction of the time and money you invested to create them, and you really don't have a business.

So what's the solution? How can you make sure that the products and services you've been dreaming about delivering to your clients and customers are the ones they truly want? It's actually quite simple: ask them. Here are a few simple steps for defining your target market and then asking the people in that market which products and services they really want and need (and will therefore be willing to buy):

1. **Decide which market you're going to target.**

    Who, potentially, are your best customers – the people in the market you want to target? Do you want to sell your products and services to busy businesspeople, to retired people, to parents of pre-school children or to people who like to go on long overseas holidays to exotic places? Whichever product or service you hope to create, first decide whom you're going to try to sell it to. All the steps that follow depend on this one, so take your time deciding which market you want to target.

2. **Ask the members of your target market which products or services they want and need.**

    You can do this in person, over the telephone, via written surveys sent through the post, by email, or through your website or blog. The key is to collect as much data about the wants and needs of your target market as you can – the more data, the better.

3. **Use the results of your survey when designing your products and services.**

    Using the data you collect from surveying your potential customers and clients, determine the design of the products and services you offer. Make sure that you address – and at least consider – every feature mentioned as important by the people you surveyed. Some may not make financial sense, but others may be essential to include, whatever the cost. Not only do you end up with better products and services, but you also sell a lot more of them because they match the wants and needs of your customers and clients.

4. **Test the market.**

    After your products and services are available – but before you roll them out to the public at large – test them out on a few selected people, businesses or not-for-profit organisations. What's their reaction? Are they satisfied with the results? Do your selected customers have suggestions for improvements or changes? What about price? Are your products and services priced realistically? Will your potential clients be willing to pay what you ask? Incorporate the feedback you get by tweaking your product or service or the prices you plan to charge.

5. **Market, market, market.**

   By going through the preceding four steps, you can be reasonably assured that you have a product on your hands that you can not only sell, but that you can sell a lot of. Now get ready for the ride of your life!

Researching your idea

Proper research is one of the most powerful tools to attract customers that you have at your disposal. It can spell the difference between creating a business which has real potential and one which is destined to go nowhere.

Research doesn't simply mean asking your friends and family whether they'd buy one of your products. It means analysing in depth your potential market, your competitors, trends within the industry, forecasts of its growth and likely direction. The basic question you are trying to find the answer to is: Are there enough people out there who will want to buy my product or service, at the price I want to sell it to them, to make my business viable?

The good news is that many resources are available to help you, much of them free. Here are some great ways to research your idea:

- ✔ **Go to the library.** Visit the Business and Intellectual Property Centre (BIPC) at the British Library (www.bl.uk/bipc) to find an enormous amount of resources available. You can find market-research reports giving details on the major players in a market, the size of their market share, the sector's potential for growth and so on.

   You can book a free 30-minute session with a BIPC adviser who can show you how to access all the free data and market reports in the Library. The Business and IP centre also runs free events and workshops for start-ups. City Business Library (www.cityoflondon.gov.uk) is another useful place to visit, offering free information and free workshops for entrepreneurs and start-ups.

   If you're unable to get to London, other libraries with good business resource centres include Norfolk and Norwich Millennium Library, Birmingham Central Library, Manchester Central Library, Scotbis at the National Library of Scotland in Edinburgh, Leeds Central Library and Belfast Central Library. And make the most of your local library, which may hold back issues of trade magazines for your industry.

✔ **Find out what customers are looking for online.** Google's free search keyword tool (go to www.google.com/adwords and click on 'Reporting and tools') tells you how many people were using particular search terms to find things on the Internet in the past month. Typing in the phrase 'plastic garden sheds', for example, reveals that in an average month over the past year 5,400 people in the UK were looking for these, compared with 3,600 people who were looking for wooden garden sheds.

✔ **Research your competitors.** Search the Internet for firms already doing what you want to do. Remember to search as if you were a customer rather than in the industry – for example, search for 'drain unblocking' rather than 'high-pressure jetting' because customers tend to use descriptive terms rather than industry jargon.

Scrutinise your competitors' websites, order their products, use their services. Look at how and where they sell their products and services and how much they charge. Search online for reviews of them and their products. Study their accounts – if they're a private company you can access a copy of their filed accounts on the Companies House website for a small fee (www.companieshouse.gov.uk). If they're a public company you can request a copy of their latest annual report (you may be able to download a copy from the company's website). Try to find out what your competitors do well, so you can do the same or better; and what they do badly, so you can do better. Try to find out what they've missed – whether in terms of products, market or geographical location – so you can fill the gaps.

✔ **Access free advice.** The government has a useful website at www.businesslink.gov.uk, providing free advice on every aspect of starting up a venture.

✔ **Ask potential customers for their views.** Go to where you think potential customers are most likely to be – in the gym, if you're creating a health drink for example, or in the playgroup, if you're creating a baby product – and chat to them. The research you gain can give you enough to either support or demolish your gut feeling. After that, you can start to get some quantitative research, by asking 100 people whether they'd buy your product and, crucially, how much they'd buy it for.

Research can be fun! When three friends from university wanted to find out what people thought of their pulped fruit drink they set up a stand at a local jazz festival and put two bins outside. Customers were asked to vote on whether the budding entrepreneurs should give up their jobs to make their drinks full-time by throwing their empty bottles into a bin marked 'yes' or a bin marked 'no'. By the end of the weekend the 'yes' bin was overflowing – and Innocent Drinks was born. The founders later sold a 58 per cent stake in the business to Coca-Cola for £95 million.

✔ **Find your gap.** Look at what other products or services are currently sold in the market you wish to enter and where your product or service might fit in. Are you aiming to be the cheapest, or the most expensive, or somewhere in between? Who will be above and below you in terms of price and quality? Draw up a mental picture of who your target customer is and how you can make your product most appealing to them. Think about who your customer will be; their age, gender, lifestyle, family situation, income, job, how often they'll buy your product and why.

✔ **Do it yourself.** Never employ an agency to do your market research for you, unless it really is the most basic kind, such as counting footfall. If you're trying to interpret what's going on through the conduit of someone else's experiences and impressions you can easily end up with a confusing and murky picture. You have to be out there yourself listening, talking, absorbing the mood and acting accordingly.

Never bring out a product before you find out for sure that your target market really wants it enough to pay for it. Otherwise you may waste far too much time and money, and delay your ability to create a positive cash flow while creating a negative perception of your company. Better to wait a few months to fully explore your customer needs and wants than to rush through a great idea that ends up going nowhere.

Finding Your Niche by Specialising

To attract customers, people need to know exactly what business you're in. Our advice is to find a business niche and specialise in it. An expert is worth a lot more to clients than someone without specific experience. Would you rather have your silk shirt cleaned by someone who has years of experience working with silk or by the local launderette? Chances are you're willing to pay more for someone who specialises in cleaning silk.

Being one in a million

In business, people want to work with people who know what they're doing. So you need to be one in a million, not one of a million, which often means you need to specialise.

Follow these five steps to find your business niche by specialising:

1. **Assess and outline your current expertise.**

2. **Identify your strengths and weaknesses.**

3. **Build on your strengths and fill in the gaps in your experience.** This might mean learning new skills, taking more qualifications or being formally assessed and accredited in certain areas.

4. **Think hard about your personal unique selling point (USP).** What do you do better than others, that people might be prepared to seek you out and pay you money for?

5. **Now look at the industry sector and market in which you have expertise.** Where are the gaps that you could fill? What customer needs aren't currently being met that you could provide?

As your expertise increases, you make yourself easier to market and so are able to make more money. As you develop and progress from a specialist to an expert to an authority, the greater your earning power becomes.

Carving out a niche

In most economies around the world, competition is a good thing. More competition is better for consumers, causing companies to push technology to the limits while reducing prices to gain advantage over other competitors. But although competition is almost always a certain win for consumers, it can mean big problems for the businesses that get caught up in it – especially small and home-based businesses.

Why? Because small and home-based businesses are often thinly capitalised; in other words, you don't have a lot of cash to spare, so your marketing budget, as well as your time, needs to be aimed well.

To avoid the problems that come with competition, carve out your own niche by providing your clients and customers with unique products and services that they can't obtain anywhere else.

Here are a number of tips for carving out a niche of your own:

- ✔ **Offer a product or service that no one else offers.** When Nick Grey sat down at a desk in the spare room of his home near Worcester and invented a cordless sweeper that could clean carpets without the need for electricity, he had no idea how successful it would become. But when he began selling it on a television shopping channel under the name Shark Sweeper, the impact was instant; customers loved it and the sweeper started flying off the shelves. Within months Grey was getting an income of £250,000 a month from his share of sales and he has since sold more than 20 million sweepers.

- ✔ **Specialise in only one business area or industry.** You can't be everything to everybody. Instead of spreading yourself too thinly with too many unrelated products and services, focus on the one or two kinds of products or services that you do best.

✔ **Serve an unserved market.** Believe it or not, not every market has yet been tapped by companies eager to sell their products. If you take the time to identify these markets and serve them, you can carve out a niche that others will be hard pressed to match. Chances are you'll find yourself with little or no competition for months or even years.

When you carve out a niche in the market, you're doing nothing more than getting in touch with your potential clients, and providing them with exactly the products and services they want and need. And when you offer that market something it really wants and needs, marketing your product and attracting customers becomes easy.

Marketing: Taking Different Roads to Meet Your Goals

The topic of marketing covers an incredibly broad spectrum of activities, all with one final goal in mind: to spur clients and customers to buy your products and services. When you start your home-based business, marketing should take up most of your time. After all, your business isn't going to get very far down the road until you start selling your products and generating the money you need to give it life (and to pay yourself for all your hard work). As you gain clients and customers – and start doing paid work – you can reduce the amount of time and money you devote to marketing, but never forget about it. When you own your own business and rely on it for your livelihood, it's important to keep a steady flow of new business in the pipeline, ready to pick up the slack as you complete your work for current clients. For most home-based business owners, making an ongoing commitment of at least 20 per cent of your time to marketing activities is about right.

For loads more in-depth advice about marketing, get your hands on *Small Business Marketing For Dummies* by Paul Lancaster (Wiley).

The good news is that you can promote your business in a variety of ways. If you decide to tackle even just a few of them, you can easily create a successful marketing campaign that can take your home-based business to the front of the pack. In the following sections, we show you some of the most popular and effective ways to do just that.

Four approaches to promoting your products and services

When you're promoting your products and services, you have an almost unlimited number of approaches to choose from. Each approach can be grouped within the following four categories:

✔ **Personal contact.** Whether knocking on your prospective customer's door to pitch your product's advantages face to face, cold-calling on the phone or buttonholing an acquaintance in the local supermarket, when you market your products directly to your customers one-on-one, you're making personal contact. If you have a great personality (always a plus when you're trying to sell something), if your product is complex or if your product is best demonstrated live and in person (like that incredible kitchen knife that slices thick parsnips and squashes with ease), personal contact is definitely the way to go.

✔ **Contact through others.** Although you can personally sell only a finite number of products or services – after all, you only have 24 hours in a day – you can leverage your efforts and sell far more by selling through others. Selling through others involves creating a buzz around your products and services by getting people to talk about them (through word of mouth or through your promotional efforts), obtaining referrals from satisfied customers and generating interest in the media.

✔ **Written communication.** Brochures, advertisements, newsletters, targeted email messages, sales letters, proposals and thank-you notes are all different ways of using the power of the written word to sell your products and services. If you're not comfortable selling your company's products and services personally, or if you'd have difficulty giving your potential customers samples of your products and services (for example, giving a potential customer a sample of your car-cleaning services without actually cleaning a car), try selling your product through written communication. Again, properly used, written communication can leverage your own direct-selling efforts and generate far more leads and sales than personal contact alone.

✔ **Proof of what you can do.** Sometimes a demonstration of a product or service can spark sales like nothing else. Product samples, demonstration video clips on your website, house parties, product displays, photos and trial subscriptions are all ways of showing what you and your business can do for your clients-to-be. When your prospective customers want to try your product before they buy it, or if you know that after your customers have a chance to actually use your products or services they'll be hooked, showing them what you can do with proof of your services is the right approach.

Which approach works best for you depends on a variety of factors, including the nature of your business, the likes and dislikes of your typical customer, your customers' buying habits and the complexity of your product or service. Make sure you keep each of these considerations in mind as you decide which approach to take in marketing your own products and services.

Generating word of mouth

Word of mouth means getting people to talk about you, your company and its products and services in a positive light. Of course, the more people talk, the better your company looks as a result and the better it is for your business. That's exactly why any good promotional campaign starts off with a heavy emphasis on generating positive word-of-mouth excitement. There's nothing like a little bit of buzz to get your sales to take off.

Here are some of the best ways to get people talking about your business:

- ✔ **Networking.** Everyone has a circle of friends and acquaintances – both in their work and personal lives. Or you may belong to a sports club, or a community service organisation such as Rotary or Lions Club. Your networks of friends and acquaintances are probably the first and best places to start a word-of-mouth campaign for promoting your business. They know you, they like you (at least, we hope so) and they're likely to be willing to tell *their* friends and acquaintances about you (who will then tell others, and on and on). Your local chamber of commerce is a great way to network with other local businesspeople. Most sponsor a variety of networking events and lunches specifically geared to support your networking efforts (www.britishchambers.org.uk).

- ✔ **Volunteering.** Why not give something back to your neighbourhood by offering some of your products or services for no charge to support a good cause? If you have a baking business you could provide cupcakes to sell at the local church fete; if you have a beauty treatment business you could offer a manicure or pedicure as a prize in the school fair raffle.

- ✔ **Offering sponsorships.** Sponsoring a kids' football team, local charity, summer fete or other special event can be another good way to generate word-of-mouth promotional opportunities. Be careful, though, that you're not just one sponsor lost in a flood of others – if you are, your message will be ineffective. Choose your opportunities carefully so that your business is featured and particularly noticeable to your target audience.

- ✔ **Using business cards and letterheads.** These basic pieces of stationery are the mainstays of most businesses' promotional efforts and are passed around between those needing and those recommending you. Your letterhead and business cards can convey a lot of information to your prospective clients and customers and get people talking about your business. Invest a few pounds in a professional logo design to make a great first impression on your prospects while conveying the right kind of message to your current customers and clients.

Word of mouth costs your business little, but the payoff can be great. Look for opportunities to generate a buzz about your business wherever and whenever you can. If people aren't talking about your business, you can be sure they aren't buying from it, either!

Acquiring referrals

Getting *referrals* – when people you know direct clients and acquaintances to your business – is the number-one way that many home-based businesses obtain new business. Although current clients are your bread and butter, not to mention the best possible sources for vital repeat business, new clients provide opportunities to grow your business while covering financial short-falls if current customers decide to shop elsewhere – or not shop at all.

Referrals are extremely powerful because when referred customers come to you, they've already been sold on your business and your products or services. You've already got a piece of their goodwill – which is an extremely valuable commodity to have in your business dealings. Here are some other advantages:

- ✔ **Referrals are less expensive than many other kinds of marketing.** No costly newspaper adverts to run and no extravagant mail-order campaign to launch. Referrals cost little or no money to obtain. And maintaining a favourable relationship with the people who give you referrals means simply doing good work for them and letting them know from time to time that you appreciate their business (perhaps with a discount on your products or services, a small gift or some other token of your appreciation).

- ✔ **Referred customers trust you.** People turn to their trusted friends and business acquaintances for advice on whom to employ for a particular job or to provide a particular product. As the saying goes, you have only one chance to make a first impression. When someone recommends you, you've already made a positive first impression with your client-to-be.

- ✔ **Referred customers are ready to buy from you.** When people ask their friends and business acquaintances for referrals, they're ready to buy. People wouldn't ask if they weren't. And because people trust the opinion of those they ask, most people go no further in their search for sources than the person or business recommended to them.

Identifying potential referrals

So where do you find referrals? Here are the most common places:

- ✔ **Family and friends.** If you don't yet have current clients, family and friends are a great place to start for getting referrals. Make sure that everyone you personally know is familiar with your new venture – what it is and what you do – and knows that you're looking for customers to help get it off the ground. Most will be more than happy to help.

- ✔ **Current clients.** If you're doing good work for your current clients (and of course you are!), they'll refer friends and business acquaintances to you when asked for recommendations. Just make sure you don't let your work with your current clients suffer as you take on new work – you need to keep a very fine balance in your business between delivering on your current work and developing new work.

To help ensure that your clients want to share you with others (don't laugh; some may want to keep you all to themselves), make sure you meaningfully thank them for the referrals they make and consider providing additional incentives for making more in future. Examples of incentives depend on the kind of business you have but might include a discount on their next order or a free additional service.

✔ **Business associates.** Suppliers and other non-client business associates can be another rich source of referrals. If you have a good reputation in your field, and if they like you, they'll gladly tell their business associates about you. Of course, they'll be equally happy if you send some business their way, too.

✔ **Other home-based businesses.** Many home-based businesses are one-person operations and, as such, can have a hard time dealing with the inevitable business peaks and troughs. Sometimes work is plentiful, sometimes not. In those times when another home-based business is overwhelmed, a good option is to farm the extra work out to a trusted and proven company – yours. Why not become the company of choice for other home-based businesses in your industry?

The best way to approach other businesses is in person at local business networking events.

✔ **Web-based referral services.** Some businesses can benefit from web-based referral services. Many of these services are run by professional or trade associations. Others are independent, such as Yelp (`www.yelp.co.uk`).

Getting referrals for your business

Okay, now that you know where to find your referrals, exactly how are you supposed to get them? The best way is simply to ask. When you do good work for clients, thank them for choosing you and let them know that referrals are welcome and appreciated. The following is a list of five other great ways to get referrals:

✔ **Do great work.** By far the best way to get great referrals is to do great work. People are proud of themselves when they find businesses that provide them with above-average services and products, and they want to tell others of their good fortune (and their good business sense). Do great work, and your clients and customers will be the best marketing tools you could ask for.

✔ **Create a mailing list.** A mailing list of all your referrals can be a powerful tool in your promotional efforts. Because they already like you and your business, your referrals generally welcome hearing from you on an ongoing basis. A variety of great Internet email-based services enable you to send periodic newsletters to your referrals for a nominal fee (or perhaps even for free if you're a small user). Some of the most popular services include:

- iContact (www.icontact.com)

- Campaign Monitor (www.campaignmonitor.com)

- Constant Contact (www.constantcontact.com)

- MailChimp (www.mailchimp.com)

With just one click, your message is sent to your entire mailing list – whether it consists of one person or a thousand – in a matter of seconds. Your clients can opt into and out of your mailing list easily, and with the barest minimum of effort or fuss. You can also track a variety of statistics if you like, such as actual click-throughs, messages sent, forwarded, bounced and delivered, and unsubscribed emails. Search for 'email marketing' at www.dummies.com for articles and cheat sheets to help you.

✔ **Keep your mailing list informed.** Many home-based business owners have discovered the value of keeping their referrals up to date with the latest news about their products and services. Not only do past and present clients enjoy reading such stories, but they also really enjoy reading about themselves. Make a point of playing up customer success stories as much as possible (with their permission of course!).

✔ **Always send a thank-you note.** People appreciate it when you take the time to thank them for sending you referrals. Whenever a new customer is referred to you, make a point of immediately thanking the referrer personally, perhaps by sending them a handwritten thank-you note, or by sending them a small gift or discount voucher for your client's next purchase. People remember gestures like this and are much more likely to be inclined to refer more customers to you in the future.

✔ **Make referrals yourself.** As your business grows, you soon find that people come to you seeking referrals. Pick out several high-quality and trusted companies to use for referrals and make sure you let their owners know when you've sent a client their way. Not only will your clients be thankful for the referral, but the companies to which you make referrals are also more likely to make referrals to you. And don't forget to post positive reviews on social networking business review sites, such as Yelp (www.yelp.co.uk) and TripAdvisor (www.tripadvisor.co.uk).

Making use of public relations

In general, *public relations* (PR) means the release of information to the general public to favourably influence its opinion about you, your business or your products and services. Because of the nature of PR – and the potential for information to be broadcast over a wide area through print or electronic media – its successful execution can lead to your message being communicated to an amazing number of people. If you handle your own public relations, the cost is minimal. If you farm it out to a consultant or PR firm, expect to pay upwards of £2,000 a month for their services.

Here are some of the most common – and effective – forms of PR:

- ✔ **Publicity (newspapers, magazines, Internet and other media).** Have you ever seen a newspaper article about some fantastic new local business or a special-interest TV news story about the 'latest and greatest' home-based business opportunity? It's no accident that particular piece of news made it to your eyes and ears – the business being highlighted is likely to have spent money on hiring a PR firm to make sure it showed up on the media radar screen. The media thrive on interesting stories, especially human-interest ones with uplifting messages. By creating an interesting and positive story around your business – and getting it in front of the media – you can generate the kind of publicity you seek, attracting potential clients and customers in the process.

  When Rob Law appeared on the television show *Dragons' Den* seeking investment for his ride-on suitcases for children, called Trunkis, he didn't get the money he wanted after one of the judges pulled a strap and it broke. However, viewers loved the product so much that monthly sales of his suitcases trebled after the programme aired.

- ✔ **Press releases.** *Press releases* are brief summaries of company news that are specifically targeted at the media. The hope is that newspapers, magazines, radio, television and other media outlets will find the press release newsworthy and give it exposure. The good news is that if the media pick up on your press release and publicise it, you'll get wide distribution for free. To have the best chance of gaining the kind of reaction you seek from the media, make sure your news release is tailored to the particular interests of the media outlet you seek. A pitch to *The Sunday Times,* for example, is going to be quite different from a pitch to a local newspaper, which will be different again from a pitch written for a breakfast radio show.

- ✔ **Blog entries.** You can submit information about your business to other people's blogs that relate to your market. To build and keep traffic, blog sites need to update their content daily, so they usually welcome content.

- ✔ **Letters to the editor.** Anyone can write a letter to the editor of a newspaper or magazine about almost any topic. Doing so is easy and offers a unique way to get your message in front of thousands of readers at a price that's hard to beat: the price of a stamp (or nothing, if you send an email). If, for example, you own a home-based business that specialises in home security systems (alarms, deadbolt locks and so on), you can comment on a recent article about a rise in crime rates while throwing in a plug for the products and services that your company happens to sell.

✔ **Speeches.** Have you ever thought about making a speech to a local service club – say, a Rotary or Lions Club – or to local business organisations? All kinds of business associations, clubs and other organisations exist in every city, and they tend to have lots of meetings. Guess what every organisation needs for every meeting? A speaker. Whether you speak to your local chamber of commerce or your local industry trade association, you have a great opportunity to promote yourself and your company by sharing your expertise with others. You can also consider organisations such as the Women's Institute (WI). And you may just get a free lunch or dinner out of it, too.

Writing a press release

A press release is a standardised and recognised way of communicating with journalists. Its purpose is to tell journalists something newsworthy and interesting. Follow these dos and don'ts when crafting your press release:

✔ Do keep your press release short, clear and straightforward. Provide some context so the journalist can understand why it's relevant. Journalists receive dozens of press releases every day so yours needs to get the message across instantly.

✔ Don't tenuously link the launch of your product to a current trend or phrase if there's no obvious connection – this will backfire and make you and your product look silly.

✔ Do include a two or three-sentence quote from the most senior person at the company (probably yourself, as founder). The quote needs to provide a comment on the information already provided and illuminate what you're announcing without being too self-serving. Ensure each sentence of the quote makes sense on its own so that journalists can use just one or two lines from it if they want to.

✔ Do back up your claims with statistics and express figures as both percentages and fractions so journalists don't have to work it out for themselves; for example, 'Four-fifths (80 per cent) of the small firms surveyed said they would use the service again'.

✔ Don't use overblown language, exaggerate, twist the facts or use exclamation marks. An interesting newsworthy story doesn't need embellishment, and a poor story doesn't become a good one simply by using the word 'groundbreaking'.

✔ Do keep your press release to one side of A4. Journalists won't read page 2.

✔ Date your press release very clearly at the top, with an 'embargoed until' date if you don't want it to be written about until a certain date.

✔ Provide clear contact details at the end, including your full name and title, mobile number, email address and an out-of-hours number. Ideally include the details of a back-up person, listed second, in case the journalist can't get hold of you.

Take a look at www.press-release-writing.com, which provides 40 free guides on a range of PR topics, as well as templates to help you craft your press release.

✔ **Seminars.** Seminars are a way to generate new customers and clients. Home-based financial planners, for example, often use seminars to generate business. Here's how they work: you send out announcements for a free seminar, usually held at a nice local hotel, to prospective customers and possible referral sources. Rent out a meeting room at the hotel and arrange for the seminar to be catered with light refreshments. During the course of the seminar, you provide attendees with a lot of usable information, and pass out brochures, pamphlets and other promotional material – all emblazoned with your company's name and contact information. After the seminar, guess who the attendees' first choice is whenever they have questions about the subject matter of the seminar or need help setting up their own personal financial plan?

One of the great things about public relations is that if you have a bit of time to spend, you can generate your own PR materials and make your own contacts. And the more PR work you do, the better you'll get at it. Not only do you become more confident in your abilities and savvy in how the system works, but you also make contacts in the media and in your community that you can keep coming back to.

Collaborating without getting lost

Q: We're a new small home business. We offer public relations, marketing and fundraising. A local advertising agency has outsourced several small jobs to us and now the owner wants to include our names on his marketing materials, but doesn't want to use our company name. Is this standard business practice? It seems like he's using our services to market his business.

A: Business-to-business collaboration is one of the major trends increasingly common among small businesses today. Many small business owners team up in some way with other small businesses and even more are likely to do so in the future.

In your situation, the advertising executive evidently believes that including your names and expertise on his marketing materials will help him get more business. For you, this arrangement could mean an inflow of new business with no marketing costs. The problem for you though is that this arrangement does absolutely nothing

to promote your own business brand or identity, and implies that you and your colleagues work for him. You need to find an arrangement that you are happy with or the relationship between your business and his business will ultimately founder.

Why not suggest a reciprocal arrangement, whereby he mentions the name of your business as a partner organisation on his marketing material and in return you mention the name of his business as a partner organisation on your own business marketing material? That way both businesses can potentially bring in work that could benefit the other and you both help each other grow. If you prefer, you could both agree to pay a referral fee for any business that comes in as a result of the marketing material. Coming to an arrangement that both sides are happy with is important, otherwise resentment will fester and overshadow any goodwill generated.

Taking advantage of direct marketing

Direct marketing means making direct contact with potential clients, most often by mailing or emailing them promotional messages. However you do it, the point is to get your message squarely in front of a decision-maker in a way that captures their interest in just a few short seconds. Any longer and your prospective client will probably throw your message in the bin – at no small expense to you and your business. Here are just a few ways to direct market:

✔ **Direct mail.** Although direct mail – also known as junk mail – can be a major headache for many who receive it, when it's targeted precisely to potential customers and clients, it can be a cost-effective way of getting your message in front of the people most likely to buy your products and services. You can target your prospective customers very precisely by buying mailing lists of people within specific demographic groups. Do you want to reach human resources managers only? No problem. People who live within a particular postcode? Easy. People who recently bought a house? Piece of cake. For a fairly reasonable fee, you can buy hundreds or even thousands of up-to-date addresses for exactly the kind of people you want to reach with your message. Regardless of how much people complain about receiving direct-mail solicitations, enough people usually respond to make direct mail worthwhile. For more information on direct-mail marketing, check out the Direct Marketing Association website (www.dma.org.uk).

✔ **Circulars and flyers.** With a computer and a printer or photocopier, you can create all the circulars and flyers you could ever want, make thousands of copies and blanket your clients-to-be with them. Drop them in your direct-mail envelopes, deliver them around your local neighbourhood and put them up on noticeboards in public places. With a little practice, you can create circulars and flyers in minutes, and at little cost. You probably won't get as good a response as you would from a direct-mail campaign, but it's certainly worth a try.

✔ **Giveaways and competitions.** One of the tried-and-tested methods of attracting the attention of potential clients is to give something away – the more attractive the prize, the more attention you'll get. And that's really the whole point of promoting your business: to attract your potential clients' attention long enough to show them the benefits of your products and services. Advertise your giveaway or competition on your flyer.

✔ **Incentives.** Businesses commonly use incentives to get prospective clients and customers to buy. Whether you offer two for the price of one or give a discount voucher offering 10 per cent off the next purchase, incentives are a standard tool in the marketing campaigns of many regular businesses, and they work just as well for home-based businesses.

✔ **Newsletters.** If you're ready to get a bit more sophisticated in your direct-marketing efforts, consider creating a newsletter. Businesses create newsletters to provide customers and clients with value-added tools and information, while also serving as a platform for promoting the company's products and services. If you run a pet-sitting business from your home, you can create a one- or two-page newsletter with the latest trends in pet care, along with plugs for your business. If you're a cook who specialises in wedding cakes, you can keep your clients up to date on the latest developments in the cake-decorating field. Sending your newsletter by email lowers your costs and time investment.

If you have neither the time nor inclination to create a quality newsletter yourself, consider hiring a home-based desktop-publishing professional to do it for you.

You can spend as little or as much as you want on direct marketing, but the results you get will be directly proportional to the amount of money and effort you put into preparing your direct-marketing pieces and precisely selecting the individuals who receive your message. Investing some quality time and money now pays off later.

Investing in advertising

When many people think about marketing, they're thinking about advertising. Advertising your products and services can be an effective way to get the word out, but it can also be expensive (and, frankly, a waste of money for many home-based businesses). The key is to make sure that your advertisements are specifically targeted and that you advertise in places where your potential clients are most likely to read or hear your message. Consider advertising in the following places:

✔ **Yellow Pages.** For many businesses, running a Yellow Pages advertisement is still a really good way of bringing in customers. The large directories are still distributed free around the country. It can be expensive – in the thousands of pounds for a large advert – but effective, because even though business is moving increasingly online, many people still turn to the Yellow Pages first to find a plumber, hairdresser or local gardening business. And of course also consider advertising in the Yellow Pages' online edition, Yell.com (www.yell.com).

✔ **Business directories.** Business directories, such as Thomson Local are another good way to get the word out about your company, as long as your potential clients and customers are likely to see your listing. Most directories are available in printed form, but an increasing number are now just on the Internet. With just a few mouse clicks, your clients-to-be can find out more about your company and discover what it has to offer them.

✔ **Website.** Creating a website and/or blog to market your business and its products and services is a must for most businesses today, whether small or large. The good news is that starting up and maintaining a website is easier and less expensive than ever. (See the 'Going hi-tech with websites, blogs and e-commerce' section later in this chapter and Chapter 11 for more information.)

✔ **Website advertisements.** Although banner advertisements have long been the standard method for advertising businesses on the Internet, another increasingly popular way of getting your message across online is targeted advertising on search engines such as Google (in Google's case, called AdWords) that's geared to specific keyword searches. This is also known as search engine marketing (SEM) or pay-per-click (PPC). If you're a home-based plumber, for example, you can arrange for your business to show up at the top of the list whenever someone does a keyword search for *tap repair*. You don't pay unless the person doing the searching clicks on your listing. Relative to print, radio and TV ads, website advertisements are a bargain. Better yet is getting links to your site from as many other high-traffic websites as you can. Head to Chapter 11 for more about pay-per-click.

Going hi-tech with websites, blogs and e-commerce

More businesses than ever are moving to establish a presence on the Internet, and being e-commerce-capable is rapidly becoming the standard worldwide. Despite the challenges facing a business that markets itself on the web (getting your site noticed in a sea of millions is just one challenge), having a website or blog is still a great idea for many home-based businesses; without one your business is invisible. If your business doesn't yet have its own website, you need to get one – fast. Building and maintaining a website or blog is now an essential part of any organisation's marketing plan. It's just as important as printing brochures, placing adverts in targeted publications, networking with potential clients and performing other, more traditional marketing activities.

Saying 'I do' to Google AdWords

Rob Hill is the founder of The Eventa Group, an online business which provides stag and hen weekends and holidays through the brands The Stag Company and Hen Heaven. Hill decided that most people looking for this type of holiday would begin by searching online, so right from the start he focused all of his efforts on developing search engine optimisation (SEO) (turn to Chapter 11 for more on SEO) and pay-per-click Google AdWords (head to Chapter 11 for more on these strategies). Within three weeks of starting up his home business, he got his first booking via Google AdWords worth £1,500 and his firm, based in Brighton, now has a turnover of £6.9 million and employs 60 people.

At its heart, a company website or blog is the online equivalent of a glossy, full-colour brochure – with a twist: the website is available to potential clients instantly, anywhere in the world, at any time, day or night. It can be interactive (as in the case of a blog, where you can post your thoughts any time and visitors can post their responses), and it enables you to respond to visitor queries, communicate with clients in real time through online chats and message forums, and provide customers with a place to research your products – and buy them.

ASK THE EXPERTS

Growing a repair business

Q: I do carpentry and household repairs, and although I have some business, it's just not enough. I don't have any money left to do the kind of advertising I know I should. I'm not much of a salesman. Is my business doomed? Is there hope for me?

A: Yes, there's hope. Many people don't have much sales and marketing experience before starting their first home business and can feel quite overwhelmed by the relentless chore of finding enough business. Surveys show that getting business remains the number-one concern of small and home-based business owners year after year.

Advertising is expensive because, to be effective, it must appear again and again in publications where your targeted customers are looking when they need your services. Fortunately a growing number of low-cost ways to advertise your business exist online. Firstly, check out www.thebestof.co.uk, a regional business directory, and also find out if your local neighbourhood has a business directory (such as the one in Balham, south-west London: www.balham.com). Also look at a low-cost listing on Gumtree (www.gumtree.com) and Craigslist (www.craigslist.co.uk). If you can afford it, taking out an enhanced listing in the Yellow Pages and its online equivalent Yell.com (www.yell.com) is a good investment. Get yourself listed on Checkatrade (www.checkatrade.com), which lists over 10,000 vetted tradespeople and is hugely popular with

the public. In addition, you can actively market yourself in several other low-cost ways, including the following:

- ✔ **Build a list of all the people who have regular interaction with potential customers who want and need services like yours right now – not 'one day'.** For example, estate agents who have just sold new homes, or who have clients trying to sell a home but need to make improvements to get their asking price, may fill the bill. Or how about landlords who need to freshen up the flats they let out in between tenancies? Contact these people by phone or in person, and let them know about you and your service. You aren't selling when you contact them; you're just getting acquainted and making sure they know how to reach you.

- ✔ **Put these people's names and contact details into a database and send them something monthly.** Consider, for example, a tips newsletter, a postcard about a special offer, or a news clipping related to home improvements.

- ✔ **Offer mini-workshops or seminars at hardware and DIY shops on home improvements.** You may be surprised by how many people realise they need help after hearing from you – especially if your mini-workshops or seminars are free.

- ✔ **Arrange to leave a flyer or newsletter at hardware shops for buyers to pick up.**

ASK THE EXPERTS

Is creating a website a good idea?

Q: I'm a photographer and sell most of my work through art fairs. Recently, more and more people are asking me if I have a website. I don't, but I'm starting to wonder if I should. What would the advantages really be, and would they be worth both the time and the money?

A: Having a website for any kind of business is common today. Most home-based businesses have websites, and the numbers are growing fast, because customers increasingly find the products and services they need by looking online, and if your business isn't on there, then they simply won't find you. All kinds of home-based businesses from crafts to home maintenance services get a growing amount of their business via their websites.

Because photographs are visual, selling your work via a website is a natural fit. You can sell your images on your own website and use it as a way of keeping in contact with your customers and keeping them up to date with what your business is doing. Or to save you having to build a website from scratch, several companies now offer website templates specifically designed for photographers who need a website to sell their work. You pay for the website by monthly subscription. Check out sites such as Luxipics (www.luxipics.com), Clikpic (www.clikpic.com) and Photoshelter (www.photoshelter.com).

However, you do need to be prepared to commit some time to regularly maintaining and updating your website. A web address that yields an error message or is obviously out of date works against you, particularly if you're using your site to attract photography clients. So if you're not ready for your own site, you can sell your images on such sites as Photobox Gallery (www.photoboxgallery.com), which displays your photos and takes a commission on sales.

Even if your business is a local one, a website or blog is important because:

- **It increasingly serves in place of a printed flyer or brochure – one you can update immediately.** A website or blog is a much faster and generally more convenient way for your potential customers to get information about your products and services. Instead of waiting to receive a brochure by post, or happen to come across a flyer, they can type in your business name and obtain the information they're looking for in seconds.

- **With the vast majority of homes and businesses having Internet access, increasingly people are going online to check out businesses they've heard about or been referred to.** If they can't find you online, you've lost their business. For this reason, using your business name as your website address is ideal, because it makes finding your business on the web as easy and intuitive as possible.

- **The web is becoming the new Yellow Pages.** Getting listed in search engines and exchanging links with sites that people are likely to turn to when looking for your kind of business is good business for you.

But what if you know nothing about creating a website or blog? How do you go about making one happen? Will you have to spend thousands of pounds to get your website up and running, or do you have more affordable options? We address these and other questions in detail in Chapter 11.

Developing a Marketing Plan – Now!

Whenever you want to achieve a measurable goal within a specific period of time, you greatly enhance your chances of doing so by having a plan. Plans make your goals real: they organise and prioritise your actions, and they tell you how close you are to achieving your goals.

A *marketing plan* summarises all your marketing goals and strategies, along with the actual methods you can use to achieve them, and states milestones and deadlines for achieving your goals. A marketing plan is not the same as a business plan, which takes a much broader look at your business goals and plans. In essence, a marketing plan answers the following questions:

✔ Who are your target customers and clients?

✔ What are your unique product or service attributes and advantages in the marketplace?

✔ Where will you focus your marketing efforts?

✔ When will you implement each step in your marketing plan?

✔ How much revenue do you expect your marketing plan to generate, and how much will it cost you to generate that level of sales?

If you've read through some of the earlier sections of this chapter, you're probably already thinking of lots of ways to start marketing your products and services. You may be ready to start up a website, seek referrals or create an email newsletter for your current customers and clients.

You can make your marketing plan as simple or as complex as you want. If you're just starting, a one-page or even a one-paragraph plan may be just right. As your company gets bigger, you may see benefits in expanding your plan to meet its growing needs.

The following sections review the five key parts of a good marketing plan.

Part 1: Overview

Also known as an *executive summary,* the *marketing plan overview* provides a glimpse of your overall plan without bogging yourself down in the details that are presented later in the document. The overview gives a pretty good idea about your overall marketing strategy, market focus, product focus and the tactics you plan to put into effect. *Projected revenues* – the estimated amount of money you intend to bring into the business during the period of the plan, as well as the budget required to achieve that level of sales – are also important parts of the marketing plan overview.

Part 2: Marketing objectives

Marketing goals and objectives define the targets that you hope to achieve in your marketing efforts. Your goals may be modest (to increase sales by 10 per cent a year for the next three years, for example) or quite ambitious (say, to be the company of choice whenever anyone in the UK needs a dog groomed).

This section of the marketing plan should, at a minimum, include:

- An **overall objective** for your marketing efforts (for example, to become the preferred source of Internet solutions for dentists).

- Several **specific marketing objectives**, such as units sold, *market share* (the percentage of the overall market that your company commands) or distribution channels (planning that 25 per cent of your sales will be through Tesco supermarkets, for example).

- Basic **financial objectives**, such as total sales and profit for the year.

Part 3: Situation analysis

This part of the marketing plan reveals what's going on in the marketplace: who your competition is, which products are similar to yours, what their relative success is, what the market trends are and so on. The idea is to develop a good understanding of your customer base, its needs and wants, and your strengths and weaknesses relative to the competition. Make sure you include the following:

- **A summary of the *demographics* (the characteristics of a population, such as age, gender, income and so on) and economic, technological and social trends that affect your customers.** You can get this information through the Internet or the reference section of your public library.

- **A list of your key competitors, including their strengths, weaknesses, products and services, market share and other key information.** See Chapter 7 for how best to collect this kind of information.

- **A brief description of your target customer, as well as his or her wants and needs.** You need to know your customer better than you know the back of your hand!

- ✔ **A summary of your key products and services.** This summary needs to include a list of your product's advantages and disadvantages versus those of the competition.

- ✔ **A discussion of your current distribution channels (if any).** This discussion needs to address how they help or hinder the product marketing process.

Part 4: Marketing strategies

For every key marketing objective listed in your plan (see the 'Part 2: Marketing objectives' section), include one or more marketing strategies for achieving it. Include a minimum of the following:

- ✔ **Specific features of your products and services that you can use to help you market them, such as convenience, speed, ease of use and so on.** Consider why people will buy your products and services instead of someone else's.

- ✔ **A pricing strategy for your products and services.** To find out more about the fine art of product pricing, check out Chapter 7.

- ✔ **Specific strategies to promote your products.** For ideas on promoting your products, see the 'Marketing: Taking Different Roads to Meet Your Goals' section.

- ✔ **Specific strategies for getting your products and services into the hands of your customers and clients.** These strategies include using e-commerce and developing relationships with distributors, for example.

Part 5: Financials

This part of the marketing plan takes all the words in the previous sections and turns them into numbers – specifically, pounds and pennies. An annual marketing plan gives financial information for an entire year, perhaps broken down into months or quarters. Make sure you include the following:

- ✔ **Detailed projections of anticipated revenues and percentage growth (or decline) – by product or service – from the previous period.** For example, you may anticipate total revenues of £30,000 for the year, growing at a rate of about 3 per cent per month.

- ✔ **Detailed projections of expenses required to obtain the projected revenues.** For example, you need to account for expenses such as petrol, phone and broadband fees, stationery, post and packaging and perhaps attending industry conferences.

Putting an idea into action

Q: I've drawn lots of sketches of jeans and now I'm satisfied with a design I think the public would rush to buy. How do I proceed with manufacturing and finding a buyer?

A: Some business experts may view the idea of a solo novice designer like yourself going head to head in a highly competitive field of giants like Levi's and Lee to be a pipe dream. But we've seen too many people defy the odds to discourage you from proceeding if you're sufficiently passionate, committed and determined. The novice designers we've seen succeed have done so in two ways: by carving out a highly specific niche, such as designing specialised clothing for yoga devotees, pregnant women or people with physical disabilities; or, for a mainstream item like jeans, by starting small and building up an enthusiastic following for a unique design that makes their line desirable to sales reps and retail stores.

So before leaping into mass production here or abroad, we suggest that you offer your jeans directly to what you hope will be a mad rush of keen buyers by making (or employing someone to make) several pairs and selling them yourself. You can do this by hiring a stall at a street market or craft fair, or by placing them in a few select boutiques. After your jeans begin selling rapidly and attracting growing numbers of customers, you can arrange for mass production and contact reps or buyers – if they haven't sought you out already.

You can contact reps in the UK and Ireland through the Manufacturers' Agents' Association (www.themaa.co.uk).

When putting your marketing plan into action, make sure you're very focused about bringing in enough new customers into the business to grow it to where you want it to be. If you have little or no business yet, you need to pursue several different avenues for reaching prospective clients on a daily basis, initiating contact and following them through. If you have some work but need more, you need to be doing this on a weekly basis. If you have enough business but want to ensure you sustain this level of activity, you should be trying to reach new customers on a monthly basis.

Chapter 5

Creating a Sustainable Income in Challenging Times

Starting a new home-based business doesn't come with any guarantees that it will succeed. No matter how many hours you put into it or how much money you throw at it, if you don't have the right business idea at the right time, for the right customers at the right price, it may not become a sustainable source of income for you over the long run – it's that simple.

The trick is to come up with a business idea that matches your passion with the realities of the marketplace.

In this chapter, with both past and recent history in mind, we identify home businesses you can start and do well with during an economic downturn, as well as those that do better in good economic times – when people are earning enough money to buy creative and everyday products and services from others instead of doing without or making or doing them for themselves. We also take a look at a few businesses that can survive both good and bad economies.

No matter what the economic environment may be, you can find plenty of home-based business opportunities out there that match your passion with an income that can sustain you and your family for as long as you like. We hope this chapter inspires you!

Recognising that People Behave Differently in Bad Times

What people will pay for and how much they'll pay for it varies according to both their own personal economic situation and the state of the economy as a whole. For example, in bad times, most people buy more basic goods and services but less of everything else. Sales of premium-quality items and services like holidays and meals out at restaurants go down with the economy, as do everyday expenditures on haircuts and petrol. The number of discount vouchers used and everyday value items bought, however, goes up.

Still you may ask, 'Is an economic downturn really the time to start a home business?' The answer may surprise you because it's 'yes'. First, consider past experience. Burger King, FedEx and Microsoft were all started in tough economic times. James Dyson launched his vacuum company in the downturn of the early 1990s. Rowan Gormley co-founded online wine retailer Naked Wines in 2008, just as the current collapse started, and is still going from strength to strength.

So what is it about a downturn that makes the creation of new and successful companies possible? First, such company start-ups have to consciously make cost-effective decisions, and be innovative in their products and processes. Second, many of their competitors may have disappeared. Third, you can acquire technology at low prices during economic downturns, which lowers the overall cost of getting a business under way.

People today are having to relearn a life lesson that their grandparents and great-grandparents learnt long ago – that they can't always count on a growing economy. Yes, everyone hopes the economy will do well, but with competition from countries like China (already number one in car sales), India, Brazil and Russia, the future will most definitely be different from the past. Whether the economy goes up as fast as it went down or continues to slide, you need to start a business that can ride the waves of the economy.

Identifying Businesses That Work Well in a Low-Growth Economic Climate

The economy naturally cycles between boom and bust – it always has and it always will. Regardless of what kind of economy you find yourself in when you read this book, however, you can find plenty of business opportunities that work in any kind of market. In this section, we focus on the opportunities that are particularly effective during low-growth economic times. For more examples of great home-based businesses that last, make sure you check out Chapter 15.

Helping others reduce and reuse

Tough times bring a variety of diverse business opportunities out of the woodwork, especially businesses that focus on helping people become more resourceful and environmentally friendly in their lifestyles and homes. Some of the best and fastest growing of these opportunities include the following:

- ✔ **Environmental remediation or clean-up.** Problems like mould, leaks, lead paint, asbestos, moisture, radon, contaminated soil and buried hazardous waste demand attention. Home and building owners may discover such problems themselves, or the issues may turn up in the environmental assessments that most domestic and commercial property transactions now involve. For this reason, the need for environmental remediation and clean-up businesses is always present. People in the environmental remediation business assess the nature and extent of certain environmental risks on homes and other buildings and then get their hands dirty cleaning up the less-than-hospitable environments. Check out the Remediation and Environment Directory (www.remediation.co.uk) for examples of what kind of services businesses can offer. The Environmental Protection Agency (www.environment-agency.org.uk) and Public Health England (www.hpa.org.uk) are also useful resources.

- ✔ **Environmentally friendly services.** Businesses providing environmentally friendly services are in demand, and the consequences of climate change and energy costs will continue to spur their growth even more. Dozens of different ways exist to tap in to this demand, including businesses that provide bicycle commuters with a place to store their bikes, environmentally friendly holidays that use low-energy travel and respect the communities they visit, environmentally friendly burials that use cardboard coffins – the list is potentially endless.

- ✔ **Home extensions.** The most active market for people in construction in a low-growth economy is converting or extending people's homes. That's because when economics require people to stay where they are, instead of moving up, they extend or convert what they currently have. This typically involves adding extra bedrooms or bathrooms to accommodate a growing family, digging out the basement to provide a play-room or extending the back of the house to create a new kitchen and family space. Older people, too, may need their homes altered to enable them to stay independent for longer, perhaps by adding an en-suite bathroom or by moving a bedroom downstairs. Check out the home building and renovating website www.homebuilding.co.uk for advice and articles on converting and extending homes.

- ✔ **Sewing.** When the economy is poor, people want to alter or repair their clothing rather than buy new stuff, so sewing is always a way to make money when times are tough. Sewing for money can take many forms. For example, many people want to sew their own clothing, so you can teach sewing in classes or private sessions. People with special physical problems, such as spine curvature, mastectomies, severe arthritis, preemies (premature babies) and wheelchair-bound people want clothing that's suited to their requirements. Other markets for custom sewing and design include making clothes for special occasions like weddings and parties, theatre costumes, uniforms and clothing for members of religious groups with rules for what they can wear. Check out The Sewing Forum, a UK-based online community (`www.thesewingforum.co.uk`) or iSew (`www.isew.co.uk`), an online resource for people who sew.

Fulfilling day-to-day business needs

The majority of businesses need support services of all kinds every day – regardless of whether the economy is good or bad. Hence, businesses that fulfil these day-to-day support needs for other businesses can expect not only to work well in bad economic times, but also to thrive in good ones. Here are some of the most lasting business-support opportunities:

- ✔ **Bookkeeping.** When times are tough, businesses frequently outsource bookkeeping to cut back on staffing costs, which increases the demand for independent bookkeepers. In addition to relieving business owners of the daily duties of handling the books, bookkeepers can also help identify errors that creep into accounting software. Some bookkeepers have other specialisations, too, such as payroll or accounts receivable. Still others serve only specific types of clients like chiropractors or restaurants. Check out the International Association of Bookkeepers (`www.iab.org.uk`) or the Institute of Certified Bookkeepers (`www.bookkeepers.org.uk`) for more information about becoming a professional bookkeeper.

- ✔ **Business support services.** The business support services field encompasses all forms of administrative work needed by small companies and professionals – anyone, in fact, who's without the time, desire or resources to do their own administrative work. Support services include preparing spreadsheets or databases; word processing; editing, formatting and proofreading documents; transcribing; drafting correspondence, proposals and reports; and much more. As with bookkeeping, businesses frequently outsource their support services to independent providers during economic downturns. Some people who provide support services to other businesses call themselves 'virtual assistants' because they can do much of their work electronically. Check out the UK Association of Virtual Assistants (`www.ukava.co.uk`) for advice on how to set yourself up as a virtual assistant.

- ✔ **Computer consulting:** Almost all businesses depend on technology, but many small business owners don't have the ability to deal with the problems of installation, upgrades, compatibility, repairs, malware, spyware, viruses, worms or the crisis of the company website going down. So computer consultants keep busy even during low-growth economic times. They may even get calls from business owners who are eligible for their manufacturer's technical support but need support faster than the manufacturer can provide. Resources for computer consultants include The Chartered Institute for IT (www.bcs.org) and the Institute of Consulting (www.iconsulting.org.uk).

✔ **Web services.** The Internet provides constant business opportunities for web designers, programmers, search engine optimisers, content writers, web promotion specialists and website developers. Everything you see and do on the Internet requires someone to design it and others to maintain it. The Internet holds countless opportunities for people interested in starting their own businesses. For example, you can specialise in a particular type of work, such as creating video content for social networking sites, or you can serve a single industry or profession. Check out Floodlight (www.floodlight.co.uk) for details of website and internet courses available near you.

Selling affordable luxuries

Although the overall luxury-goods market is one of the first things to feel the pain in low-growth economic times, *affordable* luxury goods and services become even more popular. After all, everyone likes to treat themselves to something nice every once in a while. Consider some of these business opportunities tailor-made for home-based businesses:

✔ **Direct selling.** Direct-selling organisations grow during economic downturns. Although the Internet – particularly social networking – can support direct sellers, a large proportion of all direct selling is still done one to one or at party events (group selling) at people's homes. Such party events are a low-cost way for your customers to socialise and have a good time – with a chance to shop, of course. While a range of products are sold this way, the most popular products are personal-care items like cosmetics, jewellery, skincare, clothing and baby products. All these items are affordable luxuries. For most people, direct sales is a part-time business with low start-up costs. In fact, be wary of companies charging more than a few hundred pounds to get started. Take a look at the Direct Selling Association (www.dsa.org.uk) website for some ideas and advice. (Also check out Chapter 2 for a lot more information about direct-selling opportunities.)

✔ **Holistic treatments.** Spending on alternative healthcare therapies such as massage and reflexology tends to stay very resilient during economic downturns, probably because in addition to making people feel better, evidence shows that massage lowers tension and fatigue. Many people increasingly use massage as an alternative to traditional medical and pharmaceutical treatment for common chronic health problems, such as neck and shoulder pain, and stress. For more information, check out the Complementary Medical Association (www.the-cma.org.uk) and the Complementary Therapists Association (www.ctha.com).

✔ **Travel services.** Economic downturns and high petrol prices may restrain the urge to travel, but they don't eliminate it. To fill this ever-present urge, people replace trips to faraway places with holidays nearer home, dubbed 'staycations'. Day trippers love historical towns, quaint villages and easy-to-reach beaches; they love short-break high-action activities such as surfing and canoeing; and they also love visiting theme parks, zoos and museums. This opens up fantastic opportunities for travel businesses that can cater to this demand by offering bed-and-breakfast accommodation, fun local tours or surfing lessons. Check out www.toursbylocals.com for some ideas of what can done. The Bed and Breakfast Association (www.bandbassociation.org) also has useful information.

Ecotourism is another potential opportunity in the travel industry as growing numbers of people prefer to travel in an environmentally friendly and ethically aware way. The International Ecotourism Society (TIES) offers online courses on its website (www.ecotourism.org) that lead to a certificate in sustainable tourism management. People have a huge appetite for travel, even in challenging times, so the key is finding out how to make travel possible and affordable.

INSPIRATION

'I've had a hot idea!'

Tony Curtis was undaunted by the idea of starting his home-based business selling heated sports gloves during a recession because he knew he had invented a product that people would want to buy regardless of the economic climate. Instead he concentrated on keeping his overhead costs down and setting up distribution channels so he could sell his gloves overseas as well as in the UK.

A former educational behaviour specialist, Curtis came up with the idea for his heated sports gloves while watching his son's hands turn cold and blue while playing rugby. He patented the process he invented and his Bristol-based business Alago now sells three products – rugby gloves, football gloves and gardening gloves. The heating pads within the gloves are activated by putting them in a microwave or by pressing a button on the glove and the heat lasts for an hour.

He said: 'If I was just going to sell direct in the UK then I'd be beholden to that market only. But I can sell to Europe, Canada and Japan too. Starting up in a poor economic climate means that I can start comfortably and then build a strong brand for when the economy recovers.'

Alago now sells to customers in 10 countries and has an annual turnover of £250,000.

For more ideas of the type of businesses to start when times are tough, check out Rachel Bridge's book, *How to Start a Business Without Any Money* (Virgin Books).

Creating a Business That Can Ride the Economic Waves

In the first part of this chapter, we identified the kind of home-based businesses we believe have the best potential to prosper in economic downturns. But one lesson we've learned from the past is that no one has a foolproof crystal ball. New opportunities from new technologies continue to arise, some technologies that showed promise don't gain market acceptance and established businesses fade or require such a drastic overhaul that they don't go by the same name. That's the process; change is normal and some dreams disappear as new ones arise.

But even though you can't know exactly what the future holds, you can build a lasting business that can ride the waves of the economy for years to come. In the sections that follow, we explore some of the approaches you can take.

Cushioning yourself locally and virtually

Some home businesses are inherently local, meaning that your customers are located within your local neighbourhood or within close driving distance. For example, no one has discovered a way to put up shelves, provide beauty treatments or do pest control via the Internet, so those businesses have to be local. On the other hand, you can provide web-design services or business-support services for clients anywhere in the world.

In addition to determining the kind of marketing you do, your choice of whether to build up your business locally or virtually determines where your income comes from. In a recovering economy, home businesses that can derive income from both within their local neighbourhood and from elsewhere via the Internet have more potential to be resilient.

Fortunately, the Internet enables more and more businesses to serve both local and distant customers. You can expand many primarily locally focused businesses, such as sewing and tutoring, simply by providing services and selling information and products online; for example, tutoring globally via Skype and selling your sewing mail order via the Internet.

Crowdsourcing locally and virtually

Crowdsourcing enables businesses to capitalise on an Internet version of an old adage that has proven correct again and again when tested with research: there's wisdom in crowds. Crowdsourcing starts with putting up an announcement on a website and asking a large number of people to get involved in or respond to some task. Wikipedia (for information), YouTube (for videos) and Flickr (for photos) are all forms of crowdsourcing.

Some crowdsourcing sites allow people with specific skills to bid on projects that customers put up on the web. A few online marketplaces for creative services include `www.conceptcupboard.com`, `www.99designs.co.uk` and `www.crowdspring.com`.

For other recent examples of crowdsourcing, check out `www.wikipedia.org/wiki/list_of_crowdsourcing_projects`. For more on crowdsourcing in general, get your hands on *Crowdsourcing For Dummies* by David Alan Grier (Wiley).

Telescoping your niche

When times are good, specialise in a niche you can cultivate; when times aren't so good and money is tight, telescope that niche. *Telescoping* is our term for extending or adding to the range of services you provide to existing customers without undermining your reputation for the business specialism you've developed. Telescoping your niche means offering to do work for your customers that they ordinarily would've had to do themselves or would've had to turn to another specialist for. Because your customers are already working with you, why not have them turn to you for additional services you know you can provide? For example:

- ✔ If you prepare tax returns for small businesses and you notice a client is downsizing his bookkeeping staff, you may offer to do his bookkeeping as an outside service.

- ✔ If you're an estate agent and your potential client is concerned about whether her home will sell, you can also offer to tidy and de-clutter the home, and temporarily fill it with gorgeous furniture and accessories so it's presented in a way that is most attractive to buyers. Dressing a home like this results in a quicker sale and a higher price, which makes your customer (and you) very happy.

- ✔ If you're a travel agent helping a bride and groom with travel arrangements for a destination wedding out of the country, you can offer to coordinate with the wedding organiser at the venue to ensure that the travel plans of the couple, family and guests go smoothly.

As you can see, telescoping enables you to expand what you offer in a low-growth economy and then to narrow your services again when the economy improves.

Cashing in on Barter and Trade

Bartering means trading goods or services without exchanging money. Even though it doesn't involve a direct money transaction, bartering still has implications for your cash flow. You may be wondering how home-based businesses can benefit from bartering. Well, we're here to tell you!

Taking advantage of bartering

Short on cash but long on time when you're just starting up? Then bartering your products and services in exchange for the products and services of another business may be just the ticket for you and your home-based business. After all, bartering allows you to keep more cash in the bank – cash you can use to help grow your own business instead of someone else's. For example, if you need a bookkeeper to keep track of your gardening business's financials but don't want to pay the hourly fee, give bartering a try. Find a bookkeeper who needs their garden tending on an ongoing basis and barter your services for the bookkeeper's.

Don't forget to take into account that *barter is considered a form of income and has tax consequences*. You must report the fair market value of all the goods and services you exchange as income in the year you receive them, but you may deduct costs incurred to perform the bartered work.

Bartering in action

Over the years a number of local communities in the UK have set up collective bartering schemes to enable residents to swap skills without payment changing hands. In one of the longest-running schemes in Stroud, Gloucestershire, for example, members include a taxi company, a café and a registered nurse. Known as Local Exchange Trading Schemes (LETS), the schemes generally use a barter currency to enable indirect swaps to take place – in Totnes, Devon, for example, the currency is called 'acorns', while in Reading 'readies' change hands. Local community barter schemes have met with varying degrees of success – at the peak in the 1990s more than 400 such groups with 20,000 members flourished around the country. But while some barter schemes have continued to thrive and benefit home-business owners, others fell by the wayside after the initial wave of enthusiasm waned.

Trading time and goods when cash is short

In addition to everyday bartering, other forms of non-monetary exchange can keep your business going when times are tough. These alternative means of exchange can play a valuable role for many businesses in both good times and bad – getting your business started when cash is short; obtaining goods and services your cash budget may not cover; and developing relationships in your local area. The primary types of alternative exchange are:

✔ **Time banks.** A *time bank* tracks the time its members spend doing something for other members. As one member provides a service for another member, he accumulates *time credits*, which he can then spend on time for services he needs from other members.

Unlike bartering, in which everything exchanged is valued at market price, in a time bank, all time is valued equally. One hour of service provided equals one hour of credit you can use for another service. So a bookkeeper who charges £35 per hour can get advice from a solicitor who bills at £250 per hour. Their time is valued equally, which makes for a great deal for the bookkeeper and an improvement on what the solicitor gets for doing pro bono work or having empty hours on the calendar.

Time banking is occurring in towns and villages worldwide. One may already be in operation near you. Check out the Timebanking UK website to find out more information: www.timebanking.org. The organisation already has 250 member time banks across the UK.

✔ **Local exchange trading system (LETS).** LETS is a type of local exchange system that eliminates coins, tokens, notes, or any other form of printed money usually required for exchange of local goods and services. Instead, members of LETS centrally track and record transactions, usually by using computer software available specifically for this purpose. For example, a massage therapist may earn credit by giving a massage to another LETS participant and then use that credit to acquire a service from a handyperson or any other participant.

Saving money and keeping your overheads down

One of the best ways to build a sustainable business is to keep your costs (also known as your *overheads*) down. When's the last time you took a close look at your expenses with an eye to becoming lean and mean? We suggest you take a good look now – here are some of the best places to start:

Phone expenses:

✔ Consider using voice over IP (VOIP) services such as Skype rather than a landline. But be aware that landline services may be more audible at times and that you lose VOIP service during power failures. So you may want to have one landline on hand.

✔ Regularly compare broadband, landline and mobile phone tariffs and packages to make sure you're getting the best deal for your business. If you aren't, switch as soon as your contract comes up for renewal. Visit www.uswitch.com to find out more about the best deals.

Utility bills:

✔ If you're working from home, you're spending more money on utilities than when you were working elsewhere. Make sure you're getting the best deal on your gas and electricity bills by using a comparison site such as www.uswitch.com, www.moneysupermarket.com, www.comparethemarket.com or www.confused.com.

✔ Ensure your home is properly insulated.

✔ Use a programmable thermostat to save energy costs; a programmable thermostat allows you to lower or raise temperatures at various times of day or night based on need.

✔ Replace conventional light bulbs with energy-efficient light bulbs.

✔ Check out – and use – the numerous energy-saving tips on the Energy Saving Trust's website: www.energysaving-trust.co.uk.

Businesses Best Suited for an Improving Economy

Although each of the businesses we describe in the following sections can also work in times of economic downturns, we consider them more vulnerable to economic forces than the businesses we list in the previous sections. We aren't suggesting that you rule out the following businesses during a poorly performing economy, but look long and hard at these opportunities before committing to them.

At the same time, when the light at the end of the tunnel begins to get brighter, bear in mind that these businesses often offer great opportunities as the economy gains strength and prosperity returns.

Offering services to other businesses

The first expenses that many businesses cut out of their budgets when times get tough are outside services. However, when the good times return (which they always eventually do), the need for business-to-business services surges. Here are a few examples of great businesses to get into as the economy improves:

✔ **Business coaching.** Business coaches help companies improve performance by working with managers and directors, giving them feedback on their management styles, and developing skills they need to do well in their companies and get ahead in their careers. Coaches help key personnel communicate more effectively, make intelligent decisions and deal with burnout. According to the Chartered Institute of Personnel and Development (CIPD), 90 per cent of companies in the UK use coaching, with 51 per cent saying they consider coaching to be a key part of learning development. Business coaches charge a lot of money per hour, and it's one of the highest paid and fastest growing areas of coaching. For more information about becoming a business coach, visit the CIPD website (www.cipd.co.uk).

✔ **Consulting.** Consulting appeals to a wide variety of people because it offers you a way to turn your expertise, experience and years of accrued wisdom into a livelihood when salaried jobs are no longer available or no longer appealing. Sometimes becoming a consultant is as easy as having your former employer retain you on a contract, enabling you to develop other clients while you bring in income that may be more than you earned as an employee. As an indication of the many possible consulting opportunities out there, dozens of associations of consultants offer membership to consultants in different fields, including business review and planning, computing, creativity, crisis control, organisational development, financial advice, introduction of new technology, marketing, strategic planning, training, business turnaround and all forms of technical assistance.

Regardless of which field they're in, effective consultants are part counsellor, parent figure, therapist, stern disciplinarian and, of course, problem solver. Check out *Consulting For Dummies,* 2nd Edition, by Philip Albon, Bob Nelson and Peter Economy (Wiley), for more information.

✔ **Editorial services.** Editorial services take many forms – copy-editing, proofreading, indexing and more. In addition to working as an independent contractor for publishers and corporations, the digital age has brought new editorial opportunities. Each year hundreds of thousands of self-publishers share their information, opinions and stories with the world in both print and e-book form. Many of these self-publishers turn to independent editors for help; still more need to be enlightened to the value of well-edited material. Every journal, business report or proposal, and technical training manual, whether it's published in print or electronic format, requires editorial work.

An as-you-wait editing service (take a look at the US website www. gramlee.com, for example) is entirely web based and can easily be done in a home office. Your customers submit documents to you electronically and you return them, editing complete, charging them a set fee per word. If you don't have publishing experience and editing is a new career for you, copy-editing and proofreading are good fields to break into. The Society for Editors and Proofreaders (www.sfep.org. uk) provides details of training courses in the UK.

✔ **Grant and proposal writing.** Many non-profit organisations fail or succeed on their abilities to obtain grant funding. Often people who form non-profit organisations don't have the time, desire or skill-set needed to write effective grant proposals. So if you have good writing skills, can write logically and are able to grasp a subject quickly enough to be able to explain it, you can create a niche business writing grant proposals. Grant writers usually work on an hourly or project basis.

✔ **Technical writing.** Constantly changing technology brings with it the need for manuals and other materials that introduce it to consumers, sell it, explain how to use it, service it, assemble it, install it and so on. The pace of innovation has been accelerating for more than a hundred years, and it'll continue to do so as innovation shifts abroad, particularly to China, which is investing heavily in science and technology. Companies often contract out for technical writing projects, some of which can extend over several months or more. Technical writers can also find work making technologies created abroad understandable and usable by English-speaking sales engineers and technicians. Check out the Institute of Scientific and Technical Communicators (www.istc. org.uk) for more information about this field.

✔ **Translation services.** Translation services are essential in a global economy – contracts, instruction manuals, software menus and commands, scripts for dubbing, subtitles for films, and much more, all require translation. Accurate machine-based translation is still years away, but the web allows a translator to respond instantly to a request for services. Lingo24 (www.lingo24.com), for example, hires home-based translators who can translate between 600 language combinations for clients. Working for a site like this is one option for translators, but you can also work as an independent home business. Translating technical documents in growing technology fields and web content are two high-demand specialist areas for translators. If you prefer oral interpretation and are willing to work from places other than your home, courts and hospitals need accurate interpreters to work on site. Check out the Institute of Translation and Interpreting (www.iti.org.uk) for more information.

✔ **Web writing.** The Internet has opened up new markets for writers. Some pay quite well, as is the case when you write blog and website content for many companies or organisations; others require a lot of work to produce much income. Writing projects that offer the best pay are business writing, such as annual reports, company newsletters and speeches for executives; ghost writing; and copywriting for selling and promoting products and services. Writing e-books is also a growing market, especially if you can find yourself a niche of interest to a wide group of readers.

To get started as a professional web writer, choose a topic or focus that motivates you to become an expert in that topic; then develop that expertise. Quill (www.quill-company.co.uk) for example, provides content for websites around the world and is building a database of specialist writers who can write everything from bite-size news pieces to full-length features.

Appealing to clients who have money to spare

No matter what the economic climate may be – sunny, stormy or partly cloudy – people love to shop. And when clients have money to spare, you can bet that money won't stay in their wallets for long. The following are two big items people are likely to spend money on, when they have extra money to spend, that you could start as a home business:

✔ **Functional art.** Functional art brings together the aesthetic with the practical. Artists who create functional art apply their skills to creating everyday objects imbued with a handcrafted beauty and artistry that factory manufactured products can't attain. In addition to creating original work, functional artists also turn existing items that were once simply functional into something artistic, like transforming file drawers or key holders into unique furniture or accessories, for example.

The key to functional art is that when people perceive something as handmade, they're willing to pay a higher price for it than they would for any machine-tooled version of the same item. For current examples of such handcrafted work, check out www.folksy.com, www.notonthe highstreet.com or www.jonnyssister.co.uk.

✔ **Home entertainment systems installation.** Unlike the sales of most consumer electronic products, sales of home entertainment components not only held their own during the recent economic downturn – they increased. Many people try to install their own home entertainment systems but find the task overwhelming or the result unsatisfying. These people often turn to experts in the field for help.

If you have experience in the relevant skills for home entertainment systems installation, an understanding of how sound works combined with a penchant for precision, and decent customer service skills, you can build a business largely fed by word-of-mouth referrals.

When people have extra money to spend, they're also likely to spend money on products and services designed to help them with day-to-day living or family events. Here are some quick-fire examples for you to consider (along with some resources to check out if you're interested):

✔ **Animal training:** Training dogs and other animals (The Kennel Club: www.thekennelclub.org.uk)

✔ **Cake baking and decorating:** Creating custom cakes for special occasions such as weddings (Le Cordon Bleu UK: www.lcblondon.com)

✔ **Candle making:** Making handmade candles (Candle Makers Supplies: www.candlemakers.co.uk)

✔ **Chair making:** Making classic chairs of heirloom quality (The Windsor Workshop: www.thewindsorworkshop.co.uk)

✔ **Dog walking:** Walking dogs once or twice a day (Association of Professional Dog Walkers: www.apdw.co.uk)

✔ **Errand services:** Running errands and doing nearly any other chores – small or large – that people want done (International Concierge and Lifestyle Management Association: www.iclma.org)

✔ **Family childcare:** Providing childcare in your own home (Professional Association for Childcare and Early Years: www.pacey.org.uk)

✔ **Feng shui practice:** Helping people evoke harmony in their surroundings (The Feng Shui Society: www.fengshuisociety.org.uk)

- ✔ **Financial planning:** Advising people on managing debt, buying a home, planning for the future and more (Institute of Financial Planning: www.financialplanning.org.uk)

- ✔ **Home staging:** Making a home look its best when it's up for sale (Home Staging Consultants: www.homestagingconsultants.co.uk)

- ✔ **Image consulting:** Helping clients improve their appearance and personal style visually and vocally (Federation of Image Professionals International: www.fipi.com)

- ✔ **Interior design:** Designing the interior of homes, businesses and other buildings (British Institute of Interior Design: www.biid.org.uk)

- ✔ **Landscape gardening:** Designing and installing gardens (British Association of Landscape Industries: www.bali.org.uk)

- ✔ **Life coaching:** Helping people develop their individual potential (The Society of Holistic Therapists and Coaches: www.societytherapistscoaches.co.uk)

- ✔ **Mediation:** Assisting people in settling disputes (The Professional Mediators Association: www.professionalmediator.org)

- ✔ **Money management:** Teaching others about financial management (Learn About Money: www.learnaboutmoney.org)

- ✔ **Pest control:** Blocking or eradicating pests (British Pest Control Association: www.bpca.org.uk)

- ✔ **Pet grooming:** Bathing, ear and teeth cleaning, styling and claw clipping for dogs and cats (British Dog Groomers' Association: www.petcare.org.uk)

- ✔ **Pet sitting:** Caring for pets when their owners are away, in your own home or the owners' home (National Association of Registered Pet Sitters: www.dogsit.com)

- ✔ **Professional organisers:** Organising possessions, clothing, files and more for clients (Association of Professional Declutterers and Organisers: www.apdo-uk.co.uk)

- ✔ **Web-based Teaching English as a Foreign Language (TEFL):** Providing online TEFL education (World TEFL Association: www.worldteflassociation.com)

- ✔ **Wedding planning:** Organising and planning weddings on behalf of clients (National Association of Professional Wedding Services: www.theweddingassociation.co.uk)

Fuelling the home-business engine

Because new and small businesses are the engine of the UK economy, the government and several private foundations provide resources to help you succeed. If you've decided a home business is the path you want to take, the following resources can help you get on your way. Helpful websites include:

✔ Enterprise **Nation** (www.enterprise nation.com): An online network for home-based businesses in the UK, providing support, advice, offers and resources for people starting up businesses from home.

✔ **Smarta** (www.smarta.com): A free online advice and networking resource, backed by successful UK entrepreneurs, for anyone starting and running a small business.

✔ **Gov.uk** (www.gov.uk): A government-backed resource for entrepreneurs and small businesses.

✔ **Startups** (www.startups.co.uk): A free online resource for starting a business.

✔ **British Library Business and IP Centre** (www.bl.uk/bipc): Provides free small business advice, support and resources both online and at the British Library in London.

Helpful agencies and organisations include:

✔ **British Chambers of Commerce** (www.britishchambers.org.uk): Independent business network with chambers throughout the UK.

✔ National **Enterprise Network** (www.nationalenterprisenetwork.org): Represents not-for-profit organisations such as enterprise agencies that provide impartial advice to new and emerging businesses.

✔ **StartUp Britain** (www.startupbritain.org): A private-sector-backed national campaign to support and encourage enterprise in the UK.

Part II
Managing Your Money

Top Five Tips to Get Your Cash Flow Moving

- **Get your money upfront.** If possible, ask for payment before you deliver your products or services. There's no better way to get your cash flowing in the right direction than being paid sooner rather than later.

- **Don't pay your bills any sooner than you have to.** Your cash flow will thank you if you wait to pay your bills until you're required to do so. If, for example, your electricity bill requires payment 30 days after you receive it, schedule your payment to be delivered the day before it's due.

- **Bill more often.** The more often you bill your clients or customers, the more often you'll be paid. And the more often you're paid, the better your cash flow is. Instead of billing your clients quarterly, why not bill them monthly? If you're supplying products, try breaking your deliveries into smaller chunks that you can bill sooner and more often.

- **Give prompt-payment discounts.** Everyone loves price discounts, and if you offer a small discount to clients who pay their bills quickly, you're sure to have many takers.

- **Manage your expenses.** Spend money on your home business only when absolutely necessary.

Go to www.dummies.com/extras/homebasedbusiness for free online bonus content.

In this part...

✔ Get your business bank account up and running.

✔ Decide on the right bookkeeping system for you.

✔ Evaluate how much you can charge for your products or services.

✔ Try out different pricing strategies.

✔ Discover everything you need to know about taxes.

Chapter 6

Keeping Track of Your Money

*I*f there's one thing that keeps people from starting their own home-based business, it's probably concern over money. Where will the money you need to start up your business and keep it running come from? Will there be enough to enable you to leave your current job, support your family, or at least pay some bills? How will you know whether you're making money – or losing it?

The key to answering all these questions is *financial management*. No, don't glaze over! Financial management is one of the main points of focus for any home-based business, and it requires a good system of bookkeeping, as well as constant attention to the numbers. Your business's finances aren't something you can leave to chance. In this chapter, we take a look at how to manage your finances so that your finances don't manage you.

For more in-depth explanations and advice for all things money related, read *Understanding Business Accounting For Dummies*, 3rd Edition, by John A Tracy and Colin Barrow (Wiley).

Organising Your Finances

In most large businesses, tracking cash – where it comes from, where it goes and how it's used – is one of the most important administrative functions. Large corporations like BT, Proctor & Gamble and British Airways may have thousands of people working in their finance and accounting departments. Clearly, tracking cash is important to them.

Do I need an accountant?

Do you need an accountant to help you keep track of your business's finances? The answer to this question depends on how capable you are in handling your own bookkeeping, accounting, taxes and financial strategies, and on how complicated your business is. Some business owners love to take care of the administrative tasks involved in running their own businesses; others hate it. Some home-based businesspeople are naturally skilled at doing financial tasks; however, the talents of others are better suited to delivering products and services to their customers. In addition, doing your own bookkeeping and accounting takes time and discipline – you have to update your records regularly and periodically check them for errors.

If your finances are fairly simple, you're computer savvy and you have sufficient time and interest to keep your records up to date by yourself, you can use a software package such as Sage or QuickBooks to do your own bookkeeping. Simply input your receipts and expenses, and the program performs every accounting function and trick you can imagine. You can generate all kinds of financial reports and graphs (which your lenders need to see when you want to borrow money to grow), create invoices and collect the information you need to do your taxes. (See the later section 'Choosing the Best Bookkeeping System for Your Business' for more information.)

If, however, your business isn't simple, or if you have set up as a limited liability company rather than as a sole trader, getting the help of a professional bookkeeper or accountant may be worth your time and money. When looking for professional assistance, avoid choosing someone from a random Internet search – you never know what you're going to get. Instead, ask your home-based business friends or colleagues in the area for referrals to a good accountant or bookkeeping service – preferably one that specialises in handling businesses like yours.

 Cash serves many functions in a business: it's a way to track performance, to measure the profit generated by different products and services, and a way to reflect the equity built by the company's investors and owners. Plus, it enables companies to pay employees and purchase supplies and services.

Indeed, cash is the focal point of most organisations – both large and small. When you have a small home-based business, cash – or the lack of it – can quickly make or break you.

Why do you have to worry about keeping your business finances organised? Isn't that shoebox in which you keep all your personal receipts sufficient for your home-based business, as long as you have enough money to pay your bills and yourself? Not quite. Keeping your finances organised and accurate is important because you need adequate financial information about your business to:

✔ Know where your business stands – whether it's making or losing money and whether expenses are out of line with income.

✔ Apply for loans and receive credit from suppliers.

✔ Prepare your tax and VAT returns.

✔ Provide accurate and up-to-date financial information to interested buyers in the event that you decide to sell your business.

Can your shoebox do all that? We don't think so!

Setting Up a Business Account

When you set up your company's finances, the first step is to establish a separate bank account for your home-based business. Although HM Revenue and Customs (HMRC) doesn't require you to separate your business finances from your personal finances, take our word for it: when you prepare your taxes, it makes things a lot easier. If you don't establish this separation from the start, you may spend hours and hours first trying to identify the business expenses in your personal bank account or credit card receipts and then pulling them out and classifying them.

At the very least, you need a separate bank account for your business, and a savings account may be a good idea, too. Setting up a new business bank account is fairly straightforward, particularly if you've already established a personal account at the bank or building society where you choose to set up your business account. However, before you go ahead, spend some time comparing the facilities offered by different bank accounts as some will be more appropriate for your business than others. For example, some business bank accounts charge a monthly administration fee; some provide you with a named account manager; some charge you every time you pay money in or write a cheque; some are online accounts, others are branch-based. Check out the banks' websites to find out exactly what they offer and make an appointment to see two or three bank managers in your local area to discuss your business requirements.

When you actually open the account, you need to take various forms of identification including your passport, Companies House registration number (if applicable) and a basic business plan showing an estimated turnover for the business.

Some banks can take several days to process a business account application and get your account up and running, while others can have an account open within a couple of hours. If you need to be able to use your business bank account immediately, make sure you ask how long the process takes before deciding where to open an account.

One more thing: consider applying for a credit or debit card that you use only for your business. Visa, MasterCard and American Express all have cards for small business users that enable you to buy products and services for your business and also come with special offers and discounts from relevant retailers.

Accepting Credit and Debit Card Sales

Although many home-based businesses don't need to be able to accept credit and debit card payments, if you sell products, you probably want to be able to accept payments this way. In fact, as a way to improve your cash flow, you may want to require that your clients pay you by credit or debit card *before* you deliver their product orders or services.

If you have the kind of business that's suitable for taking credit or debit card sales – perhaps you sell dolls' houses, wedding cakes or rare records – you gain many of the following advantages when you accept credit or debit cards:

- ✔ Customers appreciate the convenience of being able to use their credit or debit cards to make an immediate purchase.

- ✔ People who use credit cards to purchase items tend to spend more money per transaction than non-credit card customers.

- ✔ You get your cash from the transaction much more quickly than when you invoice your customers and let them pay later, improving the cash flow of your business. A credit or debit card payment is immediately directly deposited into your business bank account.

- ✔ You reduce or even eliminate internal paperwork that results from invoicing customers and following up on late payments.

- ✔ Your business appears more established and credible than businesses that don't accept credit or debit cards.

Being able to accept credit or debit cards is definitely a good thing. As with many other good things in life, however, accepting credit and debit cards isn't free. In fact, you have to pay a price for the privilege – particularly with credit cards.

Knowing the costs of credit card transactions

How much does accepting credit and debit cards cost you and your business? The answer depends on what kind of business you operate (retail, mail order or Internet), who processes your transactions and how much money you submit for processing (the actual amount of your transactions). It also depends on whether you want to take payments online via your website, from customers on the phone or in person, or all three. Banks typically charge less for processing debit card transactions than credit card transactions.

Here are the typical costs you can expect to pay to the company that provides your credit card and debit card processing:

- ✔ **Set-up charges.** Including application fees, these fees can range anywhere from zero to more than £100. In addition you will need to rent or purchase equipment if you plan to use a point-of-sale terminal to take payments instead of just using your computer's Internet access. If the set-up charge is free, expect to pay higher transaction fees to make up for the free set-up.

- ✔ **Transaction fees.** For each transaction made you're charged a flat fee of a few pence per transaction. Most banks charge a minimum transaction amount which you must pay even if you've had fewer transactions in a month than this.

- ✔ **Monthly fee.** You also need to pay a fixed monthly fee.

Accepting credit and debit cards is not a free service, but if your sales justify it, don't hesitate. It's a relatively small price to pay – and can be offset by the cost of just one or two fraudulent cheques. However, before you sign up for a service, carefully compare a variety of different providers. Prices and services vary widely, and some deals are definitely better than others. Take a look at www.moneysupermarket.com/credit-cards/ to compare providers.

Establishing a merchant account

Before you can accept credit or debit cards, you have to find a bank, credit card company or other merchant account provider that can grant you *merchant status* or allow you to open a *merchant account* – that is, authorisation to accept credit card payments. This process can be a bit tricky; in fact, for a new business or one that credit card companies consider to be risky, gaining merchant status can be downright difficult. Here's a list of the kinds of businesses that banks and credit card companies consider particularly risky (and that may make getting approval more difficult):

- ✔ Adult websites
- ✔ Dating services
- ✔ Prepaid telephone cards
- ✔ Online casinos
- ✔ Massage services
- ✔ Online pharmacies
- ✔ Mall kiosks (seasonal/independent)
- ✔ Ticket brokers

If you've been in business for some time (at least two or more years), you're not involved in a particularly risky business and you have a good credit history, you should have no problem getting merchant status. Of course, until you apply, you never know for sure.

Different companies charge different prices to create and maintain a merchant account for you. Do your research thoroughly and compare prices.

Obtaining credit reports

If a customer asks you to provide credit, it's always wise to first check out their creditworthiness – that is, the customer's ability to pay you back. Some high street banks now offer some form of free credit-checking service for their customers, for up to five businesses, for example; ask yours what they can offer you. You can also ask a credit-checking agency such as Experian (www.experian.co.uk) or Equifax (www.equifax.co.uk) for a credit check report. Findout (www.findoutinfo.com), the business credit-checking arm of Equifax, for example, charges a few pounds for a Business Essentials Report, which includes trade references and information on any county court judgements (a judgement issued by a county court when someone fails to pay money they owe) against a company. Visit these companies' websites or give them a call for more information.

You can, of course, also do some credit checking yourself, which is free! Ask the business customer for a copy of its latest filed accounts and up-to-date management accounts. Ask also for trade references that you can call to check if the customer pays on time and is easy to deal with.

Using the PayPal option

As a direct result of the explosion of the eBay online auction service, PayPal (www.paypal.co.uk) and a number of similar financial services companies have sprung up to facilitate online transactions. In addition to accepting cash transfers from customers with their own PayPal accounts, PayPal enables your customers to pay you using their credit or debit cards. You can then keep the funds in your PayPal account or electronically transfer them to your business's bank account.

Using PayPal to accept your customers' credit cards offers some compelling advantages over the more traditional process of qualifying for and establishing a merchant account, including the following:

✔ You don't have to fill out a lengthy application form or jump hurdles to be able to accept credit cards for your business. Simply establish a PayPal account (which just takes a few minutes) and you're ready to go.

✔ Although not free, the fees that you pay to accept credit cards with PayPal are probably less than you'd pay a bank for running charges through a merchant account, because you only have to pay a transaction fee (currently ranging from 1.4 per cent to 3.4 per cent, depending on the value of the transaction, plus 20p per transaction). You don't have to pay a set-up fee or a monthly fee, or adhere to a minimum monthly transaction amount.

If you're processing a lot of credit card payments, these savings can really add up.

When you're starting out, the PayPal option is very attractive because it's far easier than establishing a merchant account and the cash is just as real when it hits your bank account!

Choosing the Best Bookkeeping System for Your Business

Keeping track of your business's financial transactions is a must. Your business's finances aren't going to get less complicated as your business grows; in fact, the opposite is likely to be true. Start your business off on the right foot, and make keeping track of your financial transactions a regular part of doing business.

Although you may enjoy playing with Microsoft Excel, we suggest that you pick up one of the many excellent accounting software programs available on the market today instead of creating your own spreadsheets from scratch. Programs such as QuickBooks and Sage can take care of your business's every financial need – now and into the future. Take a look at *Sage One For Dummies*, by Jane Kelly, and *QuickBooks 2013 For Dummies*, by Stephen L Nelson, for more information about these programs.

For example, QuickBooks Simple Start software is an easy-to-use software program for businesses (it currently costs £119 for the desktop version or £9 a month for the online version). It enables you to do the following basic tasks (more advanced tasks, such as producing estimates, require an upgrade to a more detailed version of QuickBooks):

✔ Track sales, expenses and profit, and create business budgets.

✔ Create and send branded invoices to customers.

✔ Generate a snapshot of your company's income and expenses.

✔ Track and manage VAT (Chapter 8 explains taxes).

✔ Share information with an accountant.

✔ Track stock and create purchase orders.

The accounting method you decide to use ultimately depends on the nature of your business and on the amount and complexity of the financial transactions you incur. If you're at all in doubt as to how to proceed with your bookkeeping or accounting system, talk to an accountant for help in setting up the right way.

You'll have a great feeling when you get your business off the ground and receive your first payments for your products or services. After all your hard work and planning, these payments are what you've been waiting for. Chances are you'll be busier than you ever imagined, but make sure that you don't get so caught up in taking care of customers that you forget to take care of your business.

Successful businesses don't just happen – they require constant attention. Like a wonderfully productive vegetable garden, businesses need to be carefully tended and watched for signs of trouble. One of the best ways to keep an eye on the health of your business is to review the wide variety of financial reports available to you. Make a regular habit of generating the reports you need and reviewing them, say, every three months. Don't just assume that everything is fine – prove it to yourself regularly.

Balancing payments made and bank statements

You can do the most basic form of financial analysis once a month when you balance the payments you've made from the business, either by cheque, debit card, direct debit, standing order or bank transfer, against your bank statements. Most bank statements summarise the total amount of the deposits you made during the month (money in from your customers), as well as the total amount of the money you've spent from your account. After you've double checked to make sure the bank statements are in agreement with the amount you've paid out, subtract the amount you've paid out from your deposits to give yourself a quick idea of what direction your business is heading in financially – north or south.

Spending far more than you're taking in? Then you know you have to find ways to bring in more money while also controlling expenses. Bringing in far more money than you're spending? Brilliant! Figure out how to do more of what you're already doing.

Analysing the two most important financial statements

Financial statements take the data you've entered into your accounting system and organise it in a way that allows you to quickly gauge the financial health of your company. Although financial statements may seem a bit intimidating to many – especially for new home-based businesspeople – accounting and bookkeeping software make the process easier than ever before. It really is as simple as one or two clicks of your computer's mouse.

Two of the most popular and useful financial statements are the profit and loss account and the balance sheet. Each has its own unique role to play in your financial analysis and, ultimately, in the way you run your business.

The profit and loss account

The profit and loss account (also known as a *profit and loss statement*, or P&L) measures the *profitability* of your business – in other words, how much money is left over after you add up all your business revenues and subtract all your business expenses.

Profit and loss accounts reveal three key pieces of information:

✔ Your business's sales volume during a specified period.

✔ Your business's expenses during a specified period.

✔ The difference between your business's sales and its expenses – its profit (or loss) – during a specified period.

Table 6-1 shows what a typical profit and loss account looks like for fictional home business Frantic Antiques.

Table 6-1	Frantic Antiques: Profit and Loss Account
Profit and Loss Account – 12 Months Ended December 31, 2013	
Revenues	
Gross sales	£50,000
Less: returns	(£1,000)
Net sales	**£49,000**
Cost of Goods Sold	
Initial stock value	£50,000
Purchases	£10,000
Less: purchase discounts	(£2,000)
Net purchases	£8,000
Cost of goods available for sale	£58,000
Less: final stock value	(£48,000)
Cost of goods sold	**£10,000**
Gross profit	**£39,000**

(continued)

Table 6-1 *(continued)*

Profit and Loss Account – 12 Months Ended December 31, 2013	
Operating Expenses	
Total selling expenses	(£5,000)
Total general expenses	(£10,000)
Total operating expenses	(£15,000)
Operating income	£24,000
Other income and expenses	£5,000
Total other income and expenses	£5,000
Income before tax	**£19,000**
Less: tax	(£10,000)
Net income	£9,000

In the example in Table 6-1, Frantic Antiques had £49,000 of net sales revenue and a cost of goods sold of £10,000, leaving the company with a gross profit of £39,000. However, this gross profit was further reduced by the expenses of selling products and running the company (advertising, printing, rent, salary and so on) and by tax. The result is a net income of £9,000.

If the Frantic Antiques business is registered for VAT (which you need to do if your business has sales of more than £79,000 in a year), then the owner also has to deduct VAT from the net income (we explain VAT in Chapter 8).

The balance sheet

The entire world of accounting hinges on a simple mathematical truth, known as the accounting equation:

Assets = liabilities + capital (also known as shareholders' or owners' equity)

Assets include cash and things (like vehicles and property) that can be converted to cash. *Liabilities* are obligations – debts, loans, mortgages and so on – owed to other organisations or people. *Capital* or *owners' equity* is the net worth of your business after all liabilities have been subtracted from the business's assets.

The *balance sheet* reveals these three categories. Table 6-2 shows a sample of a typical balance sheet.

Table 6-2	Frantic Antiques: Balance Sheet
Consolidated Balance Sheet – as of December 31, 2013	
Assets	
Current Assets	
Cash and cash equivalents (cheques, money orders)	£12,000
Accounts receivable	£25,000
Stock	£30,000
Total current assets	**£67,000**
Fixed Assets	
Equipment	£20,000
Furniture, fixtures and improvements	£15,000
Allowance for depreciation and amortisation	(£2,000)
Total fixed assets	**£33,000**
Total assets	**£100,000**
Liabilities and Capital	
Liabilities	
Current Liabilities	
Notes payable to bank	£10,000
Accounts payable	£5,000
Employee salary	£19,000
Taxes payable	£6,000
Deferred tax	£3,000
Current portion of long-term debt	£1,000
Total current liabilities	**£44,000**
Long-term debt	£10,000
Deferred tax	£10,000
Total liabilities	**£64,000**
Capital	
Common stock	£20,000
Additional paid-in capital	£10,000
Retained earnings	£6,000
Total capital	**£36,000**
Total liabilities and capital	**£100,000**

The value of the assets of Frantic Antiques is exactly balanced by its liabilities and capital. Because of the accounting equation, there's no other option. The balance sheet demonstrates the fact that assets are paid for by a company's liabilities and owners' equity. Conversely, the assets are used to generate cash to pay off the company's liabilities. Any excess cash after liabilities are paid off is added to capital as profit.

For loads of detailed information, take a look at *Understanding Business Accounting For Dummies*, 3rd Edition, by John A. Tracy and Colin Barrow (Wiley).

Happiness is a Positive Cash Flow

For a new business – especially a new home-based business that you depend on to generate income – generating a positive cash flow as quickly as possible after starting the business is absolutely critical. Every new business goes through an initial period during which expenses exceed revenues (thus generating a negative cash flow), but the sooner you can make your cash flow positive, the better for the short- and long-term financial health of the business (and the easier you'll sleep at night).

Happiness in business truly is a positive cash flow! The following sections help you put your company into the black and out of the red.

Take a look at `www.businesslink.gov.uk/Finance_files/Cash_Flow_Projection_Worksheet.xls` for a cash-flow spreadsheet you can download and use.

Treating cash as king

Most home-based businesspeople who set up as sole traders (see Chapter 10 for more on the different forms of business structure) use their money to pay not only business expenses, but also personal expenses, when they're the primary wage earners. In other words, the money from your sole trader business enables you to fulfil both your business and your personal obligations, such as computer equipment and car running costs.

Should I rent or buy a van?

Q: I'm thinking about acquiring a new van for my business. Should I rent or buy?

A: The choice to rent or buy has many important business considerations. For example, leasing may enable you to get a better van than you could otherwise afford as you don't have to pay the whole lot upfront. You can then keep more working capital available for your business. Leasing may also allow you to pay for the van out of the business earnings instead of having to get a business loan (or lend the business some money from your personal savings). Another advantage of renting is that it gets round the problem of *technological obsolescence* (equipment becoming out of date) – at the end of a lease period, you can simply give back the equipment that may now be considered obsolete and have little market value, and upgrade to a newer version. Some leasing arrangements also include automatic annual upgrades.

On the other hand, a rental arrangement is likely to work out more expensive long term than buying a van outright because of the charges that are built into it.

And don't forget you have other options too – some leasing arrangements enable you to rent first and then have the right to buy the van at the end of the leasing period, for example. A whole range of financing options are available, including hire purchase, contract purchase, finance lease, contract hire and lease purchase, so make sure you understand all the various options and the implications of them before making a decision.

For your business to qualify for a leasing arrangement it must have a good credit rating. As a general rule, if you're leasing under your business name, you can expect to be required to have been in business for at least a year.

Ultimately there's no right or wrong answer as to whether renting or buying is best. If you do decide to lease, consider the following:

- The exact nature of the financing agreement (does it have conditions or restrictions?).

- The amount of each payment (are there any add-on and document-processing fees or termination penalties?).

- Who's responsible for insurance, maintenance and tax (usually, the lessee).

- What happens to the van at the end of the lease.

- Renewal options.

- Cancellation penalties, if any.

- Disadvantageous terms and conditions.

- Length of the lease period.

Whether you buy or lease, but particularly if you lease, consider getting *gap insurance* included in your lease. This insurance protects you if you find yourself in a situation in which the vehicle is stolen or written off only a week or two after you get it and the insurance company plans to pay you only a fraction of the value of the vehicle. Gap insurance covers the difference.

Put your money where your mouth is

Sylvia Tidy-Harris started up her speaking agency The Speakers Agency (www.thespeakersagency.com) in 2001 with £1,000 in cash. She has never had to take out a loan or ask for an overdraft facility, and she never has sleepless nights about whether a customer is going to pay their bill or where she will find the money to pay a speaker, award host or conference facilitator. The reason is simple – she gets the money upfront from clients wanting to book a speaker, which she puts into a client holding account and only pays the speaker after they've delivered the goods, which can be several months later. As a result, her business is always in credit, and has always been, and she's never suffered any bad debts. Now the business arranges speakers and hosts for events around the world and has an annual turnover of close to £1 million.

As Tidy-Harris says: 'There are enough concerns in business without having to worry about repaying a loan or chasing money.'

As a business, you have many different forms of money available to you, including cash, cheques, debit and credit cards – and some are better than others. For most businesses, being paid in cash – before delivering a product or service or upon delivery, at the latest – is by far the top preference, closely followed by direct debit or bank transfer. Here are the different ways you can be paid, in order from the most to the least preferred:

- ✔ **Cash.** Assuming it's not from a blood-stained suitcase, being paid in cash is ideal. You can spend it immediately if you like, and you can be sure it's not going to bounce or take five working days to clear after you deposit it in your business bank account before you can withdraw it.

- ✔ **Direct debit.** A direct debit is an instruction from a customer to their bank authorising a third-party business or organisation to collect money from their bank account when payment for the goods or services they have provided is due. The payment, which is made electronically, can be for varying amounts and can be for either a regular or irregular payment. The arrangement lasts for as long as the direct debit agreement is in place. Being paid by direct debit is a fantastic way for a business to be paid because it means that not only can you take the payment from your customer's account the minute it becomes due, you can also take all future payments as soon as they become due too. Direct debit is ideal for home businesses that provide regular services such as lawn care, hairdressing or pet grooming.

- ✔ **Bank transfer.** If you provide your customer with your business account name, sort code and account number they can make a direct electronic payment from their bank account to yours, also known as a BACS payment. Depending on whether you and the customer have accounts with the same bank or not, the money is transferred within a couple of hours or may take up to a few days. For security reasons, only give your bank details to trusted customers – don't post them on your website.

✔ **Cheques.** In many cases – particularly for large payments of thousands of pounds – being paid in cash just isn't practical, so using cheques is a good alternative. However, cheques aren't as easy as cash; you have to deposit them in your bank account, where they're usually held for five working days until they clear, to be able to obtain cash. Not only that, but cheques also introduce the possibility that the customer's account may not have sufficient funds available to pay the obligation or that the cheques are counterfeit. Insufficient funds are a very real concern, and you have to be sure your customer has the capacity to pay you before you accept a cheque. Remember too that cheques are gradually being phased out of the banking system altogether in favour of electronic payments, so they won't be around for much longer.

✔ **Debit and credit cards.** Card payments are another step down the ladder of preference for receiving money because the credit card companies take a fee for every transaction you give them to process. However, they're an extremely convenient way of processing transactions for both customers and businesses. Using an electronic terminal significantly reduces the risk of fraud as it means that payments are authorised by the bank or credit card company at the point of purchase. We recommend you also sign up to an additional layer of security such as Verified by Visa (www.visaeurope.com) or MasterCard SecureCode (www.mastercard.com). If fraud does occur, in general the card issuer or cardholder is liable, not the business selling the products or services, provided the correct procedures have been followed.

✔ **Online payments.** These payments include those paid through services such as PayPal and WorldPay for customers who don't have credit cards or who may have adverse credit (who account for about 10 per cent of online sales).

✔ **Credit.** When you sell someone a product or service and let them pay for it later, you're extending credit to your customer. Although this practice is quite common in business, it's by far the least preferred way to be paid. It may be weeks or even months before you finally get your money – perhaps well after you've sold and delivered your products or services – and you run the risk of never being paid at all. If you do decide to bill your clients for your products and services, be sure to check out their credit histories first. If in doubt, require your clients to pay you in cash, by direct debit, bank transfer or with a debit or credit card.

Creating a positive cash flow starts with bringing cash into your business. The longer you take to convert whatever form of payment you decide to accept into cash, the longer you have to wait before your cash flow is positive.

Kick-starting your cash flow

Do you always seem to be a day late and a pound short? Even though you're bringing in good money, is it already spent as soon as it arrives? If you answer yes to these questions, you probably have a problem with cash flow. Assuming you're charging enough for your products and services, either you're not collecting your money quickly enough or you're spending too much money too quickly.

But don't fret; here are some ways to put your cash flow on the right track:

- ✔ **Get your money upfront.** If at all possible, ask for payment before you deliver your products or services. There's no better way to get your cash flowing in the right direction than being paid sooner rather than later.

- ✔ **Don't pay your bills any sooner than you have to.** Your cash flow will thank you if you wait to pay your bills until you're required to do so. If, for example, your electricity bill requires payment 30 days after you receive it and you pay your bills with an online banking account, schedule your payment to be delivered the day before it's due (don't schedule payment on the exact due date – if the payment fails, you won't have enough time to fix the problem before your payment is late). If you're paying by cheque, wait until day 25 before you write out your cheque and post it. However, waiting to pay your bills doesn't mean holding your payments longer than the date when payment is due. Late payments may, at best, create ill will between you and your supplier and, at worst, damage your credit.

- ✔ **Make sure your invoices are timely – and accurate!** Send invoices as soon as you deliver a product or service – preferably with the delivery itself. And make sure they're accurate. Many payments are delayed or rejected because of honest but preventable mistakes in invoicing.

- ✔ **Bill more often.** The more often you bill your clients or customers, the more often you'll be paid. And the more often you're paid, the better your cash flow is. Instead of billing your clients quarterly, why not bill them monthly? If you're supplying products, try breaking your deliveries into smaller chunks that you can bill sooner and more often.

- ✔ **Give prompt-payment discounts.** Everyone loves price discounts, and if you offer discounts to clients who pay their bills quickly, you're sure to have many takers. You may get a little less money as a result, but this drawback is offset by the fact that you get your money sooner rather than later.

- ✔ **Manage your expenses.** The flip side of bringing cash into your company is sending it out. The less cash you spend, the better your cash flow is. Spend money on your home business only when necessary. Instead of buying the latest and greatest computer every year, for example, try to make the one you have last as long as you can – replacing it only when necessary.

> ✔ **Manage your accounts receivable.** In other words, make sure you keep track of what's owed to you and take action to collect late payments. Customers and clients have plenty of reasons why they haven't paid the money that's due to you; however, you'll never find out why if you aren't keeping track of your clients' payments. Accounting software programs such as QuickBooks can easily generate a report showing you the status of all your payments. If payments are even a day late, take immediate action to get paid.

Understanding late payments

A time comes in the life of every home-based business owner when a client forgets to pay you for the products or services you sell them or outright refuses to do so. It's one thing if the products and services you sold your client were never delivered, were supplied late or were poor in quality. Most customers have a problem paying you in those kinds of situations and they may express their displeasure by holding on to the cash they owe you. It's another thing altogether, however, if you did what you agreed to do when your client placed their order.

But why wouldn't your clients pay you the money they owe you? Or why would they drag the process out so long that it becomes almost more trouble getting your money than it's worth? Here are just a few of the possibilities:

✔ The cheque may be in the post – really.

✔ Your client may have forgotten to pay you.

✔ A mistake in your invoice may prevent your client from paying you.

✔ Your client may not be satisfied with the product or service you provided.

✔ Your client may be trying to improve their own cash flow or make a last-ditch effort to save their business before declaring bankruptcy or going out of business.

You can address each of these issues, but before you can resolve the problem, you have to find out the reason for the delay. Collecting money owed to you isn't the best part of having your own business, but it is necessary.

Follow this six-step plan and you should get even the most reluctant client or customer to pay up:

1. **Personally call your client.**

   Before you do anything else, get on the phone to your client to find out what the problem is. If it's minor, you can take care of it right then and there, over the phone. In the vast majority of cases, this initial phone call is all it takes to nudge your clients into paying you. If, however, calling your client doesn't get payment to you straight away, you need to take further action.

2. **Send a late-payment reminder letter.**

   Don't wait after a payment is due to send out a late-payment reminder letter. If payment is due 15 days after you invoice, and you don't receive it, send out a reminder on day 16. If payment is due 30 days after you invoice, send out a reminder on day 31. Don't be shy – it's your money, so go after it. In addition to sticking the late-payment reminder letter in the post, try faxing and emailing copies. You might also want to remind them in the letter that you are legally entitled to charge interest on late payments. You can use software to remind you when it's time to act on a payment. For example, QuickBooks has a reminder feature.

3. **Stop work.**

   If your client or customer drags things out longer than is acceptable to you, you may have to stop work to get their attention. If you sell products, stopping work means suspending deliveries of any further orders until your client pays their bill. If you deliver services, stopping work means putting any current projects on hold until payment is made. Stopping work shows your client or customer that you're serious about getting paid, and it's sure to solicit some sort of response. Before you undertake this step, however, be sure to give your client fair warning that you plan to take this action if you don't receive payment by a particular date.

4. **Send a 'letter before action' from a solicitor.**

   A letter on headed notepaper from a solicitor threatening court action if the outstanding amount is not paid immediately can often get results. (This may cost in the region of a few hundred pounds, so it's not worth it for small amounts.)

5. **Enlist the services of a reputable debt collection agency.**

   A debt collection agency chases debts on your behalf in return for a percentage – typically upwards of 10 per cent – of the money collected by them. However, if you decide to go down this route you need to tread extremely carefully. Debt collection agencies have a poor reputation in the UK, and you need to make sure that you don't employ one that uses heavy-handed tactics, as it could seriously damage the reputation of your own business. Check that the debt collection agency is a member of the Credit Services Association (CSA), which lists its members on its website (www.csa-uk.com).

6. **Mediate.**

   Taking a client or customer to court isn't our idea of fun. Before you're forced to take that last, most drastic step, you have one more way to get out of your impasse: mediation. A *mediator* is an impartial third party whose job is to help you and your customer work through your problems and reach a reasonable solution – one that is a win for both parties. If your client has simply decided not to pay you, mediation may not be fruitful. However, if your client is upset because of some perceived shortcoming in your performance, you may have a chance of resolution through mediation. You can find a civil mediation provider in your area by using the online search service on the government website www.gov.uk.

7. **Take them to court.**

   Taking your clients to court is always the last resort. Not only does taking a client to court take up a lot of your precious time (and, if you need a lawyer, your money), but suing a client also puts the last nail in the coffin that was your business relationship. If, however, despite all your efforts, you still haven't been paid and you decide that it's in your interest to do everything in your power to get the money that's owed you, by all means, take your client to court.

   If you're owed less than £10,000 you can go through the small claims track of your local county court where your case may be dealt with using written evidence. For claims of more than £10,000 you may need a more formal hearing. You can also make a claim online via the www.gov.uk website for money owed for amounts of up to £100,000.

The extent to which you pursue your money is up to you. In some cases, you may decide that it's easier to write off the money (and the business relationship) than to pursue it to its ultimate conclusion. In other cases, you may decide to do whatever is necessary to get paid.

Getting a Loan

Studies show that one of the primary reasons so many businesses fail in their first year of existence is because they're *undercapitalised* – in other words, they don't have sufficient cash to meet their ongoing obligations over the long haul. Depending on what kind of business you have, putting enough money aside to allow you to make it through your first year can be a daunting proposition. But it shouldn't stop you from starting a successful home-based business – because you can always apply for a loan.

For many home-based businesspeople, the first choice in lenders is a time-honoured one: F&F (friends and family). If friends and family aren't able to meet your business needs (and mixing business and family can make for an uncomfortable relationship), though, you need to look elsewhere for the cash you need to sustain your business as you become established and build sales.

In the following sections, we explain some of the most commonly used sources of loans for home-based businesses.

Discovering different kinds of credit

Banks are the traditional route to getting a loan for your business. However, you may have trouble obtaining a loan in the name of your business until it has established a track record of success over some extended period of time, particularly in tough economic times when banks can be reluctant to lend to small businesses. If that's the case for you, check out the different kinds of credit we describe in this section to find one that may work for you.

Some of the most common forms of credit for home-based businesses, along with their pluses and minuses, include the following:

- **Credit card.** Many home-based businesses are financed – especially when they're first starting up – with credit cards. Not only are credit cards easy for most people to get, but they're also convenient and easy to manage. All this convenience comes at a price, however. Credit card interest rates can be obscenely high – typically at least 16.9 per cent per year at the time of writing – and they're so easy to use that you can quickly find yourself bumping up against your credit limit and in over your head if you aren't careful. Used judiciously however, credit cards can be a terrific business tool – and may be all the credit you ever need.

- **Personal loan.** Individuals can get *personal loans* from banks, credit unions, finance companies and similar sources based on their own personal income and creditworthiness. Assuming you have sufficient income and a good credit rating, you have a good chance of qualifying for the loan you need. After you have your loan, you're free to spend the money as you please, making personal loans quite flexible. If you decide to apply for a personal loan, make sure you do so while you still have your job – *before* you leave to start your own business. Your income is likely to be higher, at least initially, improving the chances of approval as well as increasing the amount of money your bank will be willing to loan to you.

- **Business loan.** Banks and other financial institutions make *business loans* to finance business start-ups, cover ongoing operational needs or finance business expansions. New businesses are inherently risky – they often have little or no equity (value) built up, usually lack a sufficiently long track record of success and have a statistically high rate of failure within the first few years after founding. So business loans can be difficult for home-based businesses to obtain. Although rates can be reasonable – usually only a few points over the base rate set by the Bank of England – the hoops you have to jump through, as well as the ongoing reporting and bank reviews, may be enough to send you looking elsewhere for funding. You may even have to pledge your personal assets as security in the event of a loan default. To get a business loan, at a minimum, you need a business plan, and you need to establish a good working relationship with your banker. If you and your business have what it takes, however, business loans can be your best solution.

✔ **Peer-to-peer lending.** A relatively new alternative to bank lending is peer-to-peer lending, in which lots of individuals collectively lend small amounts of money to a promising business. Interest rates charges are generally slightly higher than a business loan from a bank but lending decisions are often quicker. Businesses that organise peer-to-peer lending include Funding Circle (www.fundingcircle.com) and Zopa (www.zopa.com). Crowdfunding is another possibility (refer to Chapter 3).

✔ **Bank overdraft.** An overdraft is an approved extension to your bank account: instead of getting a lump sum for the full amount of the loan, you're given approval to borrow funds up to a certain limit in whatever amounts or as often as you like. The advantage of an overdraft agreement is that you don't have to use any of the money available to you until you need it, which means you don't have to make interest payments until you actually use the money. On the downside, you may have to pay an arrangement fee for an overdraft and the interest rate is usually higher than for a standard loan.

✔ **Mortgage extension.** Extending the mortgage on your home to raise funds is similar to taking out a personal loan, with one major difference: the loan is secured on your home, which means that you could lose your home if you default on your loan obligations. Because your home is being used as a guarantee, interest rates on mortgages are generally lower than for other types of loan, and it can be relatively straightforward to extend your mortgage, provided you're earning enough in your salaried job (yes, try to apply before leaving your nine to five) to meet the monthly repayments and that you retain sufficient equity in your home to satisfy the lender's criteria. Loan terms can typically run for up to 25 years. You'll probably have a choice of a lump sum or setting up a line of credit that you can draw on – and pay back – as necessary.

✔ **Microloan.** The government has established the Start Up Loans programme (www.startuploans.co.uk) to help entrepreneurs aged 18–30 living in England and Northern Ireland to get new small businesses off the ground. The scheme provides eligible candidates with loans of up to £2,500, depending on their business plan. You need to pay back the loan over five years at a fixed rate of interest, which is currently set at 6 per cent. For thorough advice on all the government help available to contribute towards financing your business, head to www.greatbusiness.gov.uk/financing-a-business.

So what kind of loan should you get? The answer depends on your particular situation, financial goals, the amount of money you plan to borrow and your own personal credit history. Take some time to discuss your different options with your bank manager or financial adviser. Remember, however, to always minimise how much you borrow and be diligent about paying back your loans as soon as you can.

Getting the loan you want

The best way to get the loan you want is to first understand what factors go into a decision to extend or deny credit to an applicant. The five key criteria used by most banks, building societies and other financial institutions are:

- ✔ **Capacity.** Will your business have the financial wherewithal to make loan payments – in full and on time – as required by your agreement with the lending agency? Will your cash flow support this additional burden of debt on your business? If you answer no to these questions, you need to figure out how to improve revenues while tightening up on expenses. Do so *before* you apply for your loan, not after.

- ✔ **Capital.** *Capital* represents the ratio of your home business's debt to its assets or equity. Unfortunately, most business start-ups – including home-based businesses – have relatively high debt loads versus equity or assets. This is normal. You can, however, improve your chances of getting the loan you want by minimising the debt you carry, and maximising equity and your own investment in the business.

- ✔ **Character.** Are you personally a good credit risk? Do you have a history of meeting your own financial obligations, including repaying loans on time and avoiding defaults or bankruptcies? A poor credit history is an indication to a lender that your character is less than perfect. If you have a poor credit history, make sure you do whatever you can to repair your own credit before you apply for a loan. Obtain a credit report from one of the two main credit reference agencies, Equifax (www.equifax. co.uk) or Experian (www.experian.co.uk) and take action on any problems that may show up.

- ✔ **Security.** What kind of security can you pledge in case you default on your loan? Car loans require your car to be pledged as security. Home mortgages require that your house be pledged as security. What are your options for providing security or a guarantee for a loan? In many cases, lenders may require that you pledge your assets or property to secure your loan. Your ability to provide sufficient assets as security can greatly enhance your chances of getting the loan you want.

- ✔ **Conditions.** Conditions include the health and growth potential of the markets within which you operate, the demographics of the typical buyers of your products and services, and many other economic factors external to your business. Although you can do little to influence or control the behaviour of your markets or your customers, you can influence exactly which markets and customers you plan to target.

As you prepare to apply for a loan, review each of these criteria and make an honest assessment of how you measure up. Which areas can you improve in? Find them and try to improve them now – before you apply for your loan. There's no reason why – if you do your homework – you can't get the loan you want for your business.

Fixing bad credit history

Not everyone has a great credit history and, unfortunately, a bad credit history can prevent you from getting the loan you want and the money you need. Your credit history can be poor if you miss mortgage or credit card payments. The good news is that with a bit of time and patience, you can turn a bad credit history into a good credit rating.

Here are some steps you can take to improve your credit rating:

✔ Get a copy of your credit report and have any errors corrected by writing to the credit reference agency. Make sure all your debts are registered to your correct name and current address, and ensure there are no mistakes on your file such as other people's debts.

✔ Register on the electoral roll at your current address.

✔ Pay all your household bills on time.

✔ Show lenders you're a responsible borrower by paying back the amount you owe on credit cards and loans on time each month. You need to do this for at least six months.

✔ Close down any credit agreements you no longer use.

✔ Don't make too many applications for credit at the same time because lenders can interpret that as desperation. Space out your applications.

✔ Only apply for credit that you think you're likely to get.

✔ Include a landline on application forms; lenders like to see them because it shows you have a permanent address.

✔ Avoid entering into a joint finance arrangement with someone who has a poor credit rating themselves, as doing so affects your rating.

Chapter 7

The Price is Right: Deciding How Much to Charge

*P*ricing plays an extremely important role in the ultimate success of your business. Do it right, and your business will flourish; do it wrong, and your business may founder.

Here's how pricing works, in a nutshell: if you set your prices too high, your clients seek less expensive sources for the products and services you provide, and you'll soon find yourself going out of business from lack of sales. Set them too low, however, and although you'll be swamped with customers – everyone loves a bargain, after all – your profit margins will be too small to sustain your business as it grows. On the other hand, you may put some customers off if your prices are too good to be true. Not everyone is seduced by a bargain, especially if reliability or safety are key. The key is finding a compromise between these two extremes that pays you what you're worth while also generating sufficient business to keep you working as many hours as you want.

 You can set prices for your products and services in a variety of ways. In many cases, though, finding the right price comes down to good old-fashioned trial and error. In other words, do some research, check the competition, set a price and see what happens. If sales aren't high enough, you can decide whether to lower your prices as an incentive for potential buyers to part with their cash. If sales are too high and the resulting profits are too low, you can choose to raise your prices to improve your margins (see the 'Changing your prices' section later in this chapter).

The best pricing strategies are ones that strike a balance between generating the sales you need to survive and earning a reasonable profit that enables your business to grow. This chapter helps you understand how to develop the pricing strategy that's best for you, your business and your customers and clients. We help you sort out the costs that you have to cover when you set your prices and help you get a feel for what your customers are willing to pay. We also give you ideas for how to research your competition and review a number of different approaches to pricing that can aid your sales efforts. Finally, we consider the reasons why you should (or shouldn't) consider discounting your prices and how to stand firm on pricing when doing so is in your business's best interest.

Working Out What Your Prices Must Cover

Although the motivation behind your business may be to help others get things done or to provide them with the products they need to run their own businesses successfully, you can't have a business – at least not for very long – if you don't charge your customers some amount of money for your trouble. But you can't just charge them any old price; your price has to be low enough to attract the attention of prospective customers but high enough to allow you to generate a profit.

The whole idea of pricing products and services is to pay for all the expenses incurred in running a business while leaving a reasonable profit. Unfortunately, many home-based businesspeople don't fully understand the expenses they actually incur in running their businesses. Not only that, but they also sometimes forget that their home-based businesses should pay a decent salary and generate a reasonable profit – just like non-home-based businesses.

Imagine that the finances of your home-based business are a house. Just like any other sturdily built house anywhere in the world, it needs a roof, a foundation, walls, doors and windows. Your *money house* also has a ground floor and a first floor. Figure 7-1 shows the money house.

The following list describes the major components of the money house and how they relate to the finances of your home-based business:

- **The foundation – your salary.** Whenever your company sells a product or service, a portion of the cash you take in is set aside to pay you and any employees who have a regular salary.

✔ **The ground floor – your overheads.** The cash you take in also pays for your *overheads*, including all the expenses your business requires to operate, regardless of whether or not you're selling any products. Insurance, rent and telephones are examples of overhead expenses.

✔ **The first floor – your direct costs.** *Direct costs* are expenses that you incur on behalf of specific projects or products. If you drive to another town for a meeting or purchase wood to build a cabinet for a customer, for example, you're incurring direct expenses.

✔ **The roof – your profit.** *Profit* is what you're in business to try to make; it's what's left over when you've brought in all your cash for selling a product or service and subtracted your salary, overheads and direct expenses. Profit is your reward and it plays an important role in building your business.

Just like a large business such as Tesco, Unilever or BP, your home-based business can make a profit or incur a loss. Home-based businesses are real businesses, and the profit you make in your business is just as real as it is for any other business. People view profit in many different ways. Some people identify the revenue beyond what they expect to pay themselves as a higher salary. For others, it's having the money to spend on extra things, such as investing in your business without borrowing (usually a better idea than taking out loans to grow your business) or taking a long-deserved holiday. But for most people, profit is additional earnings.

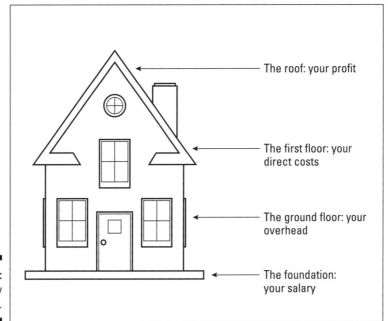

Figure 7-1:
The money
house.

The roof: your profit

The first floor: your direct costs

The ground floor: your overhead

The foundation: your salary

In the following sections, we take a closer look at the kinds of financial elements that make up each part of your money house, and we explain how they all work together to determine the prices you charge for your company's products and services.

Calculating your salary

When you set up your business as a sole trader, you probably won't pay yourself a salary because, under a sole-trader structure, the money you make in your business is automatically counted as income to you for tax purposes. When you set up your home business as a partnership or corporation, however, you may find that paying yourself a salary makes a lot of sense. But how much should you pay yourself? When deciding how much salary to draw from your business, you first have to decide which of the following three lifestyles you want your business to support:

- ✔ **Survival.** In this mode, your business is just getting by and you have little or no extra money to set aside to pay yourself. Ideally, you still work your regular day job or have a spouse or significant other to help support you while you're working to build your sales.

- ✔ **Comfortable.** Comfortable means things are going pretty well – well enough to allow you to leave your regular job and work at your home-based business on a full-time basis. You can choose to continue with the status quo – and be quite comfortable where you are – or work to increase your sales and see your business really take off.

- ✔ **Much better than average.** At this salary point, you're making more money than most people in your community. Attaining this level of income requires a lot of hard work and perhaps no small amount of luck. But for many, the rewards are worth the extra effort.

The amount you can afford to pay yourself as a salary entirely depends on how much the business can afford to pay you. If it isn't making any money, it can't afford to pay you a salary at all.

Establishing your overheads

Your home-based business's *overheads* consist of all its non-direct costs and non-salary expenses. In essence, your overhead expenses are the costs of doing business – the expenses that your business incurs even when you aren't creating products or delivering services to customers. Here are some examples of common overhead expenses:

- ✔ Computers, copiers, printers, telephones and other office technology
- ✔ Desks, chairs and other office furniture
- ✔ Internet, email and phone connections
- ✔ Website hosting fees
- ✔ Marketing costs
- ✔ Letterhead stationery and business cards
- ✔ Office supplies
- ✔ Travel for business operations, marketing or other non-project purposes
- ✔ Water, electricity and other utilities
- ✔ Newspaper and trade magazine subscriptions
- ✔ Insurance
- ✔ Licences
- ✔ Rent or mortgage
- ✔ Repairs and maintenance

 Because overheads don't directly produce revenue (or, ultimately, profit), try to minimise overhead expenses, keeping them at the lowest possible level while still providing the highest-quality services and products. To minimise your overhead expenses, you need to carefully assess every expense before you execute it. Before you spend money on any overhead item, take a moment to decide whether or not you really need it. On the plus side, your overhead (and direct) expenses are generally tax deductible. Check out Chapter 8 for more details on the tax implications of your expenses.

Incurring direct costs

Direct costs are the expenses you incur as you create products or deliver services. Generally, the more direct costs the merrier, because they directly become part of the products and services you deliver to your clients, increasing the overall amount of money you bring into your business (and ideally increasing your clients' satisfaction at the same time). Here are some examples of direct costs:

- Materials and supplies used in the manufacturing process
- Travel at your client's request
- Time spent in client meetings
- Postage and phone calls for specific projects
- Fees to consultants contracted to assist on specific projects
- Equipment dedicated to producing a specific product or delivering a service to a particular client

If you aren't creating products or working on client projects (if you're providing consultancy work, for example), you don't incur direct costs. (But you do still have to pay for your overheads – whether or not you're producing and selling your products and services – and this overhead cost can quickly add up.)

Starting a training business

Q: I know a lot about computers and for the past few years I have been teaching adult education classes in various aspects of computer applications. I also give one-day courses to students at the local college. The seminars are well received and popular. I would now like to broaden my base and start finding new markets where I can give my lectures and courses – perhaps at business conferences, or providing in-house training at big corporate businesses. Please can you give me some advice on how to go about doing this?

A: If you know a lot about computers and can explain how they work in an easily understandable way then you have a skill that many people would be willing to pay for. Your first step is to make sure you present yourself in the right way. Create a website to showcase what you can offer. Explain on the website exactly what you do and how much you charge in a clear way.

Include testimonials from satisfied customers, and explain why your courses are useful and who would benefit from them.

Your next step is to start contacting the people who might be interested in hiring you to do a course. Email conference organisers and the training managers of large corporations explaining what you do, but don't forget to include local businesses, too, who might need to train their staff. And make sure you continue to build on your existing base within the education sector. If local colleges like your courses, how about approaching local schools to see if their sixth form needs a course on computer skills? Another potentially lucrative avenue might be outplacement firms that advise people who have been made redundant from large corporate businesses – many of them would surely benefit from a computer course to brush up their skills.

Striving for profit

Although _profit_ may seem like a mysterious and complex concept if you're new to owning your own business, it really boils down to a fairly simple idea:

> _Profit: The difference between a company's revenues and its costs._

To figure out your company's profit, add together all the cash your company brings in from selling products and services and any income you earn from other sources, such as interest-bearing bank accounts and investments, and then subtract your salary, overheads and direct costs from your total income. If the profit is negative (because the money you spend for your business is more than the money you bring into your business), it's called a _loss_. Profits are good and losses are bad!

Profit is the roof on the money house we built earlier in this chapter. It's the motivation that drives many businesses to ever-greater heights. In the case of your home-based business, profit is the reward to you for risking your capital in the marketplace. If allowed to accumulate within the business, the profit becomes the _equity_ – the money put aside in savings – that gives the company real value.

Sizing Up Your Potential Customers and How Much They'll Pay

Pricing your products and services is more than simply sticking price tags on them – pricing is an integral part of the overall strategy for your home-based business. Not only is pricing important because it determines to some extent exactly how much cash your business brings in, but it's also important from a marketing perspective, and from the perspective of the overall health of your business and its ability to survive the long haul.

Set your prices too high, for example, and your sales will be few and far between. The result? Little or no cash into the business and an overall financial loss as you continue to spend money that isn't being offset by income. Not only that, but you'll also spend an awful lot of time twiddling your thumbs as you wait for your phone to ring. On the other hand, set your prices too low, and you'll set yourself up for a going-out-of-business scenario as you spend far too much time and money for too little return on your investment.

Testing the market to find the right price

When Christopher Ward was trying to decide on the price at which he should sell his hand-made watches, he came up with an unusual solution. He placed three newspaper advertisements for identical watches: one offering them for £99, another selling them for £179 and a third pricing them at £849. The £179 watch sold best, so he set the price at £179 and refunded the buyers who'd bought the watch at £849. His firm, based in Maidenhead, Berkshire – which has the advertising slogan 'the cheapest most expensive watches in the world' – now has a turnover of £4.5 million a year and employs nine people.

Before you launch headlong into your new home-based business, take a close look at your prospective customers – who they are and how much they're willing to pay for your products and services (Chapter 4 has more on recognising your best customers). What if your targeted customers don't seem willing to pay the price you need to turn a reasonable profit? You have little choice but to rethink your entire business strategy, either by creating more value for your clients-to-be to justify a higher price or by moving to an entirely different product or service that you *can* sell at the right price.

Take a moment or two to picture the kind of person who will buy your products or services. As you imagine your typical client or customer, ask yourself the following questions. To help you answer these questions, check out your competition to get a feel for what products and services they offer and how much their customers are willing to pay (see the next section for more tips).

- ✔ **What's your product or service worth to your prospective customers and clients?** Will your customers and clients see what you're selling as high value, low value or something in between? Have you targeted the right market for your products and services? If not, what is the right market, and are there enough buyers to make it worth your while? Are you providing the right products and services to your target market? If not, what are the right products and services, and can you produce them cost-effectively?

- ✔ **What price are your prospective customers and clients willing to pay?** Is the price low, high or somewhere in between?

✔ **Are you charging enough for your products and services to establish and grow a healthy business?** Will the price your customers and clients are willing to pay enable you to cover your business expenses – including the value of your time – and leave some money for profit? Will these prices enable you to grow your business, or will they cause your business to shrink – or, over a period of time, fail?

✔ **Do you have the right mix of price versus hours worked?** Are your prices set high enough to make a reasonable return on your investment of time and money, or are they so low that you have to work around the clock to make enough money simply to keep your business afloat?

Pricing can play an important role in your home business's success or its failure, and deserves your focus and attention – both in initially setting prices for your products and services, and then in monitoring them over time to ensure that they're creating the return you desire. Find the right pricing and you pave the way to increased sales at a high return – something that every home-based business owner is happy to have.

Researching Your Competition

So you've probably gathered that pricing is really important to the success of your business. But if you're new to running a home-based business and have little or no previous experience selling the products and services you now offer, what's the best way to decide what prices to charge?

By far the quickest and easiest way to determine whether your prices make sense is to research your competition and see what they're charging. After you understand what other businesses like yours charge, you have a much better idea of the prices you can charge. Want to attract more business than the competition? Just charge a little less than they do. Want to position your company as a premium brand? Charge a little more than the competition.

Luckily for you, the Internet has made researching your competition much easier than it's ever been. With a few clicks of your mouse, you can find all kinds of free information about what prices your competitors' products are selling for and about the companies you compete against – information that you can use to structure your own competitive strategies and tactics.

Here are some places to start your online search for information on your competitors:

- **Amazon:** www.amazon.co.uk
- **eBay:** www.ebay.co.uk
- **Facebook:** www.facebook.com
- **Google:** www.google.com
- **The Best Of:** www.thebestof.co.uk
- **Thomson Local:** www.thomsonlocal.com
- **Yell:** www.yell.com

The British Library Business and IP Centre (www.bl.uk/bipc) provides a wide range of free reports to help you research key industries, from construction to cake-making, from fashion to fast food. The guides highlight useful databases, publications and websites. You can download them from their website or access them in person at the Business and IP Centre in London. The British Library also runs free workshops providing a beginner's guide to accessing industry information, which can help you identify the major competitors in your industry.

The best business media

Q: I want to keep up to date with what's happening in my industry and find out which companies are doing what as well as finding advice, information and inspiration. What newspapers and magazines should I be reading?

A: The answer depends partly on the nature of your business and your clientele but to get a general overview of what's happening in the business world and how the economy is faring, make sure you read a daily national paper with a good business section, such as *The Times* or *The Telegraph*, as well as *The Financial Times,* which provides in-depth business coverage. Find out which trade magazines cover your sector and

read those – *The Grocer* and *Retail Week* are useful for the food retail industry, for example, while *Construction News* is essential reading for anyone in the, well, construction industry! Increasingly trade magazines are moving online instead of having print editions – some do both – so you may find it easier to read them that way. General business magazines such as *The Economist* and *Real Business* can also yield useful information; again, these are increasingly moving online. Finally, if your business primarily operates in your local neighbourhood, read your local newspaper or magazine, if there is one, to keep updated on local news and events.

Pricing Strategies That Deliver Sales

In an ideal world, the prices you apply to your products and services would enhance – not hinder – your ability to sell them. Pricing is a fine art and the psychology of marketing, along with how you present your products and your prices, determines much of the way your clients-to-be react to them. (Head to Chapter 4 for more on marketing.)

When your products and services are desirable and in short supply, people are willing to pay far more for them than when they're undesirable and commonly available. This is the basic law of supply and demand that you probably learned about at school. Think about what happens when a few toys end up on the top of every child's Christmas list. As a surge of parents hits the shops, the toys inevitably become hard to find and parents become willing to pay top prices to get them – often, whatever it takes to ensure the happiness of their children. And the toys that don't make the top of the list? They're plentiful and often on sale.

What does this idea of supply and demand mean for you? It means determining the best price points for your products and services. In the following sections, we explore different ways to develop pricing strategies that ease the way to sales.

Creating perceived value

Above all, your clients and customers want to feel like they're getting the best value for their money – regardless of whether the prices you charge are high or low. So by increasing the *perceived value* of your products and services (value is a subjective judgement, after all), you can increase the prices you charge for them and increase your profit at the same time.

Here are some of the best ways to create and increase the perceived value of your organisation's products and services:

  ✔ **Exceed your customers' expectations.** This dramatically increases the perceived value you deliver to them. Think about how you feel when someone goes out of their way to give you the best possible service. Aren't you willing to pay a little extra to get more of that particular kind of service in the future? The better work you do, the higher your perceived value and the higher the prices you can charge.

- **Be different.** Many markets are crowded with competitors, each one offering products and services that seem to differ little from the competition. When you differentiate yourself from the rest of the pack – whether through novel packaging, a unique sales approach or the product or service itself – you increase your value to your clients and customers.

- **Focus on customer service.** The bad news is that every industry has more than its share of businesses that don't provide good customer service. The good news is that this shortfall gives you a terrific opportunity to provide the service that's lacking in your industry. Take advantage of it, and you greatly enhance the perceived value of your organisation's products and services. Believe us – most people vastly prefer buying their products and services from companies that provide good service than from ones that don't.

- **Add value.** If you and a competitor offer the same item for the same price, why would a customer decide to buy exclusively from you? Well, in truth, they wouldn't – unless, of course, you add value to the transaction. Perhaps you provide better after-sales support, or maybe you're willing to take returned items for 30 days after an item is sold rather than the 10 days your competitor allows. By adding value to the items you sell – value as perceived in the eyes of the buyer – you create value for your clients (and they'll value you for it).

- **Build long-term relationships.** All business is about relationships, and your customers and clients value the long-term relationships they develop with you and other trusted suppliers. By building relationships with your clients and customers, you become more than a place to buy something – you become a trusted friend and adviser, someone to turn to when your customers have questions or need help. Help a few times, and you'll have a customer for life.

Always keep your customers' perceived value of your products and services in mind when you develop and set your prices. Adding value in your customers' eyes gives you much greater flexibility in the prices you ultimately choose.

Setting your prices: Five approaches

Pricing is integral to the marketing process, and it can have a dramatic impact on whether potential customers choose to buy from you or from someone else. The right price can generate more sales, and the wrong price can send potential customers and clients looking elsewhere to fulfil their needs.

Selling the eBay way

Many home-based businesspeople have found success on eBay (www.ebay.co.uk), the popular auction website. Why eBay? Because it's the most successful auction site with the widest reach to a global audience of buyers. In recent years, eBay has introduced fixed-price listings for sellers who want to sell their products for a set price without going through the hassle and uncertainty of an auction. Some home-based businesspeople have discovered that they can get more than enough business just by selling on eBay, while others have used eBay as a stepping stone to bigger and better things. Whatever your long-term goals may be, selling your products on eBay is extremely easy, and your listings can reach a worldwide audience – exposing your products to a much larger number of potential buyers than if you sold them only in your local area. This increased exposure translates to higher prices and more profit in your pocket.

Here are a few recent eBay success stories:

- ✔ Lisa Thomas used to be the manager of a recruitment agency but when her son was born in 2003 she decided she wanted to work from home so she could spend time with him. So she began selling second-hand baby clothes through eBay and soon moved on to selling traditional wooden toys and home interior products, running the business from her home in Exeter. She was so successful that in 2008 her husband gave up his job to join the business, which now has a turnover of £500,000.

- ✔ Shazina Wallington started selling personalised invitations on eBay in 2008 after leaving her job in IT and accountancy to look after her children. She quickly expanded into selling party supplies, running the business from her home in Farnborough, Hampshire, and by 2009 was selling so much that her lounge had become a warehouse and she couldn't close the garage door because it was so full of stock. Shazina opened her first retail shop in 2011 and now sells via eBay and through the shop, calling her business The Personalised Party Company.

- ✔ Husband and wife Stuart and Melinda Kirkwood starting trading on eBay in 2004 when they decided to sell some of the clothes their two daughters had grown out of. The clothes sold so well they started selling clothing, lingerie and accessories, running the business from their home in Rye, East Sussex. When Melinda was made redundant from her job with a vehicle recovery company in 2005 and Stuart stopped running the IT consultancy business he'd set up, both joined the business full time. Their business now employs 19 people and operates from two warehouses.

Although eBay can be a great place for home-based businesses to sell their wares, remember to factor in the fees you need to pay eBay to sell on their site. These fall under two broad categories: insertion fees and final value fees. You pay *insertion fees* to run your auction or fixed-price listing – whether or not you sell the item. You pay *final value fees* only when you sell the item; these fees are a percentage of the price for which you sell your item. You can find much more information about eBay fees on the website www.ebay.co.uk.

If you don't feel like dealing with eBay yourself, a number of companies and individuals can sell your items on eBay for you. Known as *trading assistants*, some specialise in selling particular items or services. You can find a list of those operating in your area by using the search function on the Trading Assistant Directory page on eBay, which enables you to search by postcode. Of course, you have to pay such companies a fee for their services, but some people use them to save time and to attract more buyers, thanks to the greater amount of traffic many of the service sites attract.

The following list describes five of the most common approaches that home-based businesses use to set their prices. As part of determining your pricing strategy, carefully consider which approach (or combination of approaches) makes the most sense for your business.

- ✔ **Start-up pricing.** If you're just getting started in your business, offer your customers an introductory rate that's set at a point somewhere between what other established businesses charge and the amount you would be paid if you were doing the work on salary for an employer. Just don't forget to increase your pricing to bring it in line with the rest of the market after you get past the start-up phase and establish a track record. To avoid unpleasant surprises, don't forget to let your early customers know that prices *will* rise in the future. Otherwise, they may turn elsewhere when your prices go up.

- ✔ **The going rate.** In some businesses, almost every company charges a *going rate* for particular products or services. For example, the typical carpet-cleaning business in your area may charge £100 to clean three rooms and a hallway. You can choose to set your price at the going rate and differentiate your business through things other than price, such as better customer service or an extra service that your competition doesn't provide. As some business owners have discovered, finding something that differentiates you from the competition can be as simple as a brightly painted van that advertises your business everywhere you go, or an easy-to-remember phone number.

- ✔ **Splitting the difference.** When you survey your competition, you may find that they offer a range of prices for the same products or services: some high, some low and some in between. By splitting the difference between the top and the bottom of the range, you can be sure that your price is neither too high nor too low. After seeing how your customers react, you can make further adjustments later (see the 'Changing your prices' section later in this chapter for tips on how to do so).

- ✔ **Bargain-basement pricing.** If you really want to generate a lot of business quickly, you can dramatically undercut your competitors' prices. However, before you try this approach, understand that some potential clients may be wary of buying products and services that are priced substantially below the competition because they may think they'd get a below-standard product or service. To offset this wariness, you need to find some way to make them feel like they aren't taking a risk by hiring you (great references from previous clients can do wonders here). Understand, too, that you may not be able to keep up this approach for long without doing serious financial damage to your company.

✔ **Premium pricing.** At the other end of the spectrum from bargain-basement pricing is pricing at a premium, *above* your competition. This approach works well when firstly, you differentiate the products or services you sell from those offered by your competition and, secondly, add value your clients and customers can see and appreciate. Consider a fancy dog-grooming service that doesn't just come to your home but that arrives in a brand-new stainless-steel van, customised with all the latest tools of the trade, hot water and big fluffy towels for your dog. Because you want only the very best for your pet, paying a few extra pounds for first-class service like this is a no-brainer.

After you set your prices, keep a close eye on what your competition is doing. Are they raising their prices? Lowering them? When your competition moves, be prepared to adjust your prices accordingly.

Changing your prices

After you decide on a specific price for a product or service, your clients expect to pay that price for the foreseeable future. No one likes buying things from a company that changes its prices every other week. However, at some point you may need to change your prices, whether up or down. If the changes translate into price increases, you may have to overcome the resistance of your clients and customers. If the changes are price decreases, of course, it's unlikely that anyone is going to object.

In the following sections, we look at price increases and price decreases – and how each affects your business.

Increasing your prices

Price increases aren't usually pleasant events for the company making them – no company wants to tell its clients they have to pay more money for the same product – but they're often necessary. Some of the most common reasons for price increases are:

✔ **You've under-priced your products.** After you set a price and begin to sell your products and services, you may discover that the money you're bringing in isn't enough to cover the expenses of the business and generate a reasonable profit. In this case, when you can't or don't want to reduce your expenses to bring your costs in line with the money you're bringing into your business, you have no other choice (assuming you want to stay in business) than to increase your prices.

- ✔ **Your expenses have increased.** If your costs of production increase, you can reduce your profit or increase your price. The choice is up to you (although if your expenses have dramatically increased, you may have to do both).

- ✔ **You need to cover a client's hidden expenses.** If you're performing services for a client and discover additional costs from working with that client that you didn't anticipate (for example, your client requires you to attend meetings twice a week instead of just once a month as you planned), you have to find a way to recoup them without reducing your profit. The easiest way is to increase your price.

- ✔ **You want to test the marketplace.** Sometimes you simply want to test the marketplace with a higher price to see whether the quantity of units you sell increases, decreases or stays the same. Airlines, food manufacturers and others test the marketplace all the time. You may discover that your customers are more willing to pay a higher price for your products and services than you thought.

- ✔ **You don't want the work.** If you don't want to do work for certain clients at the low prices you've agreed to, the best way to get out of this situation is to raise your prices far beyond your normal rates. If the customer decides to pay more, great – you just made a mint! If not, you won't miss it.

Don't be embarrassed by your prices or hesitate to raise or lower them when doing so makes sense for your business. If you decide to increase your prices, however, be as forthcoming as you can and give your customers plenty of notice so they can adjust.

Decreasing your prices

In some cases, you may have a good reason to decrease your prices. Though you may not have to decrease your prices as often as you increase them, you're bound to have to do so from time to time. The main reasons for decreasing your prices are:

- ✔ **You've overpriced your services.** If you've overpriced your services, you can choose to keep the extra money as profit (making for a very nice windfall, thank you very much), or you can give it back to your customers in the form of lower prices, refunds or rebates.

- ✔ **Your expenses have decreased.** If you've decreased your expenses, you may want to lower your prices. Then again, you can always keep the profit and increase the amount of money you put into savings. Doing so can motivate you to continue to find new ways to cut expenses.

✔ **You want to reward long-term clients.** Long-term clients always like to know you appreciate them. You can show your appreciation (and build their loyalty) by reducing prices for them on a one-off basis or permanently – perhaps in the form of a discount card, special gift or other premium.

✔ **You want to get new work.** One way to get new business is to drop your prices for new customers as a way to introduce them to your company and your products and services. Two-for-one specials for new customers, money-off vouchers and so on are all ways to get new customers to try out your company – and, ideally, stick around.

✔ **You want to extend a professional courtesy.** Certain professionals extend lower prices to colleagues as a courtesy. Why not extend lower prices to your colleagues, too? How about discounting your products and services for other home-based business owners?

As with any other price changes, make sure you lower your prices as part of an overall strategy, not just as a reaction to some momentary event unless you're having a January or summer sale. If in doubt, leave your prices where they are until the case for changing them is more compelling. Not sure whether it's the right time? Then it probably isn't.

Deciding whether to discount

When you're starting out in your home-based business, you need to get the ball rolling. Your prices can help you do so, or they can stop the ball dead in its tracks. In the beginning, getting work – regardless of how much you charge – may be more important than charging just the right price. After you build up experience and references, you're in a better position to be able to call the shots regarding your pricing.

In the beginning, you want to get known. You want to develop a buzz about your company and its goods and services. You want people to start talking about you and your company. As they do, and as more and more clients seek you out, you have the leverage to charge them what you're worth. In other words, if you're going to discount your products and services, the time to do so is when you're getting your home-based business established – not after you've developed a solid reputation, base of experience and prices people have begun to rely on.

By far the biggest mistake home-based businesspeople make is *chronic under-charging*. Chronic undercharging often occurs because first-time business owners lack confidence in their abilities so feel they need to charge a low rate just to get started in the industry. But that creates a downward spiral which slowly eats away at the foundations of your business – the longer it goes on, the weaker your business becomes. Eventually, the bottom falls out altogether, and you're left with nothing but unpaid bills.

Chronic undercharging creates the following problems in home-based businesses:

- **Price-driven clients.** You tend to attract customers who are much more interested in paying as little as possible than in buying the best product or service out there.

- **Low-margin work.** You spend far too much of your time on low-margin work and far less of your time on high-paid projects that offer the greatest return for your time and money. Because there are still only 24 hours in a day, you're working more hours for less pay – a going-out-of-business plan if we've ever seen one.

- **Burnout.** You force yourself into a situation in which you focus far more time on your business than you do on maintaining and improving your relationships with friends and family or on keeping yourself healthy and happy – a classic road to burnout. Burnout isn't unique to home-based businesses, but it can be a very real problem – especially for people who are juggling the demands of kids and family or a job that they haven't yet left behind.

Discounting is okay as long as you do it consciously and in line with long-term strategy. Don't let it become a knee-jerk reaction to every potential client who hesitates for a moment when you quote a price. If you're going to discount your services, consider some of the following approaches:

- Offer every tenth item under a certain price free of charge.

- Give a discount on your client's first order (say, 10 or 25 per cent).

- Offer volume discounts.

- Give a discount for paying before a certain date.

- Offer a variety of products and services at a variety of price points – high, low and in between. When faced with a client or client-to-be who wants you to discount your prices, you're far better off cutting the products or services delivered than cutting your unit price for those services.

  So, for example, when a client baulks at your quotation of £1,000 to develop a website, don't say: 'What if I drop my price to £750? Do we have a deal?' Instead, say: 'No problem. Here's a complete list of all the different features you get in my £1,000 plan. Which features do you want to omit to meet your budget?'

Taking a stand on prices

When you've established a price and your prospective client doesn't want to pay it, at some point you have to take a stand. You can't just give your products or services away. Often, you simply want to maintain your prices exactly where they are and deny requests to lower or discount them. Here are some strategies to help you hold the line on your prices when you think it's in your best interest to do so:

- **Understand your limits.** When you want to take a stand and hold the line on your prices, first you need to know the limitations within which you can work and the minimum prices you're willing to accept.

- **Learn to say no.** Far too many people cave in the moment their customers show even one iota of resistance to their prices, no matter how well thought out and reasonable they may be. But, luckily for you, we've found a very easy cure to this kind of reaction: just say no. Know your limits, and when someone wants you to go beyond them, be ready, willing and able to say no.

- **Be ready to explain why.** When you say no to people who think their requests are reasonable, you have to be able to explain why. Most people like to hear some rationale when someone else denies their 'reasonable' requests. Responses like 'I'll lose money on the deal at that price' or 'That's a going-out-of-business plan for me' may be sufficient.

- **It's not personal – it's business.** Separate your personal feelings from the need to conduct your business in a way that ensures its survival. Although you may like the feeling of cutting your prices and giving away your products and services to anyone who asks, you'll quickly go out of business with that approach. Remember: you've got a business to run – not a charity.

- **Be prepared with a counterproposal.** Whenever you tell a prospective client or customer no, offer an alternative that works for you. For example, if you don't want to agree to dropping your price from £100 to £75 a unit, as requested by your client, you may be able to say yes to £95 – a figure that may well seal the deal for you.

You're going to face times when you have to take a stand and hold the line against dropping your prices. Although you may lose potential customers in the process, your business will be healthier for it. And a healthy business is a business that thrives and grows – building long-term income for you and an ongoing partner for your clients.

Chapter 8

Considering Taxes, Deductions and Benefits

. . . .

In This Chapter

▶ Knowing what you need to pay in taxes and when

▶ Investigating deductible expenses

▶ Collecting VAT

▶ Providing yourself with your own benefits package

. . . .

*W*orking out what tax you need to pay, and when, is easily one of the most unappealing aspects of running your own home-based business.

Is it any wonder that the first thing many savvy home-based businesspeople do when they start their businesses is hire an accountant to help them work out and file their taxes? For many home-based business owners, the investment in a good tax planner can pay off many times over as the business grows and evolves. (And of course, being a tax adviser is generally a popular and lucrative home business to run!)

This chapter covers taxes: who pays them, when to pay them and how much to pay. And although our intent isn't to make you an expert on the subject of taxation (we don't want to put any accountants out of business), we do want to provide you with a basic understanding of the topic – enough to help you get your business started and talk intelligently to any tax professionals. (If you do want to know more about business taxes and finances, check out *Understanding Business Accounting*, 3rd Edition, by John A. Tracy and Colin Barrow; Wiley.)

We also cover deductible expenses, as these can be a boon to home-based businesses and determine how much tax you actually have to pay. Finally, we look at how to create your own benefits package.

Knowing Which Taxes to Pay – and When to Pay Them

Just like any other business, home-based businesses are required to pay tax – *income tax* if you're a sole trader or your business is a partnership, or *corporation tax* if your business is a private limited company. The forms you use to calculate and file your taxes and the kinds of expenses you can deduct depend on which of these business types you select (see Chapter 9 for details about each of these business structures).

If you fail to pay all the taxes you owe, pleading that you were confused by all the forms and schedules won't earn you any sympathy with HM Revenue and Customs (HMRC), the government tax office that deals with all aspects of taxation in the UK. In addition to being billed for all the taxes you failed to pay, you can expect to pay interest and penalties on top of them. In some cases, the interest and penalties alone can amount to thousands of pounds. If in doubt, ask an accountant.

How do I file my tax return?

In the UK, all active businesses are required to file an annual income tax return, regardless of whether they make or lose money.

HMRC encourages you to file your tax returns and other forms online, and you can do everything you need to at www.hmrc.gov.uk. All corporation tax returns must now be filed online, for example, and individual tax returns for sole traders are likely to follow shortly. However, if you're a sole trader or partnership and prefer to fill in paper forms for the time being (which you download and print out from the website), then Table 9-1 shows you which forms you need to submit when you file your tax return by post. If you set up your business as a private limited company, you also need to do your own separate *personal tax return* showing, for example, what salary and dividends you received from your business.

If you hire an accountant to do your tax return for you, you need to fill in Form 64-8 authorising HMRC to talk to your accountant, known as your *tax agent*, about your tax affairs.

Websites that can make your job less taxing

Several useful websites can help guide you through the taxation maze. Here are some of the best:

✔ **HMRC** (www.hmrc.gov.uk). HMRC's own website is the very best place to start. It provides useful information on every aspect of business taxation and all the forms you need are available to download.

✔ **Gov.uk** (www.gov.uk). The government's business advice website also contains lots of information about the UK tax system.

✔ **Smarta** (www.smarta.com). A great free online resource for start-ups and small businesses, Smarta has lots of useful articles explaining how tax works for small businesses.

Table 9-1	Taxes to Pay and Forms to File
Taxes to Pay	*Forms to File*
Sole Trader	
Income tax return	Form SA100
Supplementary form	Form SA103S (short version) or SA103F (full version)*
National Insurance Contributions	Form CA5601
Partnership	
Tax return	Form SA800
Partner in a Partnership (Individual)	
Income tax return	Form SA100
Supplementary forms	Form SA104S (short version) or SA104F (long version)*
National Insurance Contributions	Form CA5601
Private Limited Company	
Corporation tax	Must pay online

* You can only use the short (simplified) version of these forms if HMRC specifically tells you that you can. Most people need to complete the full version.

When do I have to pay?

The UK financial year runs from 6 April to 5 April the following year, so if you're a sole trader – or self-employed – you need to fill in a tax return at the end of the financial year, in other words, any time after 6 April. If you're filing your tax return online you have just over nine months in which to do it before the deadline of 31 January. If you file a paper return, the deadline is three months earlier on 31 October.

If you set up a private limited company then the financial year for the company runs from the end of the month in which you originally incorporated the business. If you incorporated it in June, for example, then your tax year runs from 1 July to 30 June the following year, every year. You must then file your corporation tax return within nine months and one day after the end of your financial year, so in this example, by 1 April.

If the end date of your company's financial year is very inconvenient for your business – if you run a seasonal business and the end of the financial year falls right in the middle of your busiest trading period, for example, making stock-taking a nightmare, you can apply to HMRC to have it changed.

How much do I have to pay?

Every business is different and every business has its own unique tax situation. One thing is for certain, though: the kind of business entity your business is has a definite bearing on the amount of tax you pay.

If you run your home-based business as a sole trader or as a partnership, your taxable business income is combined with any other source of income you receive, such as income from a property you're renting out or interest from investments, and taxed at the current personal tax rate. At the time of writing, personal income tax rates in the UK range from 20 per cent to 45 per cent. You don't need to pay tax on the first £9,440 you earn (correct at time of writing), an amount known as your *personal allowance*.

If you set up your business as a private limited company, you pay corporation tax on the profits you make, which at the time of writing is 20 per cent. If you pay yourself a salary from the business, or choose to take money out of the business in the form of a dividend, you may also need to pay income tax on that money, depending on the amount of the salary or dividend and your own personal income tax status.

ASK THE EXPERTS

Changing business structure

Q: My business partner and I set up our software company as a partnership many years ago. Since then we have managed to build a successful business that is doing really well and has strong cash flow. The problem is that because the business is set up as a partnership, we do not have to publish our accounts at Companies House and so our clients aren't able to see how strong the business is, other than to take our word for it. We want our clients to see that we are very solvent and profitable, and have good reserves of working capital compared with our competitors because, particularly in the current uncertain economic climate, we feel that this would be a strong selling point in marketing the company. The other problem is that many of our clients are big corporations or government departments, and we find that they don't really understand the concept of partnerships. We feel this is a potential obstacle to doing business with them.

A: The good news is that you don't have to stay being a partnership forever – you can turn your business into a private limited company. It involves some cost and a lot of paperwork, and you need to hire solicitors and accountants to guide you through the transition. You also need to have your business valued by external company valuers. However, you benefit not only from being a more transparent and visible business, but also from the tax savings you make from becoming a private limited company and from having limited liability.

What if I can't afford to pay right now?

When your business gets into full swing – and you start bringing in a lot more income – you may be surprised at just how much tax you owe at the end of the tax year. You may be especially shocked if you're not using an accountant to keep an eye on your finances and to warn you to start putting aside some cash for such an outcome.

So what can you do if you can't afford to pay the income or corporation tax you owe? The first thing to do is contact the HMRC's Business Payment Support Service (phone 0300-200-3835) as soon as you realise that you aren't going to be able to pay all the tax you owe. Don't wait until the payment is overdue. The Business Payment Support Service assesses each case individually and may give you more time to pay. Pay as much of the tax you owe as you can, even if you can't pay the full amount, as this reduces the amount of interest that's calculated on the amount still outstanding.

TIP

If HMRC agrees to give you more time to pay the amount you owe, you'll be advised to set up a direct-debit payment plan to make sure you don't miss any payments. If you fail to make the agreed payments, HMRC can cancel the arrangement and take legal action to recover the outstanding amount.

What if HMRC decides I'm not actually self-employed?

You've started your own home-based business and you're starting to deliver services – say, interior design – to a client. Chances are you consider yourself to be a business separate from your client's business – in other words, an *independent contractor*. But what if we told you that HMRC may not agree with your particular view of your business and instead decide that you're performing your services as an employee? 'Okay, that's interesting,' you may say to yourself, 'but what's the big deal?'

You may be in for an unpleasant surprise if you think you're a home-based business – and take advantage of all the deductions for business expenses that you're entitled to – but HMRC decides that you're really an employee of your client. This unpleasant surprise includes disallowing all the deductions you've been taking for your home-based business and recalculating your taxes without them. The amount of National Insurance Contributions you need to pay will change – possibly resulting in a substantial amount of money (plus penalties and interest) now owed to HMRC. Believe us, this is one surprise everyone could do without. The good news is that you can take a few steps right now to ensure that you're not surprised come tax-paying day.

The lines that separate an independent contractor from an employee can be blurry, so HMRC has developed guidelines to help you determine whether you're an independent contractor or an employee.

If the answer is 'Yes' to all of the following questions, it usually means that HMRC classes you as self-employed:

- ✔ Can you hire someone to do the work or engage helpers at your own expense?

- ✔ Do you risk your own money?

- ✔ Do you provide the main items of equipment you need to do your job, not just the small tools that many employees provide for themselves?

- ✔ Do you agree to do a job for a fixed price regardless of how long the job may take?

- ✔ Can you decide what work to do, how and when to do the work and where to provide the services?

- ✔ Do you regularly work for a number of different people?

- ✔ Do you have to correct unsatisfactory work in your own time and at your own expense?

Here are some of the key factors that HMRC considers when making a decision about whether you're employed or self-employed. To prove you're self-employed, HMRC expects to see:

- ✔ **Personal service.** You must provide your services personally.

- ✔ **Right of control.** You can show you have the freedom to do work when and where you want.

- ✔ **Right of substitution and engagement of helpers.** If you have to engage a helper, you, not your client, have to pay that person.

- ✔ **Provision of own equipment.** You provide whatever equipment you need to do your job.

- ✔ **Financial risk.** You risk your own money by, for example, buying assets needed for the job, bearing the running costs, and paying for overheads and materials.

- ✔ **Opportunity to profit.** Your profit (or loss) depends on your capacity to reduce overheads and organise work effectively.

- ✔ **No employee-type benefits from your clients.** You don't enjoy benefits such as paid leave, membership of a firm's pension scheme, right to a parking space or canteen facilities of any of your clients.

- ✔ **Personal factors.** You work for a number of clients throughout the year and have a businesslike approach to obtaining engagements.

Be constantly aware of how you do business and guard against conducting business in a way that may cause HMRC to believe you're actually an employee of a client instead of an independent contractor. The differences are often subtle, and the line between them is easy to cross. With a bit of forethought and planning, however, you can make sure that you're always on the right side of that line. For more information, visit www.hmrc.gov.uk/employment-status/#1.

Taking a Look at Tax-Deductible Expenses for Your Home Business

When you run a business from home you can claim as an expense against tax the proportion used by your business of the costs of running your home, such as lighting and heating, landline rental and Internet broadband subscription. You can work out the percentage of the bill that has been used by your business by calculating the percentage of space in your home that the business uses – in terms of number of rooms or square feet – or by working out the percentage of time the business uses a utility, or a combination of both. The HMRC website contains several examples of how you can calculate business use using either of these methods.

If part of your home is used exclusively for your business, that part of your property used for work may be liable to business rates, while the remainder of the house, which is used for living in, continues to be liable for council tax. To decide whether or not your home should be liable to business rates, the Valuation Office Agency (www.voa.gov.uk) considers a number of factors, such as the extent and frequency of the business use of the room or rooms, and any modifications you've made to the property to accommodate that use. In addition, be aware that if part of your home is used exclusively for your business, you may have a capital gains tax liability on a proportion of any profit you make when you sell your house in the future.

You must also inform your insurance broker that you're running a business from home because the level of household and contents cover you have may need to increase to cover the equipment and stock kept in your home.

Reviewing Other Important Tax Deductions

Home-based businesses can also deduct a wide variety of other business expenses from your income in the same way that other non-home-based businesses can. The type of expenses that you can claim for depend on the nature of your business – while a vintage electric guitar may be an allowable deduction for a professional musician, it wouldn't be for a software designer! As a general rule, expenses must have been incurred wholly, exclusively and necessarily for your business.

Here are the kinds of expenses that you can generally claim for:

- Accountancy and professional fees
- Advertising
- Bank and credit card charges
- Business cards and stationery
- Business travel expenses including petrol for car trips
- Internet access
- Office furniture
- Office supplies
- Postage
- Professional journals' subscriptions

As you may imagine, some expenses are *not* deductible. For example:

- ✔ Clothing
- ✔ Entertaining customers
- ✔ Lobbying expenses
- ✔ Penalties and fines
- ✔ Personal expenses
- ✔ Political contributions

HMRC has guidelines on its website detailing which business expenses are tax deductible and offers examples on how to go about calculating your business share of the costs of running your home. Make sure you check them out at www.hmrc.gov.uk/incometax/relief-self-emp.htm.

When in doubt, ask an accountant or tax adviser about which expenses you're allowed to deduct and which ones you aren't. It's far better to be sure about your allowable deductions *before* you take them instead of years later when your business expenses are disallowed by HMRC. Because of the complexity of the tax rules and the fact that they change – sometimes substantially – every year, hiring a professional tax lawyer or accountant can really pay off, and it's deductible, too.

Of course, evading paying your taxes is against the law, but you can avoid paying more taxes than you're legally obligated to. HMRC isn't going to give you any gold stars or special privileges for paying more taxes than you have to – you're throwing away your money if you do. And that's the last thing any home-based businessperson should ever do. However, if you end up overpaying HMRC can refund you with a tax rebate.

Tax software to the rescue

As a home-based businessperson, when you prepare your tax returns, you have two key options: pay someone to do them or do the returns yourself. If you decide to do your own tax returns, you may find that tax software makes the process much easier and far more accurate. HMRC provides a list of commercial software suppliers on its website (www.hmrc.gov.uk) and says it accepts valid tax returns and supplementary attachments for the products listed.

These suppliers and products include:

- ✔ TaxCalc software: www.taxcalc.com
- ✔ Sage Taxation software: www.sage.co.uk
- ✔ Taxfiler: www.taxfiler.co.uk

The ABC of VAT

VAT stands for *value added tax,* and if your home-based business has sales of more than the VAT threshold in a year (£79,000 at the time of writing) or you expect it to reach that figure during the current year, you need to register for VAT with HMRC and charge your customers VAT. VAT is charged on most goods and services sold in the UK. Here's how the VAT system works:

- ✔ VAT is charged when a VAT-registered business sells something to another business or to a non-business customer.

- ✔ At the time of writing, the standard rate of VAT is levied at 20 per cent, with a reduced rate charged on some goods (such as mobility aids and energy saving materials) of 5 per cent. A few goods and services, for example, children's clothes, are zero-rated, meaning that no VAT is charged on them.

- ✔ If you're a VAT-registered business, in most cases you charge VAT on the goods and services that you provide and you can reclaim the VAT you pay when you buy goods and services for your business.

- ✔ You need to file a VAT return online every three months showing the VAT you've charged and the VAT you've paid, and then either pay HMRC the amount you owe or reclaim the amount they owe you.

- ✔ HMRC also offers some accounting schemes to help you simplify your VAT. The one most relevant for home-based businesses is the *Flat Rate Scheme*. If your turnover is less than £150,000 per year, you're allowed to calculate your VAT payments as a percentage of your total VAT-inclusive turnover, rather than having to record how much VAT you charge on every individual sale. This arrangement can save you a lot of time on bookkeeping! Under the Flat Rate Scheme you can't reclaim VAT on purchases your business makes, but this may not be an issue if your business doesn't make many purchases. Check with your accountant – or study the HMRC website – to see if this would be a wise option for you.

Considering the Need for Benefits

Most full-time employees take their benefits for granted. Sick leave, holidays, maternity leave, pension plans and more are an expected part of any full-time job. However, when you start your own home-based business, you quickly discover that benefits aren't something to take for granted. In fact, some benefits aren't even available to home-based businesspeople at all, and those that are have real and substantial costs.

If you currently work – or have worked in the past – in a regular business, you know the advantages of the benefits that often come as part of an employee package. In this section, we discuss ways you can provide yourself with some of these same benefits in your home-based business.

Income protection

Imagine that you're a professional writer. And imagine that you depend on your physical ability to use your computer keyboard to do your writing. Now imagine that you're diagnosed with carpal tunnel syndrome or a repetitive-strain injury that prevents you from using your computer for weeks or even months or years. What can you do, and how can you and your family survive the loss of income that such an injury causes?

The idea of *income protection insurance* is that the insurer pays you a regular income – typically a fixed percentage of your salary – if you can't work because of sickness or disability, until you return to work or until you retire. Several different types of income protection insurance are available and include:

- ✔ **Accident and sickness cover.** This provides cover if you're unable to work due to accident or illness. You can have it as long-term or short-term protection.

- ✔ **Unemployment cover.** This type of insurance provides a fixed amount of income if you lose your job through no fault of your own.

- ✔ **Critical illness cover.** This provides you with a lump sum payment if you're diagnosed with certain serious illnesses or disabilities such as cancer, a heart attack or loss of limbs.

As a home-based business owner you need to be extremely careful about examining the precise circumstances in which an insurer will pay out. Although the idea of having accident and sickness protection, for example, may sound reassuring, the reality is that even if you become sick and are unable to carry on your normal line of work, the insurer may not pay out on the claim unless you're incapable of performing *any* kind of paid work.

For most home-based businesses, critical illness insurance is really the only form of income protection benefit you need to seriously consider. If you eventually hire employees, other kinds of insurance may be a requirement for your home-based business.

Life assurance

Of course, no one likes to think about dying and leaving loved ones without a source of income – but if you die without having established some sort of retirement fund or a life assurance policy, that's exactly what you'll do. Life assurance pays whomever you designate as your beneficiary a lump sum of money if you die, providing some peace of mind that that person's financial needs will be taken care of in the event of your death.

General life assurance policies are widely available, affordable and easy to get. Find a good broker and ask him or her to explain the advantages and disadvantages of the different kinds of life assurance available to you, including term and whole of life.

Life assurance is an essential part of the benefits package of many home-based businesses. Although the money paid out in the event of your death doesn't do you any good personally (remember: a shroud has no pockets!), the peace of mind it provides knowing that your loved ones will have the financial wherewithal to continue without you is often well worth the price.

Retirement plans

Planning for retirement is a regular part of most businesses, and it can and should be part of your home-based business. As we discuss in Chapter 7, the prices you charge for your products and services should be high enough to provide you with a decent income and benefits.

You probably already know that, on their own, the state pension and any social security benefits you may be entitled to simply can't fill the bill for ensuring a comfortable and worry-free retirement. Unless you have a retirement plan or pension from your previous employer, the only way you're going to have any sort of retirement plan for your home-based business is if you create one yourself. If you want to provide yourself with a reliable source of income after you leave the world of work behind once and for all, you must start and grow a retirement fund.

If you run your own business, you need to start a *personal pension scheme*, which you set up yourself. You can buy one from a regulated financial organisation such as a bank or insurance company that manages it on your behalf.

Here are some characteristics of personal pension schemes:

- You can pay regular or lump sum contributions to the scheme, which the financial organisation administering the scheme invests on your behalf.

✔ You can pay as much as you want into a personal pension scheme.

✔ You can get tax relief on your pension contributions of up to 100 per cent of your UK earnings if you pay in less than the annual allowance, which at the time of writing is £50,000. If you pay in more than this you may have to pay tax on the excess.

✔ Your personal pension provider sends you a statement every year telling you how much your pension pot is worth.

In addition to standard personal pension schemes, two special types of personal pension scheme may be worth considering:

✔ **Self-invested personal pension (SIPP).** With a SIPP you have greater choice about where you invest your pension pot. You can choose your own investment strategy or you can appoint a fund manager or stockbroker to manage your investments. You can start a SIPP from scratch or transfer funds from other pension schemes.

✔ **Stakeholder pension.** A stakeholder pension works in the same way as a regular personal pension scheme but it must meet certain standards set by the government. This means it must accept contributions of as low as £20 and there's a cap on management charges of 1.5 per cent. There's no charge for stopping or altering your pension contributions or transferring your funds elsewhere.

Each of these options has its pluses and minuses, and one may be better for your business than another. Consult an accountant or professional tax expert before you decide on a particular plan as changing after you've committed to one can be hard.

Time off

Most regular businesses provide a wide variety of different forms of time off, including public and bank holidays and individual holiday entitlement. As the owner of your own home-based business, you get to decide which days you take off. In a home-based business, however, time off works a bit differently than it does in a regular job. In a regular job, you usually get paid for public holidays and your personal holiday entitlement – even though you don't actually work while you're away. In a home-based business, if you don't work, you don't get paid.

Even though you don't get paid, however, make sure you set aside some time off to get out of the office and recharge your batteries with family and friends. The two main forms of time off you need to consider as a home-based business owner are:

- ✔ **Public holidays.** A number of public holidays and bank holidays are available for you to choose from: two at Easter, May Bank Holiday, Spring Bank Holiday, August Bank Holiday, two at Christmas and New Year's Day. You decide whether you're open for business on those days.

- ✔ **Personal holiday entitlement.** Many small business owners find themselves working far harder than they ever did in a regular job, which makes setting aside holiday time away from the business even more important. Whether you take two weeks every summer, or don't work on Fridays, decide on your holiday days and try to stick to them.

Make taking time off a regular part of your home-business life and an established part of the way you do business – your attitude, as well as your relationships with friends and family, will benefit.

Childcare

Working at home offers you a unique advantage that working outside the home doesn't – you can be at home with your young children every day of the week if you want to. For parents who want to work but who don't want to sacrifice their family lives to do so, working at home is truly the best of both worlds. However, if you work at home and have young children, you need to work out how to keep them out of your way (and out of the way of your clients and customers) during your normal working hours. To do so, you generally need to obtain some sort of childcare or else you'll face ongoing challenges meeting deadlines.

When it comes to childcare, you basically have two options:

- ✔ **On-site childcare.** You can hire a nanny to take care of your children in your home for a fixed number of hours each day. If you have relatives living nearby – perhaps your children's grandparents, aunts or uncles – even better. In-your-home care is often ideal because you're nearby if needed, but you're still able to close your office door and leave your family life behind while you work.

- ✔ **Off-site childcare.** Numerous off-site childcare facilities are available to the home-based businessperson. These include childminders, nurseries, nanny-share arrangements in the other family's home, and before- and after-school clubs. Make sure you research your options thoroughly and choose one that you feel comfortable with, and that fits in with your business needs.

Check out Chapter 12 for information on developing your own thriving home-based business while maintaining the contact and good relationship with your children that you desire.

Part III
Avoiding Problems

Top Five Trade Accounts to Set Up to Save Hassle

- ✔ **Product wholesalers.** If you sell products on a retail basis, you have to buy them from wholesalers or purchase the raw materials from suppliers. Establishing trade accounts with such wholesalers makes your life much easier; you can place orders now and pay for your purchases later – usually up to 30 days after you receive your invoice.

- ✔ **Warehouse superstores.** Warehouse superstores offer everything most home offices need – from appliances and furniture to office supplies – at great prices, so setting up a trade account with one of these superstores is a good idea for many businesses.

- ✔ **Copying/reproduction centres.** If you constantly find yourself using the services of a printing or copying firm, you may want to establish a trade account with your printer so that you receive a monthly bill instead of having to pay every time you need something done.

- ✔ **Office equipment repair companies.** Having an established relationship with a good computer/office equipment repair person *before* – not after – your equipment goes down can really pay off.

- ✔ **Courier/messenger services.** When you establish an account with an overnight courier service, or with a local messenger service, you receive pre-printed multipart shipping documents or air-freight bills. Even better, most of these companies now enable you to set up your shipments online, making it easy to track your package's progress – from your home office to your customer's front door.

Go to www.dummies.com/extras/homebasedbusiness for free online bonus content.

In this part...

- Get savvy with legal know-how, including trademarks and copyright, and licences and permits.

- Ensure your business has the right legal structure.

- Register your company name.

- Use the know-how of outside experts when you need a helping hand.

- Find a solicitor, accountant and insurance broker.

Chapter 9

Knowing Your Legal Do's and Don'ts

....

In This Chapter

▶ Choosing the right legal structure for your business

▶ Selecting and registering your business's name

▶ Dealing with trademarks, copyrights and patents

▶ Complying with licences, permits and registration requirements

▶ Avoiding fraudulent business opportunities

....

As you'd expect, running a business from home means complying with certain rules and regulations. Doing so may not be fun, but when it comes to the law, you've just got to grin and bear it.

Laws and regulations determine where you can locate your home-based business and during which hours you can operate it – and whether customers are allowed to visit your premises. Depending on what type of business you set up, they may also require you to get a licence, permit or registration. In some cases – if you're a masseuse, for example, both you and your premises need a separate licence.

You also need to consider what legal structure you want your business to take (sole trader, partnership or private limited company), and this in turn has financial and tax implications for your business.

In this chapter, we discuss a wide variety of legal issues that every home-based business owner faces, including how to choose the legal structure that's right for your business, how to select and register a company name and how to consider the potential impact of licences, permits and registrations on your business. We also take a look at trademarks, copyrights and patents and how they may affect your business. Finally, we briefly visit the potential impact of tax considerations on your home-based business (see Chapter 8 for the complete lowdown on taxes).

Our aim isn't to turn you into a lawyer or an accountant but to arm you with enough knowledge to take care of the basics and to know where to turn when you need more information.

Understanding the Major Business Structures

An important decision you have to make after you decide to start your own home-based business is what *form* of business – that is, what *legal structure* – it will take.

If a business has the initials *Ltd* after the name, for example, this indicates that it has been set up as a *private limited company*. The letters *LLP* after the name of an accountancy or legal firm indicates that it is a *limited liability partnership*.

Each of the different forms of business (and the accompanying alphabet soup of letters) comes with a wide variety of legal implications for many facets of your business, including legal liability in case of being sued, tax structure and more. So take the time to understand all these implications upfront as you make and implement your business plans.

Which form of business is right for you? This section gives you some basic guidelines to consider as you weigh up the different options available to you. Although these guidelines are certainly sufficient to help you get your business off the ground and to help you become an informed home-business owner, our advice is to first contact a solicitor or accountant. You can then determine the specific advantages and legal requirements of each form of business and decide which is best for your specific circumstances. The money you save over the years will probably pay for this advice many times over.

Consider the following issues when you're deciding which legal form of business to use for your home-based business:

- **The impact on your business's image.** Becoming a limited company means you can put 'Ltd' after your business name, which portrays professionalism.

- **The impact of planned business growth.** If you're planning to grow the business to a substantial size you'd be wise to limit your personal liability by setting up a limited company.

- **The cost to start up your business.** Setting up as a sole trader is much cheaper than forming a limited company.

✔ **The cost to maintain your business.** Maintaining a limited company costs more because you need to prepare a separate tax return and accounts for the business, for which you'll probably need to pay an accountant.

✔ **Your financing needs.** Raising finance is generally easier if your business is a limited liability company.

✔ **The amount of personal legal risk you're willing to take for your business.** As a sole trader you're entirely responsible for the debts and liabilities of your business.

In the sections that follow, we consider the three main forms of business that are relevant to home-based businesses, discussing the pros and cons of each one. As you review each form, think about the kind of business you want to run – not just today, but years into the future.

We know it may be difficult to picture what your business will be like a couple of weeks into the future, much less a couple of months or a couple of years. The good news is that it is possible to change the status of your business, particularly if you go from being a sole trader to being a private limited company. However, choosing a form that can carry your business for many years into the future is easier in the long run.

Surveying sole traders

By far the vast majority of home-based business owners are *sole traders*, which means there's only one business owner – in your case, that one owner is you. You're the boss, the leader, the one to congratulate when the business does well and the one to blame when the business does badly.

As a sole trader, you need to register with HMRC as being self-employed and you report the income you derive from your business on your personal tax return along with any other personal income you make during the course of the year from, say, investments – in other words, you don't need to file a separate tax return for your business. Similarly, any debts you incur as a sole trader are the same as your personal debts.

Why do so many home-based business owners set up as sole traders? One reason is that it is by far the simplest structure to take, because all you need to do to become a sole trader is to register with HMRC as self-employed. Creating a partnership or private limited company is more difficult because you need to create a partnership agreement or register your business with Companies House.

Fortunately, being a sole trader isn't a bad form for many home-based businesses to take. After all, it's the simplest and least regulated form of business organisation, start-up costs are minimal or nil, and one person owns the business and has full control over it. As a sole trader, you're responsible for securing financing and you receive all company profits. Business income under the sole trader form of business is taxed as personal income, which works out just fine for most home-business owners.

On the other hand, being a sole trader offers major disadvantages in the areas of legal liability for the owner (who can be personally sued for any and all business-related issues) and potential dissolution of the business upon the owner's death. Table 9-1 summarises the pros and cons of being a sole trader.

Table 9-1	Pros and Cons of Being a Sole Trader
Pros	**Cons**
The owner has complete control over all aspects of the business.	A sole trader business is often considered less prestigious than some other forms of business.
Starting up as a sole trader is inexpensive.	Creating and maintaining secure outside financing can be particularly difficult.
A sole trader business is easy to start and easy to close.	The business dies when the owner does.
The owner gets to keep all profits.	The owner is personally liable in the event of a lawsuit (as a result of malpractice, product failure and so on).

Perusing partnerships

If you have two or more owners of your home-based business – perhaps you and a close friend or relative – consider choosing the partnership form of business. In a *partnership*, each partner commits to provide specific skills, expertise and effort – and to share the partnership's expenses – in return for an agreed-on portion of the company's profits. The agreement spelling out these terms is called a *partnership agreement.*

Partnerships take advantage of the different skills, expertise and resources – including cash – that the different partners bring to an organisation. And they're fairly easy to put together and administer; all you really need is a simple written agreement, which you can make more complicated if the stakes are high.

Make sure, however, that you ask a solicitor to take a look at your partnership agreement before you sign it. Because partners have a legally recognised ownership stake in the business, each is an agent for the partnership and can hire employees, borrow money and operate the business.

On the plus side, a partnership's profits are taxed as personal income, with each partner taxed on his or her portion of the profits. On the minus side, however, partners are personally liable for debts and taxes. And personal assets can be confiscated if the partnership can't satisfy creditors' claims. If you have a nice home or a car or two, bear this point in mind before you enter into a partnership. Table 9-2 shows the advantages and disadvantages of a partnership in detail.

Although it's legally possible to create a partnership with only a handshake, in the event of disagreement or when it's time to dissolve the partnership, you'll wish you had a written agreement. Remember: the money you pay now for a solicitor's help can save you many headaches and, potentially, a lot of money down the road.

In the event that partners want to avoid personal liability, they can form a special legal arrangement called a *limited liability partnership*. Limited liability partnerships can be drawn up by two or more people and are very similar to private companies, except that they're taxed as a partnership and offer the organisational flexibility of a partnership. They must be *incorporated* – in other words, established as a separate legal entity by drawing up incorporation documents, which you then file at Companies House.

Table 9-2	Pros and Cons of a Partnership
Pros	*Cons*
A partnership incorporates the skills, expertise and efforts of two or more people.	Partners don't always agree on every course of action, a situation that may eventually harm the business.
Business risks are diffused across one or more partners.	Each partner is legally liable for actions of the other partners, including hiring employees, borrowing money and operating the business.
Partners can support one another.	Some partners may think they deserve more of the business's profits than the other partners.
Partnerships provide a fairly flexible business structure.	Like divorces, when partnerships break up, things can get messy – fast.
All partners share the expenses.	All partners share the profits.

Looking at private limited companies

Private limited companies are legal entities that exist separately from their owners. Setting up a private limited company offers many advantages to a home-based business – not least, it makes your business look really professional, it provides significant tax advantages and it provides limited liability, meaning that in the event of any prosecution, the business is liable, not the business owner.

Table 9-3 gives you some other pros and cons.

Table 9-3	The Pros and Cons of a Private Limited Company
Pros	*Cons*
Private limited companies offer limited liability for the company's owners.	Private limited companies offer less privacy than being a sole trader as you need to file annual accounts at Companies House.
Money earned by the business can be left in the business until you need to take it out, potentially offering significant tax advantages.	You're likely to need a professional accountant to help you complete the company's tax return and accounts.
Private limited companies are often easier to sell than sole trader businesses.	Private limited companies cost more to set up and maintain than sole trader businesses and require more form-filling and paperwork.

Most home-based businesses in the UK start out as sole traders or private limited companies.

Working Out What to Call Your Business: Name Registration

What's in a name? Choosing the name of your company is one of the most critical decisions you make as you set up your business. We're not exaggerating when we say that the right name can help pave the way to sales and success, and the wrong name can lead to all kinds of problems for you and your business.

Here's an interesting bit of information: an average of 4,000 to 5,000 commercial messages are aimed at every person each day. Think about it for a minute – television and radio adverts, ads in newspapers and magazines, internet pop-up and click-through ads, adverts on the sides of buses, billboards, junk mail, junk faxes, junk email . . . the list goes on and on. How can your home-based business cut through all that noise and capture the interest and attention of your prospective customers? A good name can make all the difference.

The best business names:

✔ Describe the service or product that the business offers

✔ Are protected by trademark

✔ Are novel

Naming your business isn't something to do with friends over a few beers one evening – it requires careful thought and planning. Your business name should give people some idea of the exact nature of your business, and it should also project the image you want your business to have. Names can be simple, sophisticated or even silly (not too silly, though!).

Think several years into the future; try to pick a name that can grow with your business over time instead of limiting it. Tots to Travel, a home-based online business that provides child-friendly holiday homes throughout the world, changed its name from Tots to France when the destinations it offered expanded beyond France.

Here are some tips on selecting a name:

✔ Use your own name – if you have a reputation or plan to grow one. Jane's Wedding Cakes, tells you exactly what it does and who does it.

✔ Use your name with a tag line or motto ('Hannah's Handmade Jewellery: making people feel special').

✔ Use an eye-catching website name (www.itsybitsyvintage.com).

✔ Use a name that communicates the key benefit that your product or service can offer (No-Mess Chimney Sweep).

✔ Use a name that describes your speciality (Fantastic Fabric Creations).

✔ Use a made-up name that suggests what you do or how you do it (Dorset Handmade Wooden Toys).

Of course, just as you can find general guidelines about what kinds of names to use, think about the kinds of names to avoid. Here are five key qualities to avoid when choosing your name:

✔ Too vague (such as Bobby's. Who is Bobby and what does he do?).

✔ Too forgettable (names that use words like Micro, General or International).

✔ Too narrow (see the earlier Tots to France example).

✔ Too confusing (Daisy's Fun Days for example. Is this a children's party entertainer, hen night planner, bouncy castle hirer . . . ?).

✔ Means something rude in another language (pop your proposed company name into a translation service such as Google Translate to check it in different languages).

After you've decided on a name, the next step is to make sure it isn't already in use by another company. If the name you use is trademarked or otherwise legally protected by another business, not only can you be sued to stop using the name, but you can also lose the money you spent developing and promoting your brand and products.

Here are a few resources you can use to find out whether your proposed business name is already in use:

✔ **Companies House.** All private limited companies must register their name with Companies House. It's free to search through their online database at www.companieshouse.gov.uk.

✔ **Local phone books.** Check for the most recent listings, but remember that some home-based businesses don't list business phone numbers.

✔ **Business directory websites.** Check out local and national online business directories such as Yell.com to see if your preferred business name has already been used.

✔ **Domain name registrars.** You can use sites like www.lowcostnames.co.uk and www.whois.com to find out which website domain names have already been taken.

✔ **Online search engines.** Type the name you're trying to check out into a search engine such as Google (www.google.co.uk) or Bing (www.bing.com).

✔ **Trademark specialists.** Search the Intellectual Property Office (IPO) database on their website (www.ipo.gov.uk) to see what trademarks and patents have already been registered.

When you've finally settled on a name, it may be worth your time and money to obtain a trademark from the Intellectual Property Office to protect your business name and logo. If you don't, someone else may take them away from you – along with all the customer goodwill you worked so hard to build. We explain trademarks in the next section.

Along with a name, many businesses develop a logo – the graphic symbol of the business. After all, a picture is worth a thousand words. As with your name, carefully design your logo to project the exact image you want for your business. See Chapter 12 for more on creating a logo.

Differentiating Between Trademarks, Copyrights and Patents

When you think of the word *asset*, the first thing that comes to your mind may be cash, a computer, a company car, or perhaps the equipment you use to make the items you sell to customers. However, one of the most important assets for many businesses today isn't any of those things – it's *intellectual property*, the unique ideas and knowledge that give a business a competitive advantage in the marketplace.

Intellectual property can range from a unique product design or the ingredients in your award-winning chutney recipe to your company's name, a song or photograph, or the exact words you wrote in a newspaper or magazine article.

The value of your intellectual property depends on the nature of the ideas and their demand in the marketplace. But one thing's for sure: the value of your intellectual property is in jeopardy if you don't take steps to protect it from theft, which is where trademarks, copyrights and patents come in.

Trademarks

A *trademark* – signified by ™ – is a distinctive word, name, symbol or device – or any combination of the four – used to distinguish a product or service from those of competitors.

The word, name, symbol or device you select to trademark must be sufficiently unique to separate your products from their generic source. You can't, for example, trademark the generic word *cola*, but you can trademark a trade name for your unique brand of cola known as *Coca-Cola* (or you could've if someone hadn't beaten you to it 125 years or so ago).

To legally protect your trademark and prevent anyone else from using it or stealing it, you need to register it. Think about what geographical area you want to register it for – just the UK, or Europe or the world? You can register trademarks online through the Intellectual Property Office website (www. ipo.gov.uk) from £170 or you can pay an intellectual property agent to do it on your behalf.

Trademarks: The 'bear' necessities . . .

One of the first things husband and wife team Jason and Anita Pritchard did when they set up their baby and toddler clothing business Dijjie (www.dijjie.com) in 2010 was trademark both the name and the bear's head logo that they used in their designs. Doing so wasn't cheap, particularly for a start-up business – it cost them £6,000 to get the trademark and logo registered using the services of a lawyer – but the investment has more than paid off. It meant that they could be confident their brand was protected when they signed distribution deals with retailers, and it was a key factor when they sold the business two years later to the new owner Katie Bailey. Bailey, who runs the business from her home in Bedford, said: 'Having trademarks registered for the brand name and logo was one of the reasons that I bought the business. It meant that everything was in already place. I probably wouldn't have bought the business without them.'

If you're wondering whether someone has already registered a trademark, check the IPO trademark database online at www.ipo.gov.uk.

A trademark may not prevent someone from stealing (or mistakenly using) your unique word, name or symbol, but it does provide you with legal recourse in court in case someone does. In the long run, that provision may be worth its weight in gold to you and your business.

Registering a trademark isn't mandatory. If you've used your unregistered trademark for some time and it could be construed as being closely associated with your product by customers, it's considered to have acquired a 'reputation', which gives it some protection legally. However, registration makes it much simpler for you to have recourse against any person who infringes the mark.

Copyrights

Copyright is a form of protection provided to the authors of 'original works of authorship', including literary, dramatic, musical, artistic and certain other intellectual works, both published and unpublished. This book is copyrighted, for example; the script for the latest *Harry Potter* film is copyrighted; that song you were humming in the shower this morning is probably copyrighted.

UK copyright laws generally give the owner of copyright the exclusive right to copy or reproduce the copyrighted work in any way, make an adaptation of the work, distribute copies of the copyrighted work to the public, or perform the or display copyrighted work publicly.

A copyright is automatically created when the work itself is created – you don't need to fill in any forms or pay someone to copyright your work for you.

However you can take three actions to help protect your copyrighted work, as follows:

- ✔ If you can, mark your work with the international copyright symbol – © – followed by the name of the copyright owner and the year of its creation. You can also mark material on your website in this way. This isn't essential in the UK but may assist you in infringement proceedings.

- ✔ Consider sending yourself a copy of your work by special delivery (which gives a clear date stamp on the envelope) and leaving the envelope unopened when it arrives back to you. This doesn't prove that the work was created by you, but it does provide evidence to a court of law that the work was in your possession at a particular date.

- ✔ Consider lodging a copy of your work with a bank or solicitor.

The length of time your work is protected by copyright depends on the category or type of work. Copyright for written work, including software and databases, theatrical, musical, artistic and film work, for example, lasts for the life of the creator plus 70 years.

If you need more specific information about trademarks, copyrights and patents, the best place to go is the Intellectual Property Office (IPO) at www. ipo.gov.uk.

Patents

A *patent* protects new inventions and covers how they work, what they do, how they do it, what they're made of and how they're made. If you're granted a patent it gives you the ability to take legal action under civil law to try to stop others from making, using, importing or selling your invention without permission. Patents can be renewed for up to 20 years. A UK patent only provides protection in the UK, so to provide protection elsewhere you must extend your UK patent or else apply for patent protection to other national patent offices, depending on the country.

The idea of patents is to allow you, as the inventor or patent holder, an exclusive right to obtain the full financial benefits of your invention – allowing you to recover your investment of time and money – before others are allowed to make money from it.

Considering alternatives for your patent

What can you do with your inspired invention if don't have the resources, skill, time or inclination to produce it yourself? You can take one of three courses once your idea is patented:

✔ **Outright sale.** You can sell the rights and title of your patent to an individual or company. Base the price on a sound evaluation of the market.

✔ **Sale and royalty.** You can enter into an agreement whereby you assign the title and rights to produce to another party for cash but under which you get a royalty on each unit sold.

✔ **Licensing.** You keep the rights and title but sell a licence for manufacturing and marketing the product to someone else. Make sure the contract between you and the licensee contains a performance clause requiring the licensee to sell a minimum number of units each year otherwise the licence will be revoked.

Imagine that you spent ten years designing a new kind of mousetrap – far superior and more cost-effective than any currently on the market – and began selling it, only to have someone immediately copy it and undercut your price, putting you out of business in the process. In such a case, a patent is essential to protect you and your business.

If you think you have an item you want to patent, we suggest that you consult a competent patent agent. The patent application process requires considerable research, and the appropriate forms have to be submitted the right way and at the right time and place. When you're talking about something that may turn out to be your major source of income for many years into the future – and may very well make you rich – don't try doing it yourself; seek professional help. Although filing a patent isn't cheap (in the region of £200 to £300 simply to process your application), a competent patent agent can save you lots of time, money and heartache.

Determining the Need for Licences, Permits and Registrations

Depending on the type of home business you set up, you may need a licence, permit or registration before you're allowed to start trading. For example, if you're planning to start up a dog-walking business in Wandsworth, south London (well, you might be!), you need a licence if you plan to walk more than four dogs at a time.

Working your way through the maze of government regulations can certainly be one of the most confusing aspects of doing business, but it's also critical for your success in the long run. Yes, the process can be intimidating, and, yes, you'd much rather be selling your products and services than messing with all this red tape and paperwork, but it's definitely worth your while to dig in for the professionalism of your business.

Licences, permits and registrations

Most licences, permits and registrations are issued by your local council, so visit your local council premises or check the council website for details of what's required for your business and how to apply.

Licences, permits and registrations that might be applicable to your home-based business include the following:

- ✔ **Animal boarding establishment licence** if you plan to provide a boarding service for pets in your own home. The licence specifies the number of animals that you're allowed to look after.

- ✔ **Export licences** if you want to export goods to another country. You also need to comply with other government regulations. Get more information from UK Trade and Investment (www.ukti.gov.uk).

- ✔ **Food premises registration and approval** if you intend to make or sell food.

- ✔ **House in Multiple Occupation Licence** if you rent out your house to more than five tenants and your house has three or more storeys.

- ✔ **Occupational licences** for certain occupations (for example, gas engineers and childminders). Check with your local council or trade association.

- ✔ **Other permits.** Check with your local council planning department for restrictions on the kinds of business activities you can conduct in your home. Some councils, for example, restrict home-based businesses that operate in residential roads from having customers come to the place of business.

- ✔ **Scrap Metal Dealers Registration** if you're going to operate a business as a scrap metal dealer.

- ✔ **Skip permit** if your business requires a skip.

Don't become discouraged by all this paperwork and red tape. Remember that people are ready, willing and able to help if you feel overwhelmed. Contact your local chamber of commerce or go online to the government business website Gov.uk (www.gov.uk) for guidance on licences, permits and registrations; you'll be glad you did.

Regulations for home-based businesses

Different local councils have different rules and regulations governing home businesses; others may have no specific requirements in place. The best way to ensure that you stay on the right side of the law is to go and talk to someone at your council and check that they're happy with your choice of business and how you intend to run it. Bear in mind that in general councils take a dim view of any home-based businesses that may cause disruption to neighbours, block access to the street, create noise, smells or other pollution, or lower the tone of the neighbourhood. But of course you wouldn't do any of that!

Although your local council may permit you to run your home-based business as you intend, if you're renting your home the landlord, housing association or local council housing department may have rules, covenants or other restrictions on those same activities. Check your tenancy agreements to see whether such rules or regulations apply to you.

If the regulations make it impossible for you to run your business effectively, try one of the following approaches:

- ✔ **Get permission.** If you're living in a rental property and your lease restricts the kinds of business activities you can undertake, ask your landlord for written permission to do what you need to do. As long as you're not creating a nuisance or causing damage to your property, you may find that your landlord is amenable to your plans.

- ✔ **Challenge your local council's decision.** In some cases, you may have no other choice but to take action to change the rules or regulations that restrict your ability to start and operate a home-based business. A variety of approaches are available to you, from buttonholing your district's council member, to circulating a petition, to lobbying for legislative change, to filing a lawsuit. The exact action you take depends on your local area's political environment. If you have any friends, relatives or business acquaintances who have challenged a council decision, ask what worked for them.

Although restrictions can get in the way of your home-business plans, they don't have to be the end of your dream. If the rules aren't in your favour, you have legally viable options for living with them, bending them or changing them.

Avoiding fraudulent business opportunities

If a business opportunity sounds too good to be true, then it probably is. Follow your gut instinct — if a business opportunity looks like a scam, avoid it. The warning signs to look out for are if a business opportunity:

✔ Promises vast wealth in return for very little or no effort.

✔ Doesn't seem to be selling a product or service of any worth, and instead is based purely on the idea of recruiting more distributors and taking a cut from them.

✔ Demands that you invest a lot upfront. Be especially careful to check that any direct selling or franchise business you want to join is legitimate. Make sure that the franchise business you're interested in is a member of the British Franchise Association (www.thebfa.org) and that the direct-selling business is a member of the Direct Selling Association (www.dsa.org.uk).

✔ Insists you make an instant decision without giving you time to consider the proposition properly.

If in doubt, don't get involved. A sound legitimate business opportunity will still be there for you to consider in a few months, or even a year's time. Refer to Chapter 2 for more on franchises, direct selling and business opportunities.

Chapter 10

Using Outside Resources and Experts

. . . .

In This Chapter

▶ Creating trade accounts and increasing your cash flow at the same time

▶ Taking advantage of support services

▶ Looking to outside professionals for help

▶ Bartering safely and effectively

. . . .

*O*kay, so you're the boss, owner and chief bottle-washer of your home-based business. Now what? In theory, you could probably do each and every job on your own – from reviewing contracts, to picking the best insurance coverage, to representing your business in court, to designing and printing your own letterhead stationery – but you may not be the best-qualified person for every task. Specialists – solicitors, accountants, insurance brokers and others – are probably more knowledgeable about certain topics than you and using their services allows you to focus on doing the things that you do best – namely, running your business.

Beyond these outside professionals, consider using a variety of outside resources when the opportunities present themselves. Establishing trade accounts with the suppliers you rely on to sell you the products and services you need to do business is just one example.

In this chapter, we look at why, when and how to take advantage of outside resources. You can gain a real edge against your competition when you do, and provide your customers with the best products and services possible.

Establishing Trade Accounts

A *trade account* is an informal agreement between you and a supplier – such as an office supply shop, printing company or wholesaler – that allows you to purchase goods or services on credit and be billed by the supplier on a regular, usually monthly, basis. A trade account is a win-win situation for both parties – you can purchase whatever you want whenever you want, and your supplier gains a steady customer.

The care and maintenance of trade accounts is essential for almost any business, because these accounts speed up the purchasing process and often provide customers with special discounts unavailable to regular customers or with arrangements such as free overnight delivery. Companies that don't have trade accounts miss out on these benefits. Another important benefit of trade accounts is that when a company agrees to establish a trade account with you, it is essentially agreeing to extend a short-term, interest-free loan to your company – allowing you to pay your bill anywhere from a few days to a month or more after you complete your purchase and receive your goods or services. This free loan is a good deal for your company, and one worth actively pursuing and maintaining. The longer you hold on to your money, the more positive the impact on your company's cash flow.

As you continue to grow your business, you may find that some of the following trade accounts are beneficial for you to establish:

- ✔ **Product wholesalers.** If you sell products on a retail basis, you have to buy them from wholesalers or purchase the raw materials from suppliers. Establishing trade accounts with such wholesalers makes your life much easier; you can place orders now and pay for your purchases later – usually up to 30 days after you receive your invoice.

- ✔ **Office supply stores.** If you regularly purchase large quantities of office supplies, such as printer paper and ink, consider establishing a trade account with an office supply provider that can meet your needs quickly and accurately. The big office supply chains such as Staples (www. staples.co.uk) offer their own business customer credit programmes. Staples' business account customers, for example, get up to 60 days free credit on purchases and membership of a rewards programme. You can simply fill out an online application and submit it for approval. If your credit record is good, you should have no problem gaining approval.

- ✔ **Warehouse superstores.** Warehouse superstores such as Costco (www. costco.co.uk) offer everything most home offices need – from appliances and furniture to office supplies – at great prices, so setting up a trade account with one of these superstores is a good idea for many businesses.

✔ **Copying/reproduction centres.** If you constantly find yourself using the services of a printing or copying firm, you may want to establish a trade account with your printer so that you receive a monthly bill instead of having to pay every time you need something done. Getting a monthly invoice showing detailed information about each order is also a great way to keep track of your copying and reproduction jobs.

✔ **Office equipment repair companies.** Has your computer's hard drive ever crashed? If so, you know just how scary losing your work can be, and how dependent you are on office machines and equipment. Having an established relationship with a good computer/office equipment repair person *before* – not after – your equipment goes down can really pay off. In all honesty, the question isn't whether your office equipment will break, but when. Even if you don't go through the trouble of establishing a relationship with an office equipment repair company before you need it, ask around to find out who's good and who's not so good. That way, when the inevitable emergency does occur, you know where to take your poorly machine.

✔ **Support services.** Numerous support services are available to you, depending on the nature of your business. From online PAs and graphic designers to telephone-answering services, you can establish relationships and trade accounts with just about anyone.

✔ **Courier/messenger services.** Although more and more transactions are being handled over the Internet, you must physically send and receive some items, such as products and signed documents. When you establish an account with an overnight courier service, such as FedEx or UPS, or with a local messenger service, you receive pre-printed multipart shipping documents or air bills. Even better, most of these companies now enable you to set up your shipments online, printing out shipping documents on your computer and making it easy to track your package's progress – from your home office to your customer's front door.

Trade accounts are a good thing, and you can establish them with all your regular wholesalers, suppliers and service providers. Not only do they streamline your business dealings, but because you hold on to your money for a longer period of time, they also help you improve your cash flow. And because a trade account is basically a short-term loan, the fact that you have trade accounts in good standing shows that your business is creditworthy, making it easier for you to obtain other trade accounts and business credit. In the next section, we address how to decide which support services you need and then how to identify and hire them.

Trade accounts also work the other way – other businesses may want to establish trade accounts with you. Allowing them to do so may make a lot of sense because it encourages repeat business and the development of long-term business relationships. You must, however, protect yourself from customers who don't pay their bills. Check credit references scrupulously. Don't just take a business's word for it – especially when you have a lot of money on the line. Do an Internet search for *credit application form,* and you'll find plenty of sample forms that you can easily adapt for your own purposes. A credit application form asks a customer to tell you details of their bank so that you can contact it and check that the customer has the ability to pay you. The form also asks them to provide the contact details of other businesses the customer trades with so you can contact them and find out how prompt the customer is at paying their bills. Finally, the form gives you permission to check out the customer's credit rating – in other words, how good they are at paying their bills – with a credit rating agency.

For advice on dealing with late payments, head to Chapter 6.

Using Support Services

With just 24 hours in a day, if you're the sole owner and only employee of your home-based business, you may find that you have difficulty doing day-to-day support and administrative tasks while still doing the work that your customers pay you to do – which is where using support services comes in.

Support services include everything from short-term employees to temporary employment firms to professionals, such as solicitors, accountants and consultants – in fact, support services potentially include any business service you can imagine. People who provide support services are specialists at what they do, just as you're a specialist at what you do. One of the great things about using support services is that you can take advantage of as much or as little of their experience as you like – usually for a reasonable hourly fee.

Consider using support services for the following three reasons:

- ✔ **You can take advantage of people who have more experience than you do in certain areas.** Do you know how to file a patent application? Or the best way to set up a computerised accounting system? If not, providers of support services – many of whom are owners of home-based businesses themselves – do.

- ✔ **You can leverage your experience.** Using certain support services, such as hiring a temporary worker as an assistant, can enable you to leverage your own experience – greatly increasing your effectiveness in the process. After you teach another person how to do a task that brings in new business that you're an expert at, that other person can do the same thing you do, instantly multiplying the effort spent on that task and substantially increasing the financial return. For example, consider hiring someone to make cold calls to prospective customers or to create and distribute flyers advertising your business. While you're busy working, your temp can be drumming up new customers.

✔ **You can focus your efforts.** Instead of getting caught up in all the details of producing 500 copies of a 12-page brochure (finding the right kind of paper, using the right machine, dealing with jams and equipment break-downs, collating and folding), why not just drop it off at Prontaprint (www.prontaprint.com) or another copy centre and let them worry about it? You can then focus your efforts on the things that bring money into your business – such as selling products and writing proposals.

So what kinds of support services should you consider using for your home-based business? Here's a list to start you off (but keep in mind that many more are available to home-business owners):

✔ Advertising

✔ Cleaning

✔ Copying, printing and graphic design

✔ Packaging and shipping

✔ Professional services, such as accounting, legal expertise, banking and so on

✔ Public relations

✔ Temporary on-site help

✔ Virtual office support, such as telephone-answering services and PA support

Meeting clients

Q: I run a recruitment business from home and although much of my work is done on the phone, at times I need to meet people in person to discuss their recruitment needs. I don't want them to come to my home and I need somewhere more private than the local coffee shop or a hotel lobby as people need to be able to speak to me freely without being overheard. What options do I have?

A: The good news is that a number of serviced office providers such as Regus (www.regus.co.uk) and Avanta (www.avanta.co.uk) have spotted the demand from home-based businesses and now provide meeting rooms for hire by the hour, half day or day in dozens of prime locations throughout the UK, from as little as £25 an hour. You can book an LCD projector for your meeting, if needed, and even pre-order tea, coffee and biscuits. Another option, if you live near a major town, is to join a members' association such as the Institute of Directors (www.iod.com), which provides access to meeting spaces across the country. The IOD, for example, currently has 13 venues in the UK – plus one in Paris – with lounge areas and private meeting rooms.

Although you may have plenty of time to do these tasks when your company is new and has little business, after it starts to grow, you'll want to devote more time to selling and fulfilling customer needs, and less time to doing the kind of tasks that don't directly generate cash for your business.

Finding Good Solicitors, Accountants and Other Professionals

When you own a home-based business, you're responsible for just about everything. Whether you're selling your products, paying the bills or taking out the rubbish, the business begins and ends with you – without you, you have no business.

This simple fact doesn't mean, however, that you have to go at absolutely everything alone. Any number of outside professionals are ready, willing and able to help you build and expand your business and assist you to make sure you're on a firm footing – legally and financially. By leveraging the services of key professionals, such as solicitors, accountants, bankers, insurance agents and others, a small business can be just as effective and organised as a much larger organisation.

No matter what kind of professionals you decide to use, check them out thoroughly before you commit to doing business with them. Don't forget: your goal is to find someone who is not only talented and affordable, but who also can grow with you and your company and become a long-term trusted associate. Take your time when you're selecting the professionals you want to work with; believe us, the time you invest in the process now will pay off many times over in the years to come. Consider the following during the selection process:

- ✔ **Accessibility.** You may have a difficult time getting some professionals' attention when you really need them. Make sure the professionals you hire aren't already so overcommitted with other clients that they can't meet your needs quickly, when you need them the most. If they don't answer your phone calls or emails promptly or get back to you when promised, give them a wide berth and find someone else.

- ✔ **Compatibility.** The preceding characteristics don't mean much if you aren't compatible with your chosen professional. Conversely, you may be willing to give up some experience or price in exchange for someone you really get along with. The ideal situation is to find someone who meets all your criteria, and is also compatible with you and any business partners and associates you may have.

✔ **Ethics.** Hire professionals who have ethical standards that are just as high as the standards you uphold. Choosing someone with flexible ethics is asking for trouble. You can tell a lot about a person by having a face-to-face conversation and asking how they'd react in certain circumstances. If you don't like what they say, move on.

✔ **Price.** Although you should never select a professional based on price alone, price certainly does enter into the equation. With some big-city lawyers charging hundreds of pounds an hour, every pound really does count. Don't be afraid to shop around for the best combination of skill, experience and price.

✔ **Qualifications.** Hire professionals who are as qualified and experienced as possible; you don't want your business to be the place where they learn the ropes. Don't hire someone who merely dabbles in an area of professional expertise or who does it as a hobby. You need someone who's a pro and who's fully committed to your success. You could hire a friend or relative if they have the expertise you need, but be careful that working together doesn't adversely affect your relationship.

In the following sections, we take a closer look at some of the kind of professionals that home-based business owners most often turn to for help and support.

Hiring the right solicitor

A solicitor's services are an important part of any business's – including any home-based business's – support team.

What exactly can a solicitor do for your business? Here are some of the most common tasks solicitors take on for small-business clients like you:

✔ Choosing a business form (legal structure) for your business

✔ Writing, reviewing and negotiating business contracts

✔ Dealing with employee issues (if you employ anyone)

✔ Helping with credit problems (and bankruptcy in the worst-case scenario)

✔ Addressing consumer issues and complaints

✔ Working with rental or leasing agreements

✔ Advising you on your legal rights and obligations

✔ Representing you in court if necessary

Make sure you seek out a solicitor who specialises in working with small businesses and start-ups. Any other solicitor may not have the exact skill set you need. If you have a family solicitor who also has lots of experience with small businesses, start there. If he or she isn't the best person for the job, ask for a referral to someone who is. One more thing: make a point of asking your solicitor how much a particular task costs – *before* you engage his or her services. There's nothing worse than getting a bill for thousands of pounds when you expected to pay far less. If you're wary about working with a solicitor who charges by the hour, ask for a total price for the work you need done. You can avoid nasty financial surprises and keep your relationship on good terms.

The Law Society (www.lawsociety.org.uk; select 'Find a Solicitor' and then select 'Business Affairs' from the Area of Law search pane) represents some 1,400 firms of solicitors in England and Wales that have come together to help ensure that all businesses, especially the smaller owner-managed ones, get access to sound legal advice whenever they need it.

Picking a good accountant or bookkeeper

If you're not an expert in accounting – and even if you *are* but would rather devote your precious time to taking care of your customers' needs – getting a good accountant is a definite must. As the owner of your business, you need to know exactly how much money is going in and out of your business and for what purposes it's being used. This knowledge allows you to assess the financial health of your company and helps you make plans for the future. Plus, the information contained in your accounting system provides the basis for determining how much you owe the government in taxes and other fees.

Inadequate record keeping is a principal contributor to the failure of many small businesses. A good accountant can be a tremendous help in setting up a useful financial record-keeping system, as well as providing ongoing financial advice.

Here are some of the most common tasks that accountants perform for their small-business customers:

- ✔ Small-business start-up, business sale or business purchase
- ✔ Accounting system design and implementation
- ✔ Preparation, review and audit of financial statements
- ✔ Tax planning
- ✔ Preparation of income or corporation tax returns and VAT returns
- ✔ Tax appeals (if you think you're paying too much tax)

Bear in mind that you may not need the services of a full-blown accountant. You may find that for simply tracking money in and out of your business, a bookkeeper is sufficient. A *bookkeeper* is someone (often a home-based businessperson) who records the accounts and transactions of a business. He or she probably doesn't have a formal accountancy qualification. However, for many basic tasks, such as entering and keeping track of income and expense transactions in an accounting system, a bookkeeper is a more affordable option.

Make sure that a prospective bookkeeper is adequately qualified. The International Association of Bookkeepers (www.iab.org.uk) and the Institute of Certified Bookkeepers (www.bookkeepers.org.uk) are the two professional associations concerned.

If you need someone to represent you with HM Revenue and Customs for tax audits and appeals (when you believe you're paying too much tax), consider using the services of a tax adviser. A tax adviser specialises in advising, representing and preparing tax returns for individuals, partnerships and corporations, and may have more experience in taxes than a typical accountant or bookkeeper.

Find and choose an accountant in the same way you select any other professional adviser. Ask friends and business associates for recommendations. Interview at least three candidates.

When you interview your prospective candidates (in person or over the phone), make sure you get answers to the following questions:

✔ Does your candidate have specific experience working with home-based businesses?

✔ Does your candidate show an active interest in the financial aspects of your business operations (cash flow, inventory and so on)?

✔ Does your candidate have specific experience with income and corporation tax, and does he or she keep abreast of the latest changes in the tax law as it affects your industry?

✔ What do the candidate's references say about his or her performance and reliability?

✔ What is the candidate's fee structure?

✔ Does your candidate have a network of other potentially beneficial contacts within your local area (bank manager or solicitor, for example)?

✔ Are you comfortable with the candidate, and are your financial philosophies compatible?

One thing you'll notice as you search for the right accountant for your business is that some have a set of initials following their names, for example, ACA, FCA, ACCA, CIMA or ICAEW. These initials indicate that they're qualified accountants – known as *chartered accountants* – and are members of a professional accountancy body, and have passed a rigorous examination covering accounting, business law, auditing and taxes. They also undergo continuing professional development. A chartered accountant may be more expensive than a non-chartered one but, depending on your specific needs, the extra cost may be well worth your money. You must use a chartered accountant if your company needs to be audited.

Any skilled accountant – whether or not he or she has initials after their name – may be just right for you and your business. It all depends on the experience and expertise they bring to the table, as well as their willingness to be available to help you when you really need it. Don't exclude good candidates merely because they lack initials after their name.

Make sure you have at least a basic understanding of accounting and the particular bookkeeping system you're using. Even if you decide to hire an accountant to take care of the details, as the owner of your own business you have to understand how the financial side of your business works. Take advantage of the financial reporting functions of whatever electronic bookkeeping system you've chosen to use, and know how to read and interpret your company's financial reports produced by the programme. For more information on doing just that, check out Chapter 6 and read *Understanding Business Accounting For Dummies* by John A. Tracy and Colin Barrow (Wiley). If you like, ask your accountant or bookkeeper to spend an hour or two talking you through the system and financial reports.

Banking on the best bankers

You want to have a relationship with your bank already in place when you need it; after all, you never know when you may need funding. It may be when you're in the start-up phase of your business or when you get a huge order from a customer and need to pay your suppliers before you receive payment. Or it may be when your business starts to grow, and you need to finance your expansion. Even if you don't plan to expand any time soon and have no need for a loan or financing, having a relationship with your bank can still be helpful.

Establish a relationship with your banker (often known as a relationship manager) *before* you apply for a loan. The relationship you have with a banker at the time you apply for a loan can make the difference between getting approved and getting turned down.

What kind of financial institution is right for your kind of home-based business? Several different kinds of financial institutions are available to you, and each one has a unique spin on the world of money and banking. Here are the main financial institutions you have to choose from:

- **Banks.** The first choice of many home-based businesses, whether on the high street or online. Banks traditionally offer a wide variety of loans, both commercial and consumer, and they're the place to go for special small-business loans made available through schemes such as Funding for Lending and the Enterprise Finance Guarantee scheme (government initiatives to increase the amount of funding available to banks to lend to small businesses). Most banks also offer special accounts designed specifically for businesses, along with a wide array of business-oriented products and services.

- **Credit unions.** Although credit unions are similar to banks in some ways, they're owned by their members rather than public shareholders and are only open to people living in their geographical area. This member-ownership structure results in lower costs of operation, which are passed on to members in the form of lower interest rates on loans and higher savings interest rates. Some credit unions are able to offer modest business loans. North London credit union, for example, can lend up to £10,000 for business start-ups and up to £25,000 for businesses that can show accounts for at least one year's trading. You can find your local credit union by searching on the Association of British Credit Union's website (www.abcul.org).

- **Credit card companies.** As you probably already know, credit card companies offer interest rates that are often significantly higher than the rates you'd get on the same amount of money from a bank or credit union, yet thousands of companies regularly use credit cards to finance purchases. Why? Because using a credit card is usually far more convenient than applying for a loan every time you want to make a major purchase or some other financial move. Bear in mind that if you take out a personal credit card in your own name, you're liable for the outstanding amount if your business fails. You can compare credit cards at www.moneysupermarket.com.

- **Commercial finance companies.** These companies specialise in working with businesses, usually in financing equipment leasing or purchases or in acquiring inventory. The deals that commercial finance companies offer – particularly in leasing – may be attractive and are worth checking out.

- **Consumer finance companies.** These businesses specialise in making loans to borrowers who have a hard time obtaining loans from their banks or credit unions, perhaps because they've defaulted on loans in the past or because their credit is already overextended. Because those borrowers are considered higher risks for defaulting on loans, consumer finance companies generally charge significantly higher interest rates than banks and credit unions do. So consider consumer finance companies a funding source of last resort.

✔ **Peer-to-peer lending.** Businesses with a couple of years' trading under their belts and an interesting story to tell may be able to borrow money through peer-to-peer lending arrangements such as that offered by Funding Circle (www.fundingcircle.com) and Zopa (www.zopa.com). Small amounts from lots of individuals are amassed to create a large amount of capital for a small business seeking funding. At Funding Circle, for example, individuals can lend a minimum of £20 and businesses can borrow between £5,000 and £250,000 for a period of one, three or five years. Lenders receive a fixed rate of monthly interest agreed in advance by the two sides.

Make sure that you anticipate your financing needs well in advance. Waiting until the last minute to develop a relationship with your banker or to apply for a critically needed loan is a recipe for financial disaster.

Consulting business consultants

Everyone has talents in many areas, but you can't be the master of everything. Don't worry, though: *consultants* are available to assist you in the areas in which you need expert help. You can hire business, management and marketing consultants; promotion experts; financial planners; and a host of other specialists who can help make your business more successful.

If you're facing a new major problem in which you have no expertise, particularly a problem you don't expect to experience again, then hiring a consultant is an option worth considering. For example, if you're moving premises, changing your computing or accounting system, starting to do business overseas or designing an employee share ownership scheme, getting the help of someone who's covered that area several times before and who's an expert in the field may well make sense. If you do hire a consultant, expect to pay a few hundred pounds a day, depending on their level of expertise.

Regardless of exactly which kind of consultant you decide to hire, follow these steps to select the right one:

1. **Clearly define your objectives.**

   Describe the job you want done and specify the things you expect from the assignment. Understand precisely how you expect your business to benefit from the work. Decide on the time frame, scope and any constraints on the assignment. Clarify your own role and explain how the consultant's time will be spent.

2. **Research a variety of consultants, select the best three and ask for written proposals.**

   Good consultants will be more than happy to send you basic information about themselves and talk with you about your needs, without charge. Invite your best prospects to submit written proposals, which should include the following:

   - Their understanding of the problem

   - Their approach to solving the problem

   - Their experience and references

   - Work plan

   - Reports and/or systems that will be supplied to you

   - Fees, expenses and schedules of payment

   - Any input required from you

3. **Clearly explain your desired outcomes.**

   Prepare a concise brief that clearly defines the objectives, scope, time frame, reporting procedure and constraints of the project, and provide this brief to your top-three consultant prospects to use as they prepare their proposals. Remember that the cheapest price won't necessarily give you the best value for your money and that consultant fees may be negotiable.

4. **Interview your top consultant candidates.**

   Successful consulting requires goodwill. Meet the consultant face to face if you can and brief him or her well, using a written brief and any background information you think is necessary. Talk through each proposal before making a final decision to make sure the consultant has addressed all of your concerns. If you're not happy with any aspects of the proposal, don't feel pressured to accept it. Continue discussions with the consultants until you reach a full agreement on the proposal. Select the firm or individual that you feel has the best qualifications and experience, and that you feel you can work with comfortably.

5. **Ask for references – and follow up on them.**

   After you make your selection, ask the chosen consulting firm or individual for names or written references from former clients to verify the consultant's suitability for the assignment.

6. **Sign a written contract and start the assignment.**

   Get a solicitor to take a look at the contract before you sign on the dotted line.

7. **Keep in touch with your consultant as the project progresses.**

   Using consultants effectively demands a commitment of time as well as money from you. Remember that you must keep in touch with the progress of the assignment if you want to get the most from it. Consultants are likely to be most cost-effective when working on an agreed programme and time frame. Make sure that you hold regular progress meetings and that the consultant keeps you fully briefed on progress.

8. **Make sure you don't find any surprises in the final report.**

   The consultant's report is often his or her most tangible *deliverable* (what he or she provides in fulfilment of a contract), but it must be in a format that's beneficial to you. If necessary, ask the consultant to produce a draft report so you can review the findings and recommendations before the final report is produced. The final report should contain no surprises.

9. **Implement the recommendations and involve yourself as well as the consultant.**

   You may need to make arrangements for the consultant to help with the implementation of their advice. You can do so cost-effectively by involving the consultant in regular progress meetings. Get a written quotation for any implementation work, even if it follows directly from an assignment.

Hiring the right consultant for your business at the right time can mean the difference between just getting by and achieving tremendous success.

The Institute of Business Consulting (www.ibconsulting.org.uk) provides guidelines for choosing a consultant in the Purchasing Consultancy section of its website.

You can't delegate decision making, you can only delegate the analysis of problems and the presentation of options. In the end, *you* have to choose which way to go.

Working with insurance agents and brokers

A dizzying array of different insurance policies is available to you and your home business, from hundreds of insurance companies. Which company and policy offers the best coverage for you? To get an inkling of the answer, you have to extensively research insurance policies and companies – definitely not the best use of your time.

A better way to find out what insurance is available (and necessary) for your business, and which deals are the best for you, is to use insurance agents and brokers. Insurance professionals can save you precious time and money – sometimes thousands of pounds – while providing you with the peace of mind that comes from knowing your insurance needs are being met.

Not only can a good insurance agent or broker advise you about the type and amount of coverage that's best for your business, but he or she can probably also tailor a package that meets your specific needs at reasonable rates. All of these services are worth their weight in gold to busy home-based business owners who have neither an extensive knowledge of insurance and risk management nor the time to mess with them.

Ask your friends and business associates for referrals to good agents or brokers, check with professional and trade associations or use an online service like www.moneysupermarket.com, www.comparethemarket.com or www.confused.com to find a broker.

Make sure you look for someone who regularly handles accounts of your size (many agents and brokers consider one-person businesses too small to be worth the trouble to service). Expect your agent to add value to your enterprise, just as a solicitor or accountant does.

When choosing an insurance agent for your business, we suggest that you do the following:

✔ Solicit bids from two or three established agents to see who can deliver the lowest price for a specified level of coverage.

✔ Evaluate the professional experience and qualifications of prospective agents as if you were choosing a new solicitor or accountant.

✔ Interview prospective agents (in person or over the phone) with an eye towards if you trust the agent and have confidence in him or her.

The following steps can help you find the agent or broker who best meets your business's needs:

1. **Look for an agent who's knowledgeable about your industry and who regularly works with home-based businesses.**

   Different companies have different needs. A wildlife photographer, for example, has very different insurance needs to those of an estate agent. And what's good for a high-tech company may not necessarily be right for an online retail operation or high street shop. One thing is for sure: no one agent can effectively keep up with every different kind of insurance for every different type of business.

2. **Choose an agent who's knowledgeable, dependable, loyal and effective at communicating.**

   You want the agent to work well for you and know how to speed up claims when necessary. Check out the agent's support structure to make sure it's adequate to handle your account. Visit the agent's office and meet the people who handle day-to-day operations. Confidence in them will increase your confidence in the agent or broker.

Insurance is an important part of every business, and it'll pay off for you to get the best advice possible. Although most home-based businesses never have to use their insurance, if you need it – because of a theft, fire, product-liability lawsuit or other covered risk – you'll be glad you have it.

Part IV
Making It Work: Moving Ahead

Top Five Ways to Separate Your Work Life at Home

- **Use a separate room.** Having a room apart from the hustle and bustle of your regular home life – one that's dedicated *exclusively* to your business – is the first step in making your home office a real office.

- **Set a work schedule.** When you own your own business, you can work whenever you like. You may find it easier (and more productive), however, to establish a regular work schedule. That way the people you share your home with know when it's okay to interrupt you and when it's clearly not okay.

- **Consider dressing formally, as if you were going to work in a corporate office**. Some people find it helps them feel more business-like and act in a more professional way.

- **Hire a meeting room.** If your home office isn't suitable for meetings, you can arrange to meet your clients at a convenient off-site location such as a hotel lobby or even your local coffee shop.

- **Get help.** Instead of trying to juggle your obligations at home while keeping up with your work, consider getting the help you need to allow you to focus exclusively on your work when you need to do so. For example, you can hire a cleaner, nanny or babysitter.

Go to www.dummies.com/extras/homebasedbusiness for free online bonus content.

In this part...

- ✔ Make the most of the amazing opportunities the Internet offers.
- ✔ Get to grips with networking and using social media.
- ✔ Create a website for your home business.
- ✔ Balance your work and personal life.
- ✔ Maintain your motivation and avoid interruptions.
- ✔ Grow – or sell – your business.

Chapter 11

Making the Internet Work for You

The Internet has opened up tremendous opportunities for businesses of all shapes and sizes, and in all locations. Today even the smallest home-based business – located in the most remote location in the country – can sell its products and services to a worldwide customer base via the Internet. Nowadays it's easier than ever to make the web work for you, whether you create your own website; use an established site like eBay.co.uk or Amazon.co.uk to reach potential customers; or reach out using social networking tools, such as Twitter or Facebook.

But guess what? A lot of other businesses are trying to get noticed, too, and they're all trying to sell their own products and services – some of which may be exactly the same products and services *you* plan to sell. The good news is that you don't have to become a huge company to take advantage of the Internet – the costs of getting set up on the web are quite affordable for most home-based business owners. In fact, many small, home-based businesses are doing quite well selling their products and services via the web. And you can too.

In this chapter, we explore how to use the Internet to bid for work and how to get listed and noticed in online directories. We explore the best approaches and places for networking with others on the Internet, and explain how to use social networking tools to your advantage. Finally, we consider the best ways to attract clients and customers with your website.

Bidding for Work Online

Something interesting has been happening on the Internet over the past few years: a number of freelance bidding sites have sprung up with the express purpose of getting independent, home-based businesspeople together with companies (including other independent, home-based businesses) that need work done.

In this section, we take a look at what you need to know to use the Internet to expand your own business opportunities.

Taking advantage of sites that bring buyers and sellers together

So what exactly is a freelance bidding site? A *freelance bidding site* is a website where companies can list jobs they need done (anything from writing advertising copy, to building websites, to doing graphic design), and freelancers can bid for the work. The company needing the work selects a freelancer and assigns the work; the selected freelancer does the work. Depending on the site, either just the company is charged a commission by the bidding site (for example, Elance.com charges the company 8.75 per cent of the value of the project), or both the freelancer and the company are charged a commission (for example, Freelancer.co.uk charges the company 3 per cent and the freelancer 10 per cent).

In general, follow these steps to take advantage of freelance bidding sites:

1. **Visit the bidding site of your choice and register.**

2. **Build your online CV by adding your particular skills and experience to the site. Be specific.**

3. **Conduct a search for projects that are suited to your experience.**

   Look beyond the main categories and dig deeply into the subcategories and special skills.

4. **Bid on a project by providing an estimate of the price for the job and your time frame for completion.**

5. **Negotiate a deal with an interested company.**

6. **Do the work and get paid.**

For someone with the right skills, using a freelance bidding site can be a relatively easy way to develop an ongoing stream of work that may be quite lucrative. You have plenty of freelance bidding sites to choose from, but make sure you check out these sites first:

- ✔ www.peopleperhour.com
- ✔ www.freelancer.co.uk
- ✔ www.elance.com
- ✔ www.odesk.com
- ✔ www.conceptcupboard.co.uk

Working out how to win bids

You may be very well qualified in whatever it is you do, and you may have tons of experience and skills. But you're not alone. Countless other people have just as much experience – maybe more – and you'll undoubtedly have to compete with some of them when you bid on a project, which means you have to sharpen your pencil and bid to win.

Here are some tips on how to win a project:

- ✔ Become intimately familiar with how the freelance bidding site you're using works.
- ✔ Make your profile look really good. In it, show your background in the field; your education, training and credentials; the services you offer; and the range of your rates. If you need help writing your profile, consider posting it as a job on one of the freelance boards and hiring a writer to help you. You'll experience first hand what it's like to receive bids and what impresses you about the bidders.
- ✔ Create an online portfolio with samples of your work. While a photographer or graphic designer can provide samples easily, even if you're a consultant, you can still show potential clients what you've done. One way to do so is to post testimonials from customers declaring how great it was to work with you. To avoid cluttering up your profile, create your portfolio elsewhere – for example on your own website – and provide a link to it from your profile page. You can go into more depth on your own website than you can on your profile.
- ✔ Demonstrate that you have the skills and tools needed to do the job. So, for example, if you're seeking virtual-assistant-type work and you're skilled at using different types of communication systems and computer

programs, say so. Don't be shy – show the buyer everything you have to offer. You probably have only one shot, so make it the best possible.

✔ Don't place your bids automatically or base them on guesswork. Ask detailed questions of the company or person seeking bids if you need to. Often, the posted work descriptions are too sketchy or leave too many gaps to provide a full picture of the work required. Just as you don't want to overbid and lose a good job, you don't want to underbid and win a job that you later find out requires more work than you originally anticipated.

✔ Do some market research; check to see what your competitors are bidding for the kind of work you want to do. Remember that you're competing against bidders from all over the world, many of whom can underbid the prices that most people working in the UK can charge. But also bear in mind that wary buyers are apt to be just as suspicious of extremely low bids as they're turned off by high ones.

✔ Propose payment schedules that show you're motivated to get the work done in a timely manner, such as asking for a relatively low initial upfront payment of 20 or 25 per cent with progress payments based on agreed-on milestones.

✔ If at first you don't succeed . . . learn from your experience and try again!

Keeping clients and building your business with them

The best business relationships are long-term business relationships; your best clients are your current clients. Believe us: a bird in hand is definitely worth two or three in the bush. Whenever possible, work to build strong relationships with your current clients and customers that will keep them coming back to you again and again.

Here are some tips for keeping your online clients happy and building long-term business relationships:

✔ **Be on time and on budget.** No client likes to hire someone who delivers the products or services late or who wants more money to do the work than they originally quoted.

✔ **Do great work.** Great work speaks for itself, and it separates you from the home-based business wannabes.

✔ **Be flexible.** Business today takes place faster than ever, and companies must be able to change direction at a moment's notice to keep up. So be flexible and ready to change accordingly.

- ✔ **Be dependable and reliable.** Be someone your client can rely on through thick and thin – if you are, you're already ahead of most of your competition.

- ✔ **Don't surprise your client with bad news.** Keep your client informed if you anticipate any possible problems or delays.

Getting Listed in Directories

Back in the old pre-Internet days, if you were a small business and you wanted to attract customers or clients – especially if you ran your business out of your home or some other non-high street location – one of the first things you had to do was put an advert in the Yellow Pages. Having a listing in the Yellow Pages was essential for many kinds of businesses, especially service businesses, such as plumbers, building contractors, tree trimmers and many others.

Although the paper Yellow Pages aren't obsolete yet, they're also online as an *online directory*. In this section, we explore some of the most common versions of this business tool.

Online business directories

Online business directories are all over the Internet today. Like anything else in life, some are better than others. Here are a few of the best:

- ✔ www.yell.com
- ✔ www.thomsonlocal.com
- ✔ uk.search.yahoo.com/yp
- ✔ www.thebestof.co.uk
- ✔ www.touchlocal.com
- ✔ www.yellowleaf.co.uk
- ✔ www.misterwhat.co.uk

You can get your site placed on any number of online directories, but our advice is to stick with the top ones – that is, the ones that get the most traffic and the ones specifically targeted to your kind of business (for example, a directory of landscape architects isn't the best place for you to list your wedding cake business). Seek out the top-notch directories in your field and apply to have your website listed. Follow up to make sure that your listing information is correct. You may also have the option of making your business stand out more by paying for a more prominent listing – displaying your entry in bold, for example, or in a box, or at the top of the list.

Association memberships

Do you belong to an association? For example, if you're a plumber, you may belong to the Association of Plumbing and Heating Contractors. Or you may belong to your local chamber of commerce or a local business association. Whatever your affiliations are, one of the fringe benefits of belonging to many associations is the opportunity to be listed in their online member directories.

Go to the Association of Plumbing and Heating Contractors website (www.aphc.co.uk), for example, and you can search for their members by post-code, town, area of work or business name. The listings tell you what areas they specialise in and provide their names, addresses and contact details.

If you don't yet belong to an association, consider joining one and getting listed in its online directory. If you already belong, make sure to take advantage of all the promotional and networking activities your association has to offer, including being listed in its online directory.

If anything changes in your business, such as your phone number, website or email address, remember to submit updates to all your online directories to keep your listings current.

Local directories and review sites

The problem with many online search engines and directories is that they include the whole world when you just want to attract customers in your small town in Northumberland. In response to this issue, some search engines, directories and business review sites have services that focus on local offerings. When you use a local directory to do a search for a specific kind of business – say, a window cleaning or bookkeeping service – you can specify a town or county in which to search, thus providing results that are much more relevant and useful than if the entire country were included in the search.

Here are some examples of local directories specific to a particular area:

- www.allinlondon.co.uk
- www.justbillingshurst.co.uk
- www.touchliverpool.com
- www.wembleybiz.co.uk
- www.crawleysussex.co.uk

Again, follow up after you apply for your listing to make sure your business is indeed listed and accurate – business name, address, phone number, email address and website address.

Networking the Internet Way

You can make a splash – while driving traffic to your own site (more on that in the next section) – by getting noticed on *other people's* websites. If you have a particularly lively personality, or if you're knowledgeable and enjoy giving advice to others (in a polite way, of course) you may soon find yourself a very popular fixture on many different websites – not just your own. In this section, we cover the most common networking tools currently available online.

You can choose from 101 ways to use online networking to promote your home-based business. However, when using the various networking tools we describe in this section, be careful not to get so caught up in sending tweets or updating your Facebook page that you run out of time to take care of your current customers and clients, or to do the other kinds of marketing you need to do to keep a steady stream of new customers and clients walking through your door. Make sure you test the results of your networking efforts regularly. If you find that they aren't resulting in enough new business to be worth their while, quickly move on to something else.

The real beauty of making the Internet work for you is that you can quickly, easily and inexpensively change your approach – literally in just minutes. So, if at first you don't succeed, try, try again – with a new and different approach, of course.

Discovering the benefits of online forums

Today you can find lots of UK-based online forums devoted to just about every conceivable hobby, business, activity and enthusiasm imaginable: parenting; steam trains; vintage Jeeps; genealogy; politics; personal finance and investing; maths; children's book writing; knitting; and much, much more. If you can imagine it, someone probably already has a forum on it.

What sites and forums are devoted to topics that relate to your products or services? Seek them out, become a member and begin contributing. For a relatively small investment of your time, you'll definitely see a positive impact on your bottom line.

You can find lists of forums on the Yahoo! Groups site (`groups.yahoo.com`). Joining forums is easy, but remember to honour the unique etiquette for each group you join (see the later section 'Making winning relationships the right way' for more on the etiquette of networking online).

Several forums are devoted to small businesses, entrepreneurs and start-ups in the UK: check out `www.startups.co.uk/forums` or `www.ukbusinessforums.co.uk/forums`. Companies such as `www.websitetoolbox.com` and `www.proboards.com` can get you up to speed in minutes and some of their services are absolutely free.

Improving your social networking

Social networking sites are websites devoted to creating networks and communities of friends and acquaintances. As members join these sites, they bring along their own networks of family and friends, quickly creating large online social networks, some linked by common interests such as business.

In recent years, social networking has become all the rage as businesses of all shapes and sizes scramble to establish a meaningful presence on social websites dedicated to this purpose. Here are the three most used social networking sites in the UK:

- ✔ `www.facebook.com`
- ✔ `www.twitter.com`
- ✔ `www.linkedin.com`

Although the chances of developing serious business by participating in social networking sites are more remote than by participating in forums specific to your expertise or business, giving them a try may be worth your time to make your presence known.

Here are the four best ways for home-based businesses to use social networking sites to their advantage:

- ✔ **Use them regularly.** Going to the effort of establishing a Twitter or Facebook account and then never updating it is pointless. You'll just end up annoying more customers than you'll gain. Commit to updating your Facebook page once a week and tweeting on Twitter at least once every couple of days. At the same time, don't spend so long on these sites that your business suffers and your customers feel bombarded.

✔ **Respond.** If a customer or potential customer makes the effort to contact you via Twitter or Facebook, with a query, suggestion or complaint, respond immediately – and meaningfully. Don't just reply in platitudes – do everything you can to solve the problem or answer the query. Remember that social media is a very public space – many other customers will be watching closely to see how you respond too.

✔ **Don't sell your product.** Social media isn't about telling everyone over and over how great your product or service is. Instead it's about having an ongoing discussion or conversation with your customers so you can find out how they think, and you can show them another side to your business. Tweet links to interesting things you've read; hold competitions; get involved.

✔ **Do it yourself.** At least in the beginning, don't outsource your social media content to a third party. You need to find your own social media voice and customers need to be able to contact you directly – and feel confident that they're doing so. And don't schedule automated tweets to go out at set times. It looks fake and shows you don't understand how social media works.

A good way of monitoring and managing the tweets you make on Twitter is to use a free online organiser such as www.tweetdeck.com or www.hootsuite.com, which goes one step further by enabling to you manage all your social media networks in one place and gives you the ability to analyse your social media traffic.

Making winning relationships the right way

Just as you have rules of etiquette for behaving in your offline life, you have rules and norms for behaving in online forums and networks. Here are some basic rules to follow so that you find yourself a welcome participant rather than someone to be avoided (or worse, talked negatively about).

✔ **Stay on topic.** Make a point of posting only messages that are relevant to the subject of the forum or network in which you're participating.

✔ **Include the necessary information.** If you're asking a question of forum or network members, make sure you give them a complete description of what your problem or issue is. Doing so helps other readers of the forum determine a resolution to your issue.

✔ **Be nice.** If you want the welcome mat to be put out for you, refrain from inappropriate language and personal attacks. Remember the first rule of karma: what goes around comes around!

✔ **Choose a descriptive title.** A descriptive title helps subsequent visitors to the forum successfully identify your topic.

✔ **Don't spam the site!** Although most forums and online social networks tolerate a small amount of plugging your business, blatant and ongoing plugs can incur the wrath of your forum mates. Your best bet is to put a brief plug about your business (along with a link to your website) in your *signature,* the identifying line or lines tacked to the bottom of your messages.

✔ **Don't include graphics or other files in the forum posts.** Don't post attachments. Most users don't want to download a file when reading your post, for time and security reasons. Just explain your point in writing and include the URL of the file in your post so others can view it *if* they want to.

✔ **Don't duplicate threads.** Before posting messages, make sure you familiarise yourself with the forum. If possible, check to make sure your topic hasn't already been addressed in a recent thread.

✔ **Don't get too personal.** Remember, all messages are public and are viewed by others.

✔ **Don't perpetuate off-topic threads.** If someone makes an inappropriate or *spam* post, don't add more noise by replying to the thread.

Be polite, helpful and friendly – you'll attract far more business with honey than vinegar.

Building and Maintaining a Website

Okay, so you've decided to start your own website – congratulations! Now what? Well, the first step is to build it. You can hire someone to do it for you or you can do it yourself by using an online website builder such as www. moonfruit.com, www.wix.com or www.basekit.com, which provide a selection of pre-designed templates to choose from, many of which are free. Basekit can also design your website for you, for a fee. For each of these website builder sites you can choose to pay to include an e-commerce function if you want to.

Even if you decide to pay someone to create your website, make sure they build it on a widely used platform, such as WordPress, so that after it's up and running you can make small updates yourself, such as changing the text or adding more photos – and get your website developer to show you how to use it. Otherwise you'll have to ask them to make every little change and that could mean more expense and waiting days or even weeks until they find the time to get round to it.

You can create an effective store on the Internet without having a website at all. How? An increasing number of established websites such as Amazon.co.uk now host e-commerce sites for other businesses.

Hiring someone to create and maintain your website

If you have no interest in creating and maintaining your own website, or in getting to grips with an online website builder such as Moonfruit.com, plenty of website design companies (many of them home-based businesses, by the way) would love to design it for you. It probably won't be cheap – anywhere from a few hundred pounds for a simple site to thousands for a much more complex one – but if you have no interest in learning the ins and outs of websites yourself (and we can't blame you if you don't), hiring an expert is clearly the best option.

Don't hire just *anyone*. Remember that your site will be the first (and perhaps the last) thing that many potential customers and clients see regarding your business. Make sure their first impression is a good one.

Here are a few tips for finding a great website designer:

- ✔ If you see a website that you really like, find out who designed it. Sometimes the designer's name is posted on the site itself, often at the bottom of the home page, but sometimes you need to ask the site owner. Talking to prior clients is a good idea anyway.

- ✔ Interview website designers just as you would a new employee. Get references, do interviews, check them out.

- ✔ Ask your business acquaintances if they know of anyone who's good at designing websites.

- ✔ After you find some candidates, ask each of them for a list of active websites that they've developed and actively maintain – and then visit them. How do they look? Are they attractive and well produced, or do they look terrible? Are they current and up to date, or do they look like they haven't been touched for months?

- ✔ Compare the work of several different designers before deciding. Only after you have a chance to fully explore your candidates' work and compare it with the work of others should you select a website designer.

- ✔ Ask how soon your site will be up and running and how much it will cost – not just to set it up, but also to host it, periodically maintain it and troubleshoot problems.

The price of hiring someone to build a website for you has been steadily decreasing as more people learn the skills involved. Now it's relatively easy to find and engage an affordable (and, probably, home-based) website designer. Although some prefabricated designs look decent, you may be able to hire a talented website designer to establish a unique and professional-looking web presence for your business at a price that definitely doesn't break the bank.

Creating a website yourself

If you have a basic knowledge of the Internet and how it works, you may be able to create your own website and have a lot of fun in the process. Although building your own site can be enjoyable, make sure you don't have so much fun that you forget to sell your products and services, too.

Follow these steps to create a working website:

1. **Select a web-hosting service.**

   A *web-hosting service* sets up your website address (or *URL*), something like www.yourname.com (or www.yourname.co.uk), and then hosts your site on its computers where anyone with access to the web can access it. You have countless web-hosting services to choose from, and they vary considerably in price and level of service, so it pays to shop around. Most home-based businesses can get by with a bare-bones level of service, which can cost as little as £2 a month. Before you select a web-hosting service, ask around for references and make sure you visit some of the hosted sites to see how well they work. Some options to consider include www.dreamhost.com, www.hostgator.com and www.justhost.com.

2. **Build your website.**

   Some hosting services offer simple built-in software for creating websites as part of their hosting packages. This kind of package may be all you need to create the site you want, and it's probably the best option if you're new to all this Internet stuff. However, if your needs go beyond what your host provides, consider buying software specifically designed for creating websites. Microsoft Expression Web, Macromedia Dreamweaver and NetObjects Fusion are powerful and simple to use. In essence, if you can use a basic word-processing program, such as Microsoft Word, you can create your own website. Microsoft Word even allows you to save regular text pages as HTML (Hypertext Markup Language; the language of the web) documents.

3. Maintain your website.

The great thing about creating and maintaining your own website is that you have full control over the content, as well as when and how you update or modify it. Need to add a new product to your listings? In five minutes, you're done. If you have to go through a hired third party, it can take days or even weeks to make a minor update. Google offers a terrific tool called Content Experiments (formerly known as Website Optimiser) that can help you test and improve your site, by trying out different versions of your web pages so you can find out which of them results in the most enquiries or sales. You'll find Content Experiments within Google Analytics at `www.google.com/analytics`.

As the site's administrator, you also have direct access to your website's statistics: how many visitors your site has, who they are and where they're coming from. Use these statistics to find out which of your pages are the most and least popular, and adjust the content accordingly.

When creating your website, consider keeping space to write a blog on it. Writing a regular blog is a fantastic way of keeping in touch with your customers and creating a feeling of community to ensure they come back time and time again; you also benefit because adding regular new content to your website ensures that it's noticed by search engines such as Google and given priority in search listings.

A visionary idea for an online home business

The wonderful thing about websites is that you can create one to sell things you never knew were even possible to sell online. When Jamie Murray Wells decided to start a home business at the age of 19 selling prescription glasses online, everyone told him it would never work because no one had ever bought prescription glasses over the Internet and would only ever buy them in person from an optician. But he was convinced there was a gap in the market, and so started his business Glassesdirect.com from the front room of his parents' home, selling glasses for £15 a pair. He hired a student web developer at £6 an hour to help him design a website where customers could enter their prescriptions and order glasses. The business took off immediately and is a huge success. Not only that, but Murray Wells has gone on to pioneer another Internet first – selling hearing aids online at HearingDirect.com, which has a website where customers can actually check their hearing online to work out which hearing aid they need. His business, which also includes Sunglassesshop.com, now has a turnover of £30 million.

Keep your blog professional looking and appropriate; get someone to proof-read it for you if you don't have much writing experience, make sure that what you post is in line with the business image you want to project – so don't moan about difficult customers – and remember that it's your business blog, not your personal one!

For more information on creating your own website to meet your business's marketing needs, take a look at *Web Marketing For Dummies,* 3rd Edition, by Jan Zimmerman (Wiley).

Attracting and holding attention with your site

The following tips can help you create a website that attracts and holds your clients' interest and encourages them to send their money your way:

- ✔ **Be easy to find.** Don't make it difficult for your clients to find you. Your URL needs to be intuitively obvious. If, for example, your company's name is Luke's Lute Lessons, your URL should be something like www. lukeslutelessons.com or www.lutelessons.co.uk. That way, clients (and clients-to-be) who don't have your address at their fingertips can easily guess it or search for it. You can choose whether you prefer to be .com or .co.uk but make sure you buy both (you can forward one to the other so you just have one address to give to customers) to stop anyone else buying the domain name and setting up in competition with you. Also, take the time to register your website with the most-visited Internet search engines and directories, which is free (see the later section 'Knowing what it takes to get traffic').

  Of course, many domains are already taken, so you may have to settle for one that's longer and a little less direct (like www.lukeslondon-lutelessons.co.uk). Because many domain names are minimally used, you may be able to purchase a domain name you want from an online domain marketplace such as `www.sedo.co.uk`. You may even be able to buy it from its current owner. You can use an online broker service such as that offered by Sedo.co.uk to negotiate a deal on your behalf. If the domain name you want isn't being actively used and you're willing to wait for it to expire, you can back-order the name from a domain registration service.

  Another approach is to come up with a name that's catchy (and readily available), but that says nothing at all about what products or services your business sells, such as Google.com, Ocado.com and Opodo.co.uk. Whatever your approach, put on your thinking cap and be creative!

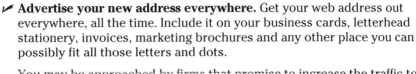

✔ **Advertise your new address everywhere.** Get your web address out everywhere, all the time. Include it on your business cards, letterhead stationery, invoices, marketing brochures and any other place you can possibly fit all those letters and dots.

You may be approached by firms that promise to increase the traffic to your website. Maybe they will, and maybe they won't. If you do decide to hire a firm to increase traffic, make sure you ask exactly what it plans to do to reach the people most likely to buy your products and services and what sort of guarantee it offers. Chances are you can do the same things on your own and save a lot of money in the process.

✔ **Give your visitors a reason to visit – and to come back again and again.** The attention span of the average web surfer can be measured in seconds. If your site is boring, or if it takes too long to load, your client or prospect will click out of the site just as quickly as he or she clicked in. Take a look at your competitors' sites to get an idea of what works and what doesn't. Use graphics, photographs and attractive backgrounds to make your site look more appealing, but be careful that these byte-intensive files don't dramatically slow the speed at which your web pages load. Above all, provide lots of fresh, value-added content in the form of news, reports, blogs, articles, surveys, industry trends, networking forums, and the like that keep your clients and prospects coming back for more. (See the next section for more tips on how to attract customers and clients to your site.)

✔ **Capture contact information.** When people visit your site, they're probably not there by accident – they're there because they're interested in what you have to sell. Take advantage of this opportunity by encouraging your visitors to give you their contact information, which you can then use in your organisation's marketing and promotional efforts. For example, you can set up a guestbook where visitors can leave comments about your site, along with their name, email address and phone number. Or you can offer to email a complimentary copy of your client newsletter to prospects who are willing to give you their contact information. Contests, special offers and surveys are all great ways to encourage your visitors to give you their contact information.

✔ **Check web stats.** A good hosting service gives you access to vital statistics related to your website: the number of visitors each day; where they're from; how long they stayed; which pages they viewed; which search engine (if any) referred them to your site; and much, much more. By analysing these statistics, you can quickly identify which parts of your site attract the most (and the least) visitors and test visitor response to site changes on a real-time basis. (Hint: do more of what your visitors like and less of what they don't.)

If your service provider doesn't offer a decent statistics package, check out Google Analytics (`www.google.com/analytics`).

✔ **Regularly visit your website.** Make sure your site is working the way it's supposed to. Some hosting services are better than others, and it's in your best interest to make sure your site is always available. The easiest way to make a habit of visiting your site is to set it as your browser's home page. That way, it pops up every time you log on to the Internet. And ask your friends and family to check it frequently and let you know if they run into any problems.

The ABC of SEO

Search engine optimisation (SEO) is the art of persuading search engines such as Google to put your website near the top of their list of search results when someone types in a request which you could fulfil. If you sell dog baskets, for example, you want your website to come out at the top of the list every time someone types the words 'dog baskets' into the search engine.

Getting near the top of the list is important because websites which appear in the top three places of a search engine's results attract 98 per cent of the traffic for that particular search, while the website in first place attracts 60 per cent of the traffic all by itself. The fact is that even though a search can generate millions of results – a search for dog baskets produces 22.4 million websites to choose from, for example – people rarely bother to look at the second results page or beyond. In fact, they often don't even bother to scroll down to see the bottom of the first page.

Exactly how Google decides to rank the websites on its search list is a closely guarded secret based on constantly tweaked algorithms. But what is known is that the results are displayed according to how relevant Google decides they are to what someone is looking for. Relevancy is determined by factors such as the content of your website (both visible and embedded), how many other sites link to yours, how many people visit the site and how often the content on your website is updated. Other factors, such as how long the website has been running for, are also taken into account.

Consider the following three crucial factors to help make your site relevant:

✔ **Meta tags.** *Meta tags* are words which you can write into the html code of your website – in other words, the unseen instruction part of your website. People looking at your website can't see them but they are recognised by Google and other search engines as they trawl the Internet looking for relevant sites. The meta tags need to indicate what your website is about by using keywords to describe its contents.

✔ **Content.** You need to include the words and phrases you want to be known for into the content of your website. There's so much competition, you can improve the chances of your website being noticed by Google – and therefore put high up the search list – if you can find yourself a niche, by highlighting any unusual or specialist products you sell.

If your website sells products for hikers and outdoor walkers, for example, you'll get a lot more attention if you highlight the head torches which you sell than if you highlight walking boots, because far fewer sites sell head torches than walking boots.

✔ **Links.** Get other well-regarded sites to mention your site and include a link to it. The simplest place to start is to create a Facebook page and Twitter account for your business which link to your site. Links from a trade organisation or local community website are useful too. You might also be able to get a blogger to link to your site, perhaps by sending them some products to review. Write a regular blog yourself on your website – basically a regularly updated online newsletter – which people can follow and link to.

For lots more advice and information about SEO, read *Small Business Marketing For Dummies* by Paul Lancaster and Barbara Findlay Schenck (Wiley).

Using Your Website to Attract Customers and Clients

Well, you've created a website; now what? Now you have to work out how to attract attention in the vast crowded space that is the Internet. At the time of writing, more than 250 million *domain names* (website names such as Dummies.com) are currently in use, many of which have their own functioning business, special-interest, personal and other websites attached to them. That's a lot of competition for customer eyeballs.

In the sections that follow, we take a look at how to attract potential customers to your website and how to get them to buy after they find their way there.

Knowing what it takes to get traffic

Traffic – that is, visitors to your website – is perhaps the key element that can make or break your online business. Generally, the more traffic the better, assuming that the traffic consists of people who may be interested in buying what you have for sale.

Just because you have a website doesn't mean that anyone is going to show up for your party. It isn't enough to simply hope that people will find your website. If you hope to be successful, you need to get more – and the right kind of – traffic to your site. Here are a few of the most effective ideas for doing so:

✔ **Register with the most-visited search engines.** Hundreds of search engines are available but, in our humble opinion, you needn't waste your time with 99.9 per cent of them. Our advice is to stick with the top search engines (based on the number of visits they get):

- Google (www.google.com)
- Yahoo! (www.yahoo.com)
- Bing (www.bing.com)

Registering is free. You can register your website address with Google, for example, by going to www.google.co.uk/addurl and putting your website address in the box provided. You can register with Bing (which powers Yahoo!) at www.bing.com/toolbox/submit-site-url. Referrals from sites such as Yahoo!, Bing and Google are a critical link in helping people find you.

✔ **Register with pay-per-click search engines.** Google offers a service where you can pay to have your company's site show up in a prominent location when someone searches a specific keyword or phrase (this service is called Google AdWords: see www.adwords.google.co.uk for how to get started). Imagine that your home-based business is wedding consulting. Using Google AdWords, for a price, you can have a small ad with a link that shows up any time someone searches the keywords *wedding consultant*. You pay only when someone clicks on your advert to go through to your website, and the amount you pay depends on how popular the keywords are – more keyword competition means higher prices.

✔ **Create unique content.** Don't make your website just a place to buy things; make it a place people want to visit to find out something new or participate in a unique experience. Take time to create unique content for your site that can attract busy web surfers and then make them want to stick around for a while. For example, if you're a dog breeder specialising in French bulldogs, why not create a website that is *the* best source of information on that breed? By doing so, you're sure to drive more traffic to your site.

✔ **Start an affiliate programme.** Offer other website owners a commission on sales they send your way. The big sites, like Amazon, make affiliate programmes a central part of their selling model – driving more traffic to their sites and increasing their sales. You can, too. Check out sites such as www.affliatefuture.co.uk or www.affliatewindow.com to see how the process works and to get ideas for how to set up your own programme.

✔ **Exchange links.** Have you found some sites out there that are somehow related to what you do but aren't in direct competition? If so, ask the site's webmaster to place a link to your site on their site in exchange for putting a link to their site on yours. For example, if you provide fishing-guide services in the Lake District, why not exchange links with fishing websites or websites devoted to the Lake District?

Making it easy for visitors to become customers

The two main reasons for having a website for your home-based business are: (1) to attract potential customers to your services and (2) to make it easy for them to buy. Although many websites do a fine job of getting people to visit, they aren't very good at converting visits to sales, often simply because they're too confusing, too slow or just too much trouble to use.

Your job is to make it easy for customers to buy what they want directly through your website, assuming you've got a product or service that lends itself to buying online. Here are some tips for doing just that:

✔ **Have a well-organised, professional-looking site.** People are reluctant to buy from an amateurish, disorganised site because they don't feel as if their payment details are safe.

✔ **If you're selling products, put up lots of high-quality photos and detailed descriptions.** People want to see exactly what they're getting before they order it.

✔ **Make sure your hosting service has ample bandwidth to load your pages quickly.** Slow servers mean your visitors will quickly get bored and leave.

✔ **Give your customers plenty of payment options.** Consider signing up for a payment service such as PayPal that also allows customers to use their debit or credit cards to pay for goods. See www.paypal.com for more information.

✔ **Provide plenty of contact information for customers who have questions.** If you can quickly address questions – via phone, email or Twitter, for example – you greatly increase your chances of converting the contact into a sale.

Not sure whether your site is welcoming or not? Give it a try yourself. Is it easy to get around? Does it load quickly? Is it easy to place an order? Get your friends and family to try it out, too. Use their feedback to fine-tune your site and make it as user-friendly as possible.

Promoting your website

A website won't do you or your business much good if no one knows about it or visits it. So what can you do to make sure people find your site and visit it? Here are just a few ideas to get you started:

- Send an email announcing your website launch (including a picture of your home page) to all your customers and clients, as well as to the media and targeted mailing lists of potential clients.

- Include your website address on all external materials, including letterheads, business cards, catalogues, invoices, newsletters, packaging, answerphone messages, advertising and so on.

- Visit Internet newsgroups and message boards pertinent to your business, leave messages and participate in relevant discussions.

- Seek out busy websites where you can volunteer to host online chats and conferences. Large sites such as `www.ivillage.co.uk` are always looking for knowledgeable hosts who are willing to share their expertise with others.

- Register your site with the most popular Internet search engines (Google, Yahoo!, Bing and so on), and make sure you optimise your site to rank high in the search results (by incorporating meta tags and other tricks of the trade). Check out *Search Engine Optimization For Dummies*, 5th Edition, by Peter Kent (Wiley), for a lot more information about these tags and tricks.

- Trade links with your customers and clients, as well as with other relevant websites.

- Create an email signature that includes your website address. A *signature* is a short paragraph that's automatically included at the bottom of every email message you send. It usually contains a plug for your business, along with your address, phone or fax number and a website address.

Chapter 12

Balancing Your Business and Your Life

. . . .

In This Chapter

▶ Having a serious business attitude

▶ Keeping your work life and personal life separate

▶ Avoiding interruptions and distractions at home

▶ Managing your time

▶ Teaming up with a friend or family member

. . . .

Many people dream about starting and running their own businesses, but relatively few actually do it – and even fewer start businesses that turn out to be successful for the long haul. What makes the difference between those who succeed and those who don't? In many cases, it's all about attitude – and not just any attitude, but a business attitude.

In this chapter we examine exactly what having a real business attitude is all about – and why it's so important. We also discuss how to keep your work life and personal life separate, at least enough to get some work done! We assess two of the most common problems facing home-based business-people – interruptions and distractions – and provide you with a variety of tips to help you beat them. Finally, we consider the importance of developing regular work routines, as well as the whys and hows of getting organised.

Starting with the Right Attitude

Most successful businesses are successful in part because the people who own and run them are serious about doing business. But why is being serious about your business so incredibly important? Well, we offer you two main reasons, both of which involve perception and both of which have a way of becoming self-fulfilling prophecies:

> ✔ **If you're not serious about your business, you probably won't put your all into making it a success.** You won't be able to imagine that your modest little enterprise will ever have the potential to provide you and your family with a liveable wage or that it will ever provide you with an alternative to a regular nine-to-five job.
>
> ✔ **If you're not serious about your business, no one else will be either.** Your potential clients and customers won't take your business seriously if you don't. And if your potential clients and customers don't take your business seriously, you have no business at all.

The first step to developing a business attitude is realising that your home-based business is no different from any other business. You may have decided to start your home-based business because doing so gives you something that working for someone else simply can't provide. Maybe it's freedom, autonomy, control, flexibility, money or any number of other reasons.

Regardless of why you started your own business, you need to realise that your home-based business is a business first and foremost. If you hope to be successful (and we're sure you do), you have to treat it like a serious business, which means recognising that your business is *not* any of the following:

✔ A hobby

✔ Something you do every once in a while

✔ A tax shelter

✔ A get-rich-quick scheme

✔ A lark

Having fun in your business is brilliant, but don't forget that your home-based business can be your ticket for leaving the rat race behind once and for all. Many successful home-based business owners have done just that, and you can, too.

Building success from the inside

Starting your own business can be daunting. If you've always worked for someone else, the thought of working for yourself can truly feel like a step into the great unknown. And in many ways, it is an unknown world for you. Will customers buy your products? Will you be able to make enough money to support your family? What will you do if a much larger competitor tries to steal all your ideas?

Having a serious business attitude starts on the inside. It starts with being knowledgeable about your services and products, and having the confidence that comes with that knowledge. Above all, it starts with a conscious decision to make the dream of starting your own home-based business a reality. Here are some of the ways you can start to build a successful home-based business from the inside out:

- **Have confidence.** Confidence – or the lack thereof – can make all the difference in the world when you're starting and growing your own business. When you're confident, you feel like you can overcome any hurdle you come up against – and you probably can!

- **Keep a positive attitude.** Most successful entrepreneurs tend to be optimistic about themselves, their businesses and the future. They see the glass as half full rather than half empty. A positive attitude can take you far in this world, both in business and in your personal life.

- **Expect the best from yourself and others.** Set your standards high and refuse to settle for less. The quality of your products and services begins – and ends – with you.

- **Care about your customers.** Would you rather do business with someone who really cares about you and who takes the time to show it or someone who doesn't? If you take care of your customers and clients, they'll take care of you.

- **Make the decision.** Plant your foot firmly on the other side of the fence and make the decision once and for all to turn your home-based business dream into a reality. Stop talking about it; just do it!

Take the time to build your business attitude from the inside out. If you already have all the self-confidence and positive attitude in the world, that's great – you have a big head start towards business success!

If you still have some way to go to build the business attitude you need, don't be afraid to work into your business slowly, one step at a time. Instead of leaving your regular job to start your own business, consider starting your home-based business while still doing your regular job. Not only does this approach take much of the pressure off you to create an immediately successful enterprise, but it also gives you the time you need to really get to know your products and services, and to network with potential customers and clients without needing to really push for sales.

What to do if you go on holiday

Q: I feel like I've been working at maximum capacity for months and really need a break before I burn out. But how can I go on holiday for a week or two and keep my home business ticking over at the same time?

A: Most new business owners forgo holidays and time away for the first couple of years of starting a business because it takes time to get to a stage where you can feel confident that your business will still be there when you get back. But if you really feel you need a break, here are some options for how to minimise the impact:

✔ Leave someone competent in charge of answering the phones, and give them enough information and resources to be able to deal with straightforward queries. If customers or suppliers ask where you are, have them explain that you're away on business. Don't say that you're on holiday as that may indicate a lack of commitment.

✔ Check messages and emails on your phone while you're away. Set aside some time each day – perhaps for half an hour after lunch – to catch up on your inbox.

✔ If you feel unable to deal with all the emails you receive, set up an automatic reply explaining that you're away on business until a certain date and will be checking your emails daily, but may take slightly longer than usual to reply.

✔ Don't go away for long. New businesses are like plants: they need attention otherwise they wither and die. If your customers sense that you aren't fully committed to their needs, they may take their business elsewhere.

Counting on the outside for help, too

Although everyone knows you can't judge a book by its cover, people still make assumptions about you and your business based on what they see on the outside. Whether their ultimate judgements are right or wrong, these initial impressions can mean the difference between getting new customers or clients and losing them.

Here are some ways to make sure what's outside (and easily seen) reflects your inner business attitude (which isn't so easily seen):

✔ **Create a top-notch web presence.** Invest some time – or money – in building a top-notch website that absolutely exudes quality and experience. The good news is that many web-hosting services offer inexpensive and easy-to-use templates that instantly give your business a professional look. And don't forget to leverage social media to your advantage. Twitter, Facebook, LinkedIn, and, of course, your own blog can be very powerful promotional tools for your home-based business (check out Chapter 11 for more on using the Internet to help promote your business).

✔ **Create a custom logo and design for your stationery, business cards and promotional materials.** The money you invest in making your business look more professional will pay off many times over in the number and quality of clients that you attract. (Check out Chapter 9 for more information on creating a logo.)

The quality of the paper and other materials you deliver to your client says a lot about the quality of your work and the importance you place on delivering a quality product.

✔ **Form a company.** Those three little letters – *Ltd* – say something about your business. They say that you're established, that you're serious and that you're in it for the long haul. Not a bad impression to leave with your potential customers. (See Chapter 9 for more information on incorporating your business.)

Also, being registered for VAT, even if you aren't quite at the threshold, looks impressive. In fact, some customers may be suspicious if you aren't!

✔ **Dress for success.** As a general rule, always dress professionally when you're meeting with a client. Wear a suit or jacket and tie (for men) or a dress, skirt and blouse or trouser suit (for women). Of course, if you're at home – and there's no chance a client will be popping by unannounced – you can wear whatever makes you comfortable.

✔ **Get a dedicated phone line.** Nothing screams 'unprofessional!' more loudly than a five year old answering a client's call. You'll make a much better impression by having a dedicated phone line for your business, which is connected to your business answering machine or voicemail system.

You can dedicate a landline, a mobile phone or both for your business. Customers do like to see the option of a landline, particularly on a website, as it makes the business seem more solid and permanent. So offer just a landline or both landline and mobile, and then simply forward all calls to the landline to your mobile phone. This way you can take calls when you're out and about, and your customers and clients can directly contact you at all times. If you want to take calls on your landline when you're back in your home office, simply forward calls to your mobile phone to your home phone line.

Never answer business calls when you're in a decidedly non-business environment, such as at a children's birthday party or in a noisy pub. Make sure the message you project on the outside reflects the high level of quality and commitment to your customers that you hold so dear inside.

Serious doesn't mean you can't do it your way

One of the most liberating things about having your own business is that you get to decide when and where you're going to work, what work you're going to do and for whom you're going to do it. Surveys of home-based business-people reveal that they often create their own way of working. For example:

✔ Choosing not to work a traditional nine-to-five working day.

✔ Preferring to dress casually, or even in pyjamas.

✔ Taking breaks during the day to do some exercise such as going for a run or a swim.

✔ Choosing to listen to music while they work.

✔ Varying their workspace, for example, working in the garden when the weather is good.

Separating Your Work from Your Personal Life

Although being closer to your loved ones is one of the big attractions to working at home, you'll definitely have times when you need to draw a line between your home life and your work life. By taking the time to anticipate this requirement upfront, you can make the transition to your home-based business smoother – not just for you, but also for your clients, customers, family and friends.

You can use a number of barriers to separate the business and personal sides of your life. Here are some of the most important ones to consider:

✔ **Use a separate room.** Having a room apart from the hustle and bustle of your regular home life – one that is dedicated *exclusively* to your business – is the first step in making your home office a real office.

✔ **Set a work schedule.** When you own your own business, you can work whenever you like. You may find it easier (and more productive), however, to establish a regular work schedule. That way the people you share your home with know when it's okay to interrupt you and when it's clearly not okay.

✔ **Consider dressing formally, as if you were going to work in a corporate office**. Some people find it helps them feel more business-like and act in a more professional way.

✔ **Hire a meeting room.** If your home office isn't suitable for meetings, you can arrange to meet your clients at a convenient off-site location. Depending on your requirements, you can hire a dedicated meeting room, complete with all the bells and whistles (see Chapter 10 for more details on hiring dedicated meeting rooms), or for smaller, less formal meetings, venues such as a hotel lobby or your local coffee shop work well.

✔ **Get help.** Instead of trying to juggle your obligations at home while keeping up with your work, consider getting the help you need to allow you to focus exclusively on your work when you need to do so. For example, you can hire a cleaner to clean your home and relieve you of that burden. Or you can hire a nanny or babysitter to watch your young children while you work. Or you may be able to get your partner or a relative or friend to help you out. The main thing to remember is that you do have alternatives available to you if you feel overwhelmed.

Bear in mind that the degree to which you separate your work and personal lives is totally up to you. You can be far more flexible than you ever could be working for someone else. You can strengthen the separation when you have a lot of work to do and loosen up when things are a bit more relaxed. In this way, you really can enjoy the best of both worlds, where you're able to do the work you love in the place you most want to be – your own home.

Getting off the school run

Q: Once when my neighbour needed help I offered to pick up her son from school. She has since asked me to repeat this favour several times. How can I explain to her, without damaging our friendly relationship, that just because I'm working at home doesn't mean I'm not working as hard as her corporate acquaintances?

A: You don't need to explain. The way to let her know that you're working as hard as her corporate acquaintances is to tell her that even though you'd like to help, you can't pick up her son because you're working. Be warm and sincere, but be clear and definite that your business is such now that you can no longer take time off during working hours. She'll probably be disappointed, as she has come to rely on you. But if you want her to take you off her emergency help list, you may need to reinforce your message several times, repeating that you're sorry and wish you could help, but because of your work, you simply can't. She may call you several more times, just to be sure. But if you continue to be clear that you'd like to help but can't, she'll eventually get the idea and find new resources.

Kate Jenkins has devised the ideal way to separate her home-based business making chocolate brownies from her home life with her husband and two young children. She deals with orders during the day when the children are at school and bakes her brownies in the evenings when they've gone to bed. Most importantly, Jenkins has created a separate area for her business within her home that contains a commercial kitchen and office – and at weekends she lets calls to the business phone go to the answering machine and firmly locks the door. Customers making orders via the website get an automated reply to confirm the order has been received. She says: 'It's hard to say no, but we're shut at weekends and people completely understand that.' Her business, Gower Cottage Brownies, which she runs from her home in the Gower Peninsula, Wales, now has a turnover of £160,000.

Avoiding Interruptions and Distractions

Every job has its interruptions and distractions. When you're in a regular office, you may have a colleague who drops in on you regularly to share his or her latest thoughts about your company's management team. Or you may have a boss who is so busy assigning you new tasks that you never seem to be able to get around to the old ones.

Without a doubt, however, working at home offers its own unique set of interruptions and distractions. From television soap operas, to your neighbour's ear-splitting power drill, to that piece of chocolate cake in the fridge calling your name, almost an unlimited number of interruptions and distractions are waiting to take you away from your work. Your job is to find ways to ignore them or to avoid them altogether, which is where the following sections come in.

Managing interruptions

You can't always prevent interruptions, but you can take some steps to remove them after they occur, and then get back on track and back to work. Here are some ways to deal with interruptions:

> ✔ **Focus on your goals and priorities.** Although you may not be able to keep from being thrown off track when an interruption occurs, you should be able to quickly return your focus to the goals and priorities at hand. How? By resolving the interruption as quickly as possible and then refocusing your full attention on your work.

✔ **Be kind but firm.** The wrong way to deal with family members' interruptions is to get mad at the person who's interrupting you. The right way is to firmly explain, in a loving and supportive way, that the interruptions need to stop while you're working. Children especially need this kind of caring treatment. They probably aren't aware that they're interrupting your work; they simply want a chance to spend some time with you.

Put a sign on your office door saying 'Danger: Woman/Man at work!'. When the sign's up, people know not to disturb you.

✔ **Take action.** Don't try to ignore interruptions – chances are they won't go away, no matter how little attention you pay them. In fact, by not taking action, you send the person doing the interrupting the message that it's okay to interrupt you – or even that you welcome it – all the while building resentment within yourself.

✔ **Stay calm.** No matter what you do, someone somewhere will interrupt you. The key is to stay calm and not let the interruption totally destroy your ability to jump right back to work. Work out how to be flexible and find ways to get back to work quickly.

Is TV the problem or the symptom?

Q: I'm often tempted to watch television during work hours. At first, I set a rule that I would watch telly for only one hour during my lunch break; however, I sometimes get sucked into a programme and watch longer than I should. Then I rationalise it by saying I'll work longer hours. Sometimes I even have the telly on in the background and then press the mute button when I get a call. Do you have any suggestions on how I can break this bad habit?

A: Take the television out of your office. Make a list of the shows you want to watch and then watch them after work hours on catch-up TV websites such as BBC iPlayer and Channel 4 On Demand. If it turns out that you don't like a show enough to actually watch it after work hours, something must be missing from your workday. Find out what that something is and replace your bad habit with new, more appealing habits that serve you better. For example:

✔ **Are you bored with your work?** What has made watching daytime TV more interesting to you than the work you do? Any business has a few tasks that are pretty mindless, and you may as well be watching TV while you do them, but you're in the wrong business if that's how you feel about most of your workday. Has your business lost its magic – or never had it? How can you make what you do more exciting and challenging? What attracted you to go out on your own in the first place? What do you like best about your work? What can you do more of in your work that will make you forget all about watching TV? Find answers to these questions and put them into action.

✔ **Do you miss the social interaction of an office setting?** Arrange to have more contact with people whose company you enjoy. Call up a former work colleague; arrange to

(continued)

(continued)

meet a useful contact for coffee; get active in a local business or professional organisation; join an Internet newsgroup; or sign up for a local business-related adult education class or an ongoing social activity you enjoy.

✔ **Are you stressed out and working too hard?** Give yourself something else to look forward to, such as planning an exciting evening for when you've finished working. Or replace your bad habit with a better one. Many home-business owners, for example, enjoy listening to talk radio or music while they work. Others walk outside at lunchtime or take an exercise break like running, swimming or an aerobics class. What do you enjoy doing most?

With a bit of practice, you'll soon be able to deal with your interruptions like a pro, and you'll find that you can take charge of them instead of letting them take charge of you.

Dealing with distractions

Interruptions generally occur when people take you away from your work – by walking into your office and demanding your immediate attention or by calling you on the phone and talking at you for half an hour. Distractions are often more subtle. For home-based businesspeople, common distractions include the Internet, a favourite soap opera or a fridge full of goodies.

Here are some ways to deal with distractions:

✔ **Remove the sources of distraction.** Is your television begging you to turn it on? Is there a long list of blogs you have to read each morning before you can start work? Are you spending more time looking through your magazines than producing billable work? One of the best ways to avoid distractions is to remove their sources. Turn them off, throw them out or move them to another room. If surfing the Internet or social media sites is the problem, set definite times – perhaps during lunch or maybe no more than five minutes every hour – during which you allow yourself to spend time on those activities.

✔ **Avoid procrastination.** Putting work off until later, sometimes much later, is a powerful enemy of the home-based businessperson. And it's an enemy that you must defeat in the short run if you hope to be successful in the long run. Plan to get your least favourite task out of the way first. Just do it!

✔ **Reward yourself for achieving your goals.** Don't forget to give yourself some sort of reward for accomplishing a significant task or achieving an important milestone. Take a day off; meet your significant other for a long lunch; go shopping; or go for a bike ride with your kids – whatever makes you feel good. Not only do these rewards make you feel better, but they also motivate you to stay focused on your work and tune out distractions.

✔ **Schedule (and take!) regular breaks.** Do you find yourself fidgeting or unable to stay focused on your work? Take a short break from your work. Forward your calls to voicemail and get out of your office. You can relax and take your mind on a brief holiday by going for a brisk walk outside or enjoying a cup of coffee or tea in the garden. Don't leave taking breaks to chance; schedule regular breaks into your daily work plan.

You can control the effect of distractions on you and your business by taking action to remove their sources, and by providing sufficient structure and motivation in your work. Don't let distractions get in the way of your doing the best job you can do – and building the best business you can build.

When interruptions and distractions get the best of you, you certainly do whatever you can to resolve them. But what happens when you can't resolve your interruptions and distractions, and they actually begin to threaten your ability to get your work done?

ASK THE EXPERTS

Resisting the call of the fridge

Q: I'm embarrassed to say that I've gained some weight since I began working at home. I think part of the problem is that I eat out of stress and, of course, the fridge is now just a few steps away from my desk. Do you have any suggestions for how I can moderate my eating habits?

A: You're not the only one to gain weight in the comfort of working from home. But although you have more access to excess at home, you also have more control over what you do and how you do it.

The best way to beat this problem is to find new ways to de-stress: take a walk, go for a swim, call a friend, or lean back and listen quietly to some of your favourite music. It may take a while to find out what satisfies you more than food, but, on the way to the kitchen, take a deep breath and think of what else you may enjoy at that particular moment.

Also, stock your fridge and kitchen cupboards with lots of low-calorie, low-fat, healthy-but-filling foods that don't make you want to eat until the bag is empty, the way that crisps and biscuits do. Apples or rice cakes are good examples. Eating regular, small, balanced snacks can help keep snacking within bounds. Make sure you drink lots of water throughout the day too – people often mistakenly reach for food when really they're just thirsty. You can remove the incentive to visit the kitchen between meals by keeping drinks and healthy snacks in your office.

It may be time to take drastic action. Here are just a few ways you can really shake things up and get back on track:

- ✔ **Change your schedule.** Work when your chances of being interrupted or distracted are minimised. If you can't seem to avoid being distracted by your noisy flatmates who party late into the night, do your work in the morning and afternoon – well before the partying begins.

- ✔ **Learn to live with the distractions.** Of course, doing so is easier said than done, but perhaps you can learn to live with the distractions – accepting them but tuning them out and ultimately ignoring them.

- ✔ **Move your work.** Sometimes a temporary change of scenery can do wonders for your concentration, especially when the source of distraction or interruption is a short-term one. Try out your local café, library or even a hotel lobby. With a mobile phone and a laptop, and for the price of a cup of coffee, you can take your work wherever you want, whenever you want.

- ✔ **Move your office.** If you have a long-term, ongoing problem with distractions and interruptions, and it doesn't appear that you can solve the problem with a temporary change of scenery, consider moving your office altogether. At a minimum, choose a different room or other location within your home. In a worst-case scenario, you may need to move your office out of your home and into a leased office space.

Don't let interruptions and distractions get in the way of your success. If you're serious about your home-based business and about the potential for succeeding at it (and we're sure you are!), take action before things get so bad that your business suffers irreparable harm.

Managing Your Time

When you work at home, getting off track is easy to do. What starts out as a day full of promise for getting things done can easily turn into a day full of detours! Good time management doesn't happen by accident. You have to work on managing your time each and every day. In this section, we consider some of the best ways to manage your time. For even more tips and ideas, get hold of *Time Management For Dummies* by Clare Evans (Wiley).

Letting routines rule

Routines are a part of life. They help you stay focused on the things that are most important. They provide the structure and continuity that you – and your clients and customers – rely on to do business efficiently and effectively. Routines are a good thing!

When it comes to running your home-based business, some routines are better than others. Here are some tips for establishing the right kind of routines – the kinds that can bring you success rather than failure:

- ✔ **Establish a regular work schedule.** Maintain regular business hours just as you would if you worked for a regular business. It doesn't matter if you decide to work from 9 a.m. to 5 p.m. or from 5 p.m. to 9 p.m. – or even 9 a.m. – as long as your schedule meets your needs and the needs of your clients and customers. As the owner of your own business, you get to decide!

- ✔ **Take plenty of short breaks.** When you work in a regular business, you have lots of opportunities to take breaks from your routine. A phone call from a friend, a visit from a supplier, a lunch break with industry contacts or a quick walk to a nearby deli all offer a break from the routine. When you work at home, such breaks are much fewer and farther between, but you have to make a point of taking them.

- ✔ **Schedule appointments for you, your friends and your family.** The everyday events that take place in a typical business – home-based or not – can quickly fill up your schedule. While you may have planned to get out for a relaxing lunch with friends, go to the gym to work out or attend your daughter's awards ceremony, you may find yourself glued to the phone or computer instead. Instead of 'trying' to do the things you want to do, schedule firm appointments to do these things. Just as you'd schedule an appointment to meet with a client, schedule an appointment to meet your spouse for lunch or to go for a walk.

- ✔ **Start your workday the same way every day.** Create a routine around starting your workday. For example, you may make a pot of coffee, check your email and voicemail, read *The Times* and then begin making sales calls. You decide what to do in your routine; the point is to have a routine and to follow it.

- ✔ **End your workday the same way every day.** So many businesspeople complain about not having enough time to sit down and really think ahead and plan, but few do anything about it. Here's your chance to do just that. At the end of your workday, take 15 minutes to go over what happened that day and then review your priorities and schedules for the next day. File away any papers that need filing and straighten up your desk so that you come back to an organised workspace on your next working day.

If you feel that your work life – and maybe even your personal life – is chaotic and out of control, step back for a moment and take a close look at how you run your life. Use the list above to create routines in your life that you can rely on day after day, week after week.

Identifying priorities

Priorities – what's most important in your business – have a significant impact on what work you decide to do and when you decide to do it. Most people think they know what's most important in their businesses, but many people don't follow through on this knowledge, and instead let trivial events and distractions rule their schedules.

To separate your real priorities from the wannabes, start by asking yourself these questions when you're trying to decide whether a particular action is a real priority:

- **What's the action's impact on your firm's bottom line?** Everyone has reasons for being in a particular business, but one of the main reasons for creating a business is to make money, pure and simple. Yes, you want to do fulfilling, creative work, but if it doesn't pay the bills, you won't be doing it for long. What kind of impact will the action have on your bottom line – will it reduce your expenses or increase your revenues? The greater the impact an action has on improving your bottom line – your profitability – the higher it rates on your list of priorities. If an action has little or no impact on your bottom line, give higher priority to other actions that do have such an impact.

- **Is the action in response to a client emergency?** Another reason why many people start their own businesses is to solve their clients' problems and to provide them with solutions. Because clients in many ways are the heart and soul of any business, solving their problems is clearly a priority. So when your clients have emergencies, the actions you need to take to solve them should be top priorities for you.

In a nutshell, you need to consciously identify your business's highest-priority actions and then take a single-minded approach to tackling them. This single-minded approach may mean ignoring the calls of a salesperson, forwarding your phone to voicemail for a day or even throwing your to-do list into a drawer and working only on your number-one priority until it's done. The good news is that prioritising gets easier with experience.

Don't forget that it's up to *you* to decide what's most important to your business and then to act on it. You're the boss now; no one else is going to decide for you.

Missing the hustle and bustle

Q: I know home-based business owners often complain about noise distracting them, but my problem is the opposite: sometimes it gets so quiet in my home office that it unsettles me. Do you have any suggestions for creating a little bit of good old-fashioned office noise?

A: You're not the only one who doesn't work well in silence, which is undoubtedly why many home-based business owners avidly listen to music or talk radio. Of course, background music helps many people stay productive and, rather than being a distraction, it can energise your brain and your work. You may like to spend part of your day working in a coffee shop or library. Or perhaps you have the option to work at your corporate client's premises several days a week.

As for office noise, if that's really what you miss, you can always ask a client or former work colleague to let you record 10 or 15 minutes of office sounds that you can then play on repeat in the background while you work!

Teaming Up with a Spouse or Other Loved One

You can find countless examples of husbands, wives, siblings, parents and kids who have pulled together to build successful enterprises. Husband-and-wife team Gordon and Anita Roddick co-founded the Body Shop, the ethical skincare business in 1976; Mary Perkins and her husband Doug co-founded Specsavers, the chain of opticians, in 1984; brothers Walt and Roy Disney founded the Disney Brothers Studio in 1923 and built it into a global entertainment business; the list goes on and on.

For many people, teaming up with a loved one may seem like the ultimate dream. And for many home-based business owners, this dream is a reality. After all, if working at home is right for you, why not see whether it's right for the people you really care about, too? Unfortunately, though, for others, teaming up can turn into a nightmare. The secret is knowing when to team up and when not to – and what to do when a good team goes bad.

In the sections that follow, we take a look at when to team up with people you care about, how to team up with them and how to build a successful, long-term relationship – both at work and away from the job.

Knowing when to team up

Here are some times when teaming up with a friend or family member is a good idea:

- ✔ **When a friend or family member has relevant skills and interests.** If you decide to start a plumbing business in your home and your close friend or relative has solid bookkeeping skills that can help you better keep track of the financial end of your business, teaming up makes perfect sense.

- ✔ **When a friend or family member purchases a business opportunity or franchise.** Teaming up is a good idea if, of course, the business opportunity or franchise is something you want to do, too.

- ✔ **When a friend or family member can make a positive contribution to your business.** It's definitely time to team up when a friend or family member is at exactly the right place in his or her life to make a positive and substantial contribution to your business, customers and clients.

- ✔ **When a friend or family member has a resource you need.** Perhaps you need a large amount of cash to get your business off the ground and your close friend or relative wants to help by providing you with a loan. Maybe your friend has a network of contacts that would be very beneficial for you to approach. Such resource synergies can make teaming up a very smart move.

- ✔ **When a friend or family member has more work than he or she can handle.** Teaming up can be a win-win situation when a friend or family member is so successful that he or she needs help – and needs it fast.

Not every business team or partnership is going to work. Working closely together – day after day – may bring out the worst in your partner (or you), and you should always be ready to break up your team if necessary. *Do not* – we repeat, *do not* – allow a bad situation to become worse because you're afraid to tell a friend or relative that your partnership isn't working out. Always be honest – with yourself and with your partner. And never team up out of weakness or pity for a friend or family member who just can't seem to get his or her act together. Finding the right time to team up is a must if you want your business relationship to be successful in the long run.

Firefighting for success

Kresse Wesling and James Henrit aren't just business partners, they're also real-life partners too, having been a couple since 2002. Their social enterprise business Elvis and Kresse (www.elvisandkresse.com) makes handbags, belts and accessories from old fire hoses that are too damaged to repair, so are thrown out by fire brigades and would have previously ended up in landfill sites. Half the profits from this range are donated to the Fire Fighters charity. They successfully manage to combine their business relationship with a personal one because they divide their roles down the middle, with Henrit taking charge of design and manufacture and Wesling in charge of sales and marketing. The company has grown from a few handmade belts to an award-winning business and their products are now stocked in boutiques around the world.

Working out how to team up

How you team up with a friend or family member is just as important as – if not more important than – *when* you team up. Doing it the right way can help reinforce your relationship and increase the likelihood of your success. Doing it the wrong way, on the other hand, can be a recipe for disaster – not only for your business, but also for your relationship.

As you begin to team up with your friend or family member, consider taking the following actions:

- ✔ **Define goals and assign clear responsibilities.** Although you may have different approaches to achieving your goals, you and your partner need to agree on definite and clear goals, and on who will be responsible for different jobs and tasks within the business. Confusion isn't a good thing in business or in relationships, so define each of your responsibilities from the very beginning and get them in writing. Talking of which . . .

- ✔ **Get important agreements in writing.** Of course, you should be able to trust your friend or family member without question, but it's always best to get your important agreements in writing. You may choose to incorporate these agreements into a legally binding contract. After all, people forget; misunderstandings arise; relationships are broken. Why not prevent these misfortunes by laying everything out on paper from the start?

✔ **Encourage each other to communicate openly.** Communication is incredibly important to the success of any business; so it's equally important that you and your partner communicate openly and honestly with each other about all aspects of your relationship and your business. Always be upfront and open with your business partners, no matter who they are or how closely you're related.

✔ **Treat each other with respect.** You treat your clients and customers with respect, and you need to treat your partner with respect, too. If you don't respect your partners enough to treat them with the utmost respect, don't team up with them in the first place – you may want to reconsider your relationships, too.

✔ **Take a break from each other whenever necessary.** People get on each other's nerves from time to time, no matter how good the relationship is. Rather than getting angry or stewing on it, take a break from each other for a while. Doing so gives you both time to get over whatever issue is bugging you and to remember why you got together in the first place.

If you do it right, teaming up with a friend or family member can strengthen and deepen your personal relationship. Work hard on bringing out the best in both of you.

Partnering with a spouse or significant other

Turning your life partnership with a spouse or significant other into a business partnership can be great for your home-based business. Or it can be living hell! Because you both live under the same roof, this new relationship can turn into a never-ending tunnel with no easy or apparent exit. The US website Entrepreneur.com (www.entrepreneur.com) suggests the following five steps for creating a home-based business with your spouse or significant other that's more heaven and less hell:

1. **Divide your roles and responsibilities.** Each of you has your own unique strengths and weaknesses. Take time to assess who is best at what. You, for example, may be great with numbers and organising your business, while your spouse may be the salesperson of the year. Have clear divisions of responsibilities so each of you knows who's supposed to do what.

2. **Develop an effective way to air differences and resolve disputes.** Don't let differences of opinion or disputes with your significant other business partner fester, unaddressed and unresolved. Deal with them as they occur and put them behind you as quickly as you can. Addressing differences as they arise not only makes for a better and more effective business, but it also helps ensure that your relationship is built to last.

3. **Put a childcare plan in place.** If you have kids, you need to find a way to do business while making sure you also meet their needs. Consider bringing in a part- or full-time nanny or au pair – students at local colleges are often available to help with childcare – or split your duties so that one partner takes care of the kids in the morning while the other runs the business, and then you swap in the afternoon. If you

have relatives living nearby who are able and willing to help, use them.

4. **Make sure both of you have enough room to work.** Working full time jammed into the same small room can eventually drive even the most lovey-dovey couples temporarily insane. If you share an office or workspace with your business partner, make sure it offers plenty of elbow room for both of you – and for your computers, files, cabinets, desks, tables, chairs and other office equipment.

5. **Agree on an exit strategy before you begin.** What happens if one or both of you decide you want to get out of the business? Or if you and your partner have irreconcilable differences and decide that splitting up your business partnership is the only way to save your life partnership? In the same way that a prenuptial agreement can make a divorce easier for both parties, taking time to decide the terms and conditions of the dissolution of your business partnership in advance of the event is the smart thing to do. Deciding on an exit strategy at the outset of your partnership may also save your personal relationship.

Building a healthy, long-term partnership

If all goes well, working with a friend or family member in your home-based business can go a long way in helping you build a deeper and even more profound personal relationship. And if you decide to team up with someone you love, nurturing your personal relationship is just as important as developing a healthy business relationship. If one suffers, the other is sure to suffer, as well.

The following tips can help you build healthy, long-term relationships – both personal and business – with your friends or family members:

- ✔ **Do be clear about who's in charge.** In most businesses, one person is ultimately in charge and has the right to veto the suggestions or actions of others, including partners. Make it clear at the outset who's in charge, but be sure to ask for the input of your partner and to seriously consider that input. If your business is a true, legal partnership – with ownership shared in equal amounts – make sure that you establish a system for making decisions when you're in disagreement with your partner. If making decisions is problematic for you and your partner, you probably shouldn't be in a business partnership in the first place.

- ✔ **Don't interfere with how your partner achieves his or her goals.** Focus on agreeing on what your goals are, and then let your partner decide how he or she will reach them. Avoid the temptation to micromanage your partner's efforts or to interfere with or second-guess them. You'll only build resentment and erode your long-term relationship.

✔ **Don't forget to nurture your private lives.** All friends or family members who work together need to take time away from the demands of their business to focus on themselves and their relationship. You can find a number of ways to be fun and spontaneous in your relationship. Close the office for a day and enjoy a long weekend at the beach or in the countryside. Take a long lunch together, or treat yourselves to an afternoon of pampering at a spa or health club. Or simply turn off the phone and sleep in late one morning.

✔ **Do seek the help of a professional mediator if needed.** Sometimes relationships break and you need the help of a professional to put them back together. Don't hesitate to seek mediation, or even counselling, if your relationship breaks down – the sooner you do, the easier it'll be to get things back on track.

Long-term relationships can be the most meaningful relationships in your life, and there's no reason why you can't share a meaningful and productive business relationship with someone with whom you share a close personal relationship. Don't be afraid to explore the possibilities!

Being clear about the downsides

Although of course we hope that your business goes swimmingly if you team up with a partner, you need to be aware of the drawbacks:

✔ If your partner makes a business mistake, perhaps by signing a disastrous contract without your knowledge or consent, every member of the partnership must shoulder the consequences. Your personal assets could be taken to pay creditors even though the mistake was no fault of your own.

✔ If your partner goes bankrupt in their personal capacity, for whatever reason, creditors can seize your partner's share of the business. As an individual you aren't liable for your partner's private debts, but having to buy them out of the partnership at short notice could put you and the business in financial jeopardy.

✔ Even death may not release you from partnership obligations and in some circumstances your estate can remain liable. Unless you take 'public' leave of your partnership by notifying your business contacts and legally bringing your partnership to an end, you could remain liable for any debts.

ASK THE EXPERTS

Working at home with a baby

Q: Though I've just had a baby, I obviously can't take maternity leave from my home-based business. How do I balance the needs of my business and my clients with the needs of a demanding newborn, each of which take an incredible amount of time?

A: Get help. Most female home-based business owners *do* take some type of maternity leave. They stagger contracts or clients so they have a one- or two-month break, hire temporary or part-time help, or subcontract work to colleagues for a period of time. Get help caring for your baby, get help running the business, or arrange for some combination of the two. Begin by deciding what kind of assistance will be most helpful. Ask yourself the following:

✔ How much time during each day do you want to devote entirely to your baby?

✔ What aspects of your baby's care can you get help with? What do you want to do yourself?

✔ Which business tasks are the most burdensome right now? Which ones demand your full attention without interruption?

✔ Which tasks must you do? Which ones can others do?

By working from home, you have many more options for tailoring childcare arrangements to your particular needs. For help with your newborn, for example, you can hire a nanny to come to your home for a few hours each day while you work. Alternatively, you may be able to line up help from family or friends, or exchange babysitting hours with other new mothers. When you feel comfortable taking the baby out, you can place him or her in a nearby nursery or with a childminder for several hours a day.

New fathers can take paternity leave. Having Dad at home, even part time, can be a big help. Mum and Dad can care for the baby in shifts, and Dad can help answer the business phone and do other business-related tasks. Taking simple steps, such as switching voicemail on and replying to only important calls, can free you to better concentrate on both family and business matters. Hooking up a baby monitor between your baby's room and your office may also help.

Set up a schedule that suits both your needs as a new mother and your work habits. For some people, doing so means working only mornings, afternoons or evenings. For others, it involves fitting work around the baby's sleep times. To keep your sanity, remember that this is a special time. It can be exhausting, but it will pass all too soon, so arrange your schedule to enjoy it while you can.

Chapter 13

On a Roll: Growing Your Business . . . or Selling Up

*T*here comes a time in the life of every business owner when you have to decide whether or not to grow the business. Some home-based businesspeople may find a few clients they like working with and decide they're comfortable with keeping things just the way they are. But if you're good at what you do and your customers love the products and services you sell them, don't be surprised if, after you start your business, they tell their friends and colleagues about you – bringing more business your way. If enough prospective customers show up at your door, you may be faced with more business than you can handle in your present state.

When your business increases to a point where you can't accommodate it in the normal course of your day, you have to make a conscious choice: reject this extra work and maintain the status quo (or perhaps even cut back the time and effort you devote to your business to spend less time working), or take on the extra work and grow.

For many home-based business owners, being in business means growing the business, pure and simple. When you grow your business, you have the opportunity to make more money, and making more money is a powerful motivator for many people.

In the case of growth, the right answer is the one that's best for you. And what's best for you may or may not be what's best for your clients and customers, your family and friends, and any employees or contractors you may have.

In this chapter, we consider what makes a business a success and examine the good and the bad news about owning a growing company. We take a close look at expanding your operations and bringing partners into your business. Finally, we explore strategies for selling your business and moving on to other opportunities.

Becoming a Success

Success is a relative thing. For example, while one home-based business owner considers himself a huge success if he makes £25,000 a year, part time, and enjoys lots of time with family and friends, another may consider that level of income a failure.

As the owner of your home-based business, *you* get to decide how to define what success means to *you*; no one else can define it for you. You may decide to measure your own success in terms of money or in terms of how many clients you can help. Or you may define it by the high quality of the products and services you deliver. You may also measure success in terms of your ability to achieve an equal balance between your work life and personal life. When you're the one who decides what success means to you, there really is no wrong answer.

After defining what success means to you, though, you have to have a strategy or plan for achieving the goals you've set for yourself – like anything else you want to achieve in life. Although anyone who puts his or her mind to it will find some measure of success, starting up a successful enterprise involves more than just working hard.

William Bygrave, former director of the Centre for Entrepreneurial Studies at Babson College in the US, describes nine keys to success for a business in his book (co-edited with Andrew Zacharakis) *The Portable MBA in Entrepreneurship*, 3rd Edition (Wiley). Bygrave calls these keys the *Nine Fs*:

- ✔ **Founders.** Every start-up must have a first-class entrepreneur (that's you).

- ✔ **Focused.** Entrepreneurial companies focus on niche markets. They specialise. (Fuzzy companies lead to fuzzy customers; people are willing to pay a premium for products and services that clearly appeal to their wants and needs, not ones that may or may not work out.)

- ✔ **Fast.** Entrepreneurial companies make decisions quickly and implement them swiftly (but never so quickly that they don't take time to understand and consider the alternatives before they implement their decisions).

✔ **Flexible.** Entrepreneurial companies keep an open mind. They respond to change. (Small, home-based businesses can often respond much more quickly to change than larger businesses – a key advantage in today's fast-changing, information-driven marketplace.)

✔ **Forever innovating.** Entrepreneurial companies are tireless innovators.

✔ **Flat.** Entrepreneurial organisations have as few layers of management as possible. (Quite an easy feat when you're a sole proprietorship and have no employees.)

✔ **Frugal.** By keeping overheads low and productivity high, entrepreneurial organisations keep costs down (which makes them more profitable).

✔ **Friendly.** Entrepreneurial companies are friendly to their customers, suppliers and employees.

✔ **Fun.** Being associated with a successful entrepreneurial company is fun. (Owning your own home-based business doesn't mean you can't have fun – indeed, if you're not having fun, why bother?)

Compare the way you do business with the nine Fs Bygrave describes. Do the two have any similarities, or are they miles apart? The more Fs you find in your own home-based business, the greater your chances of finding success at the end of your rainbow.

Identifying the Upsides and Downsides of Growth

Business growth has ramifications that extend far beyond the simple day-to-day running of an organisation, including the following:

✔ Growth means new work, new clients and new opportunities, but it also means more time, more effort and more energy from you.

✔ Growth means more money coming into your business, but it also means more money going out.

✔ Running a growing business can make your life very busy and hectic, but it can also be incredibly rewarding – both financially and personally.

What are your long-term goals for yourself and for your business? Do you want to make a certain amount of money every year – enough to enable you to support yourself and your family? Do you want to make a certain level of profit or provide services for a certain number of customers or clients? Do you want to work for a limited number of years or save enough money to travel the world – or buy a new car or boat, or retire early?

Whatever your long-term goals are, if you decide that growth is indeed what you want for your business, you can't leave it to chance – you have to have a plan to achieve that growth. But don't forget: your business will change, as will your feelings about it. Be flexible and prepared to change your plans as your goals change.

Growth has both good and bad aspects. In the following sections, we explore growth in detail so you can decide what growth means to you and whether you'd rather grow, maintain the status quo or perhaps even shrink your business operations.

Understanding why you may want to grow

Whenever a business provides quality products or services that people need at a fair price, that business tends to grow as new customers seek it out. Although the pressure to grow seems inevitable for many businesses – especially ones that do a good job for their customers and clients – growth is something that's almost completely within your power to control.

Too many clients? Trim back your client list by removing the marginal ones that cost you more to service than they earn you in profit. Too much work? Turn down new work until you reach a level you're comfortable with. Not enough time for yourself or your family? Do less work and focus more on the things in your life that are most important to you. You're in charge; you're the boss. The decision is yours.

So given the possible attraction of maintaining the status quo (having less work-related stress, spending more time with loved ones and so on), why grow? Here are a number of good reasons:

- ✔ **To increase revenue and profits.** The immediate impact of growing your business is an increase in revenue and – as long as your costs of doing business don't grow out of proportion – an increase in profit. And if we're not mistaken, increasing your profit is probably one of the reasons you're in business for yourself in the first place.

- ✔ **To build equity.** *Equity* is the amount of money you have left over after you subtract all your company's liabilities from its assets (see Chapter 6). If your business is profitable over a long period of time, or if your business catches on with the public and undergoes rapid and substantial growth, your equity can be quite large. Growing your business is likely to grow your equity as well.

✔ **To take advantage of economies of scale.** The larger your business, the more you can take advantage of *economies of scale* – that is, paying lower prices for items you buy in larger quantities. Buying a big box of printer paper at an office supplies warehouse, for example, works out far cheaper per sheet than if you bought a single pack from a high street retailer.

✔ **To feel more secure.** Having more customers makes the business safer. Losing a customer when you only have three is a disaster. Losing one when you have ten is just a problem.

Growth can be exciting and fun, and who knows – it may lead you to new and more exciting adventures down the road. However, growth brings with it its own set of headaches and problems. Many people have become home-based business owners to leave the rat race and get off the never-ending treadmill of business that devours their personal lives. Lifestyle entrepreneurs – business owners who make a conscious choice not to grow – are active and vital players in the UK economy, and they tend to be just as happy as their more growth-oriented counterparts.

Recognising the many different ways to grow

If you make the decision to grow your business by increasing your sales and enlarging your customer base, you have a number of ways to do so. The exact approach you take depends on your growth goals and plans, and on the nature of your business. The following are some of the most common approaches for growing a home-based business:

✔ **Expand beyond your local area.** If you work only for people who live within a few miles of your home, one of the quickest ways to grow your business is to expand the area in which you do business. What if you did business citywide or countywide? Or even nationally? Expanding beyond your immediate geographical area dramatically increases the number of prospective clients and customers available to you – potentially resulting in increased sales and profits. Of course, depending on the type of business you run, you need to consider the extra cost in petrol and extra time it takes for you to reach these customers, and adjust your prices accordingly.

✔ **Get on the web.** With the right Internet presence, the number of people who view your products or see your work can mushroom (make sure you check out Chapter 11 to find out exactly how to establish the right Internet presence). Many home-based businesses have seen tremendous growth after capturing the imaginations of their customers on the Internet.

✔ **Go international.** It's a great big world out there, and depending on the products and services you sell, a huge, underserved international market may be waiting for you to tap in to. Websites such as eBay (www.ebay.co.uk) and Alibaba (www.uk.alibaba.com) can turn you into an entrepreneur with global reach quite literally overnight. For many growing businesses, a plan for expanding into international markets is a key success strategy.

✔ **Expand your product line.** If you currently stock ten different products and you want to double your business, what's the quickest way to achieve your goal? Stock 20 different products. Although the exact impact your decision to carry more products ultimately has on sales depends on the products, their pricing and the extent to which you promote them, expanding your product line is a quick and easy way to grow your business.

✔ **Add employees.** Adding employees to your business by definition means that you're growing it. Just make sure that you don't hire new employees before you have sufficient business to support them. If your revenues are flat or decreasing as you add employees, you have what's commonly known as a *going-out-of-business plan*. Although hiring employees can provide your business with the capacity it needs to increase sales, it can also dramatically increase your expenses. For lots of information on the right way to interview and hire employees, check out *Starting & Running a Business All-in-One For Dummies*, edited by Colin Barrow (Wiley).

You know your business better than anyone else, so think about what you can do to grow your business. One of the benefits of being your own boss is that you can do whatever you want with your business, whenever you want. Think you have a good idea? Give it a try. Tired of providing a particular product or service? Get rid of it. Want to enter a new market or exit an old one? Just do it. The more things you try, the higher the probability you'll find something that works.

To grow or not to grow, that is the question

If you've anguished over the decision of whether or not to grow your business, you know that the decision isn't just a business decision – it's a personal one as well. Because you're the one who has to live with the consequences of your decision to grow or not, it's in your best interest to thoroughly examine yourself, your business and the marketplace to make sure that whatever decision you make is the best one for you and your business.

As you consider whether or not to grow your business, we recommend that you look in these four places to find the answer:

✔ **Your heart.** It sounds mushy, but it's true – the first place to look when you're thinking about growing your business is deep inside yourself. Take some time to get away from the hustle and bustle of your business and really listen to what your heart tells you. Are you looking forward to the excitement that business growth will bring with it, or are you secretly dreading the possible consequences of such a choice?

✔ **Your lifestyle.** Will your preferred lifestyle support or be in conflict with the growth of your business? If, for example, the growth of your business will take you away from your family – and spending more time with your family is one of the key reasons why you started your home-based business in the first place – you'll likely resent the extra time you have to devote to your business, as will your family, who will have less of your time. Growing your company changes your life. Make sure that the changes are consistent with the lifestyle you want for yourself.

✔ **The numbers.** Of course, your heart and lifestyle may say 'go', while your business (more specifically, your business's financials) says 'no'. If your company's sales are too low or costs too high, growing your business probably isn't the best thing to do. Can you somehow increase sales or decrease costs enough for growth to make sense? If not, either figure out some way to put your financials on the right track or put your growth plans on the back burner until the numbers do make sense.

✔ **The market.** You may think it's time to grow, but the market in which your business operates may not be ready for you. Before you invest lots of time, money and effort in growing your business, make sure that enough potential customers and clients are interested in buying your products and services. If they aren't, you're wasting your time and your hard-earned money – two things that are especially precious for every home-based business owner. Remember that your business can thrive only when you provide quality products or services that people actually want to buy.

All these factors play a role in the growth decision; the weight that you place on each depends on your own personal desires and goals. Many businesses have succeeded, for example, when the numbers didn't make sense or when the market didn't seem to offer broad support for a business's new initiatives. But behind businesses that succeeded in these kinds of conditions are incredibly motivated and hard-working business owners.

Diversifying your client list

Q: I've been in business for three years, and about 80 per cent of my work comes from one client. How can I find the time to diversify while still keeping my client satisfied?

A: As great as the steady cash flow is, getting the bulk of your income from just one client puts you at great risk should that client suddenly go bust or decide to work with someone else. You sound as if you not only get 80 per cent of your income from this one client, but also spend most of your time serving him or her. To free up your time to market and serve new clients, you need to get some additional help. Work out what segments of your work can be done by an assistant, associate or outside contractor. Arrange to free up at least two hours a week for marketing, and begin breaking in someone to work with you so that when you generate new business, you have dependable help to meet the demand.

In many fields of business self-employed individuals can't or prefer not to market themselves, preferring instead to subcontract their services to someone else. Such individuals like to work with people like you. Make certain, however, that all the billing and all funds come through you. Make sure you get clear, written agreements preventing associates or subcontractors from contracting directly with your clients. Also, you need to line up individuals you can depend on to do high-quality work within necessary deadlines.

To find associates you can count on, get referrals from sources you trust. Make sure you review their work and talk with them about how they approach their work and what their priorities are. Ask for – and check – references. Most importantly, start with one small, low-risk assignment. Set a clear goal and a specific deadline. Check progress intermittently and, if possible, ask the associate to turn in segments of the work as he or she completes them. Doing so can help you identify possible problems before they develop.

Bear in mind that working with someone else takes some additional time – especially at first. But by building a network of others you can subcontract work to, you can expand without taking on debt or adding to your employee or other operating expenses until you have sufficient business to cover them and hire one or more employees.

Bringing in Partners

A *partnership* is when two or more people team up in the ownership and operation of a business. If your business is growing healthily, you may want to consider getting someone else on board to share the workload. Many well-known businesses started out as successful partnerships (and home-based businesses at that), including the following:

- ✔ **Innocent Drinks:** Founders Richard Reed, Adam Balon and Jon Wright started selling their smoothies at a music festival in London and subsequently sold a stake in the business to Coca-Cola for many millions of pounds.

- ✔ **Ben and Jerry's ice cream:** Founders Ben Cohen and Jerry Greenfield met at school and took a correspondence course in ice-cream making before setting up their successful business together.

- ✔ **Google search engine and online business tools:** Founders Larry Page and Sergey Brin started their business in a friend's garage and then raised $1 million from friends, family and other investors to fund their start-up.

Although these businesses quickly outgrew their original partnership structures – eventually becoming large multinational corporations – the combination of the original partners provided the spark of creativity and energy that led to great success.

When a partnership works, the business runs like a well-played symphony. When it doesn't, it runs completely out of tune. Unfortunately, you can't really know how things will turn out until you actually create a partnership and you begin to work together with your partner – or not. A partnership is like a marriage; you really don't know how things are going to work – or even if they will work – until the honeymoon is over.

More than a few friendships and personal relationships have been destroyed by partnerships gone bad. Partners can clash in a variety of ways, and these clashes may only occur in a business environment under the pressures of deadlines and busy schedules, which is why you should always apply the same standards of care when you decide to partner with family or friends that you would when hiring a stranger.

The following are some tips for ensuring that your partnerships operate smoothly. (For more specific information on the partnership form of business – including its advantages and disadvantages – take a look at Chapter 9.)

- ✔ **Date first.** Before getting married, you probably want to date your prospective mate for a while first – a few months or even a few years are ideal. Not only does doing so allow you to develop trust and find out how to communicate with each other, but it also enables you to see both the good and the bad sides of your partner. Business partnerships work the same way: get to know your prospective partner very well before you tie the knot. Consider doing shared marketing or a specific project together first.

- ✔ **Partner only with someone you trust.** Trust is the glue that holds a partnership together and enables you to achieve great things. Don't even consider partnering with someone you don't trust or respect. The road to business success is littered with broken partnerships that fell apart as soon as the trust that kept the partners together vanished.

✔ **Don't partner until you can stand on your own.** Partner from a position of strength, not weakness. Otherwise, your business can become a co-dependency and, thus, dysfunctional. And a dysfunctional company has problems serving its customers well and making money.

✔ **Enlist partners who add to the business.** Ideally, your partner will complement you and bring positive personal value to the company. Short on cash? Then find a partner who can provide the cash you need. Need help marketing? Then find a partner who's a strong salesperson. Don't like managing the business? Then find a partner who's a strong leader and administrator. Just as you hire employees who shore up your weaknesses, choose partners to cover the skills or connections you lack.

✔ **Share the equity (and the burden of risk).** Sharing equity means sharing ownership of the company with your partners. If you don't share ownership with your partners, they won't act like they're owners – they won't value the business the same way you do, and they won't be willing to make the same sacrifices as you to keep the business alive and healthy. They may even come to resent you because you hold all the cards. But if you agree to share ownership of your company, make sure your partner shares equally in the risks associated with the business, too.

✔ **Create a written partnership agreement.** Formalise your partnership in a written agreement that spells out – clearly and unambiguously – the ownership stake of each partner, rights to business proceeds and his or her responsibilities to the business. Our advice is to spend the relatively small amount of money necessary to get a solicitor to draw up a proper partnership agreement for you and your prospective partner to sign. Many business partnerships eventually fail; when they do, a well-written partnership agreement can help protect the huge investment of time and money that you've made in your business.

Follow these tips, and your partnerships should be happy ones. Of course, there are no guarantees. If your partnership turns out not to be one made in heaven, you can always split up the partnership and try again, but you'll have a much easier (and more profitable) time if you do your homework and get it right the first time. Bear in mind, too, that partnership is only one of many ways to collaborate with others; many of the other methods of working together carry less risk than partnership (see Chapter 3).

For advice about partnering up with a loved one, head to Chapter 12.

Cashing Out and Other Exit Strategies

Although most entrepreneurs with young businesses focus on starting and growing their businesses, eventually their thoughts may turn to selling their businesses and retiring or moving on to something new. For some people, this phenomenon occurs at an early age. On the other hand, some business owners plan to keep on working right to the end.

If and when you decide to exit your business, you'll be faced with many decisions – in particular, when and how to gracefully sever your ties to the business so that you don't damage its value in the process. You can find all kinds of strategies for exiting your business, from mild to extreme. Here are some of the most common ones:

✔ **Sell it.** Businesses are bought and sold all the time (take a look at sites such as www.daltonsbusiness.com or uk.businessesforsale.com for lots of examples). If you've built a strong customer base or have a valuable inventory, or if your operations are particularly profitable or otherwise attractive to a potential buyer, you may be able to make some significant money in the process of selling your business.

✔ **Merge it.** Merging your operation with another business can create a new business that's more powerful and profitable than the two businesses were separately. In a merger, you have the option of stepping aside and letting the owner of the other company run and operate the combined companies while you maintain an ownership stake, or you can accept some form of one-time or ongoing payment or royalty while acting as a part-time consultant or adviser to the business. Either option can make a lot of sense, depending on your personal preferences.

✔ **Pass it on to a family member, friend or employee.** If you have a son, daughter, close friend or employee who's particularly interested in keeping the business going, you always have the option of passing it on to him or her. You can choose to pass it on for free, sell it or set up some sort of compensation arrangement, such as an ongoing royalty or payment based on a percentage of sales.

✔ **Close it.** Of course, you can simply close the business, unplug your answering machine and move on with your life. For many home-based business owners interested in exiting their businesses, this option is by far the simplest. If you decide on this option, make sure you take care of your customers before you call it quits. See the nearby sidebar 'Closing up shop' for ideas on how to make sure your loyal customers are looked after.

Closing up shop

Unfortunately, not every home-based business is destined to last forever, which means that, at some point, you may have to close yours – whether by choice or because of circumstances out of your control. If you decide to close your business for whatever reason, here are a few tips to ensure that your customers aren't left out in the cold:

✔ Give your customers plenty of notice. A month is about right.

✔ Refer your customers to companies like yours, including former competitors. (After all, you don't need to worry about them anymore, right?) Give your customers as many options and alternatives as possible.

✔ Offer to train your customers to do what you do. You may have a customer or two who'd like to start a business like yours or add

your business to their own. You may even decide to become a consultant – training others to do what you've been doing for so long.

✔ Subcontract the work to another company or individual in your field.

✔ If you have a contract that's legally assignable, sell or transfer it to another company capable of satisfying your client's needs. Whether required by your contract or not, preparing your client for a change in who'll be providing his or her goods or services is always a good policy to follow.

✔ Sell your client list to another company or individual in your field, letting your customers know you're doing so and introducing them to the person or company who'll be meeting their needs in your place.

Whatever you decide, make sure you carefully match it with your long-term goals. If you merge the business with another or pass it to a family member, friend or employee, you may have the opportunity to keep a finger in the business's operational pie, if you so desire. If you sell or close it, however, chances are slim (zero in the case of a closed business) that you'll be able to have anything further to do with it. Is that what you really want? Are you really ready to call it quits? Only you know the answers to these questions, and only you can make the ultimate decision.

The price is right: Putting a value on your business

If you decide to sell your business, the first question your potential buyer is likely to ask is 'How much do you want for it?' Or perhaps you'll be approached by a buyer who makes you an offer. So, do you have any idea how much your business is worth?

You can establish a price for a business using a number of different methods. If you're thinking about selling your home-based business, consider the following:

- ✔ **Your business's earning capacity.** How much money does your business bring in every month or year? Are your sales high enough to offset expenses and leave a reasonable profit behind? The higher the earning capacity of a business, the more it's worth to a potential buyer and the more he or she is willing to pay you for it.

- ✔ **The value of its assets.** The worth of your business is influenced by the money you have tied up in physical assets, such as *inventory* (the products you keep on the shelf to sell to customers); *machinery* (manufacturing equipment or mechanic's tools, for example); or *intellectual property* (trademarks, patents, trade secrets and so on). The higher the value of your assets – and the ease with which they can be converted to immediate use by a buyer or into liquid assets such as cash – the more money you can demand for your business.

- ✔ **The market value of similar firms.** The value of firms similar to yours inevitably has a significant influence on the value of your firm. You can get a rough idea of your firm's value by finding out what similar businesses are selling for. Try listings of businesses for sale in your local newspaper's classified ads or check out uk.businessesforsale.com.

- ✔ **The value of the company's shares.** If your business is organised as a corporation and you've sold (or given away) shares in the business to, say, a private investor, then those shares, also known as *equity*, have a value. And that value determines the value of the whole company. If, for example, you sold shares equal to 10 per cent of your business to a private investor for £50,000, then that values the whole business at $10 \times £50,000 = £500,000$.

Now what?

So you've sold your business or handed it over, and you've done your best to keep your nose out of how it's running. But for years, you've spent the better part of your waking hours working and, lately, running your own business. Now what?

Many people dream about retirement their whole working lives, but, after they get there, they find that they miss the action, the demands and the responsibilities of a busy business environment. Of course, others adjust to their retirement just fine and spend their days travelling the world, fishing or enjoying their hobbies. If you're ready to take the next step, but you're not exactly sure what that step is, make sure you give yourself time to think about the kind of life you want to live before making any irrevocable moves.

Whatever you decide, don't forget that you always have one option open to you: starting another business. As you now know, starting your own home-based business can be amazingly simple and the rewards can be many.

Part V
The Part of Tens

Go to www.dummies.com/extras/homebasedbusiness for free online bonus content.

In this part...

- ✔ Discover the ten top tips to help you succeed in your home business.

- ✔ Benefit from word-of-mouth referrals.

- ✔ Investigate ten home businesses that are built to last.

- ✔ Maintain your levels of savings and manage your cash flow.

- ✔ Enjoy the benefits of volunteering.

Chapter 14

Ten Tips for How to Succeed in Your Home-Based Business

*A*lthough no one can guarantee that your home-based business will be a success, if you work hard, price your products and services right, and keep your customers satisfied, you stand a good chance of building a thriving company. The results you get out of your business are directly related to the work you put into it. That relationship between work and results is one of the real joys of having a home-based business. If you do a good job, you'll be rewarded. Plus, you get the satisfaction of having happy clients and customers tell you how much they enjoy doing business with you – and buying more of your products and services.

The most successful home-based business owners – those who get the results they hoped for – share a variety of traits. We discuss ten of these traits in this chapter.

Do What You Love

All employees dream about the jobs they'd love to do if only they had the opportunity. Unfortunately, many people are in their current jobs because they have to pay the bills, not because they've always dreamed of doing their particular work. But what if you could do what you really loved to do? Wouldn't that be great? Well, it is, and it's exactly the opportunity you get by starting your own business. But to do what you love, you first have to know what kind of work you really want to do. This discovery requires deep introspection and an understanding of which kind of work gets your creative juices flowing, and which kind dries them up.

Doing what you love also sometimes requires you to ignore what other people want you to do for a living. You may decide, for example, that you'd really like to start a photography studio in your home, but your spouse or best friend may think something more practical, such as buying a successful pet shop on the high street, makes more sense. Ultimately, you must decide what you really want to do for a living.

It's *your* dream – you're the one who gets to choose it (and live it!). No one else has the right to tell you what kind of work you should love – and do.

Treat Your Business like a Business

If you want your business to be a *real* business – an organisation that generates the kind of money that enables you to become financially independent – you have to treat it like one, not like a hobby or a momentary fling. Here are some ideas to help you treat your business as what it is – a business:

- ✔ Set aside an entire room in your home – not just a corner or a shelf – exclusively for your business (see Chapter 12).

- ✔ Make sure you have the business equipment and supplies you need: a decent computer, a dedicated phone line and whatever else is required to effectively and efficiently run your operation.

- ✔ Create a marketing plan and follow through with it (see Chapter 4).

- ✔ Publicise your company's products and services to a wide audience of potential customers and clients (also in Chapter 4).

- ✔ Build a strong customer base and make plans for future growth (see Chapter 13).

Being serious about your business doesn't mean that you can't have fun, though, or that you can't make up your own rules along the way. Indeed, being your own boss means that *you* get to decide how you're going to run your business. If you want to work only on weekday afternoons, for example – setting aside mornings for exercise or spending time with your kids – you can do so and still have a serious business.

Become an Expert

People naturally respect those who know more than they do. By specialising in a particular area of expertise – whether it's how to turf a lawn, where best to go scuba diving or what to do in a financial crisis – you assume the role of a presumed expert, even if you've just started your business. It makes good business sense for your clients to hire an expert instead of someone less experienced. By avoiding the mistakes and dead ends that someone with less experience may make, you can help your clients spend less money by hiring you – even if your hourly rates are higher.

The interesting thing about becoming an expert is that the passage of time makes you increasingly more experienced in your field. As time goes on, potential clients and customers will seek you out just to get the benefit of the expertise you've developed through experience and education.

Don't Be Shy

Companies don't spend millions of pounds advertising their products in the media for no reason; they do so because media advertising is a particularly effective way to get the attention (and, ideally, the business) of potential customers. Unfortunately, far too many people believe that a good idea is all a successful business needs. In the real world, however, it takes far more than that; the world is full of good ideas that have gone nowhere fast. Even the best ideas have to be packaged, presented and sold, and the key is to identify and use marketing methods best suited to both your personality and your business.

Although you may never have had to sell yourself or your products before, you can't avoid doing so when you own your own business. After you generate momentum and build a strong customer base, you can rely more on referrals from your happy clients to do the marketing for you. But when you're getting your business off the ground, consider and attempt every possible method for selling your products and services.

For a complete discussion of the hows and whys of marketing your products and services, check out Chapter 4.

Charge What You're Worth

No matter how hard you work, if you charge your customers less than you're worth, you won't be able to stay in business for long. Some people charge less than they're worth because they don't realise exactly how much they *are* worth. Others charge less than they're worth because they're embarrassed or afraid to ask for an amount that reflects their true worth. Whatever the reason, if you don't get paid what you're worth, you may very well drive yourself out of business.

If you don't know what you're worth, find out what other companies charge for similar products or services by researching catalogues, price lists, shops, and e-commerce and auction websites. If you can't find written prices or listings on the web, call or email the companies for information. From there, develop a pricing or fee structure that can help you attain your personal goals. (Check out Chapter 7 for more info on setting the right prices.)

After you figure out what you should charge, use the following tips to get the price you want:

- **Become a master at selling the value that your products and services offer to your customers and clients.** They won't know why your products and services are better than others if you don't tell them, so tell them often and in a variety of ways.

- **Be creative in how you're paid.** Many successful home-based business owners take cash out of the equation by bartering their products or services with others. For example, Jo Sensini, who owns the successful Velvet Integrated PR in West London, was paid £1,000 in chocolate for some work she did and agreed to be paid in shoes by another client.

- **Get past any hang-ups you have about charging your customers and clients what you're worth.** Practise stating your price in front of a mirror, or with someone you trust to give you constructive criticism, just as you would practise a request for a raise or a speech. After you go through the process a few times with prospective clients – and discover that they still want to hire you – you'll find it easier to demand a price that reflects what you're really worth.

Avoid Unnecessary Expenses

Shopping for the latest and greatest business gadgets and equipment is fun – a *lot* of fun. And treating clients to expensive lunches and dinners is also fun. The bad news about all this fun is that it can be expensive (and some of it may not be tax-deductible) and detrimental to your company's financial health and welfare.

Spend your company's hard-earned money only when you have to. A good example of this is your personal computer. Every other week, computer technology makes another great leap forward, which may constantly tempt you to upgrade to the latest and greatest computer with all the new bells and whistles. Unless your older, slower and less flashy computer – and the software within it – is actually getting in the way of your ability to do business efficiently, stick with it for as long as you possibly can. Think about adding a bigger hard drive, more RAM or other upgrades that improve performance at far less cost than buying a new computer. Eventually, you'll need to replace your computer, but the longer you can defer the expense, the better for your company's bottom line.

Do your best to hold the line on all the other expenses that simply drain your financial reserves while bringing in little or no additional revenue. If you're going to eat out with clients, for example, go to less-expensive places. Save the expensive meals for your highest-paying customers or consider inviting your best customers over as dinner guests in your home.

Manage Your Cash Flow

Cash, or the lack of it, is one of the key indicators of a company's success over the long term. If you have cash, you can buy and stock new products for your customers, develop innovative new services for your clients, pay for your day-to-day operations and expand your business. If you don't have cash, your business suffers, and so do your customers and clients. You may even jeopardise your own personal or family financial situation.

Simply watching your cash flow – the money going in and out of your business – isn't enough; you also have to actively *manage* it. Managing your cash flow means looking to the future, planning and scheduling your projected cash inflows and outflows, sending invoices out quickly, staying on top of money owed to you, and paying attention to the money that goes in and out of your business. One of your most important business tools should be a rolling cash-flow projection showing you how much cash you'll receive from customers each month for a year into the future. See Chapter 6 for more ideas on managing your finances.

Keep Your Day Job

The best way to work into your own successful home-based business is to start out while retaining your full-time conventional job. Not only does maintaining your day job keep your income safe and sound while your home business's revenues increase – a process that can take months or even years – but it also enables you to keep your company pension and other benefits in place (not to mention your employer continuing to make contributions to the cost of these benefits, if applicable in your case). A rule of thumb for when to move to working in your business full time is when your business income can sustain your minimal living expenses and you feel confident that by putting in more time, you'll increase your business's earnings. (Check out Chapter 3 for more details.)

When Janan Leo started her business selling folding shoes for women to wear while commuting (the shoes are easily transportable so you can change into them from uncomfortable shoes) she had no idea if the business would take off and was keen to minimise the risks involved. So she started the business with £3,000 of savings and initially ran it in the evenings and at weekends from the spare room of her home in north London, while holding on to her full-time nine-to-five job as a product development manager for Virgin Trains. After three years, the business, Cocorose, was going really well, selling hundreds of pairs of shoes a month, so Leo was able to give up her day job with Virgin Trains to work towards her business full time.

By approaching the transition to self-employment this way, you can discover whether you've picked the right business – and whether you're right for the business – without risking unemployment if it doesn't work out.

Build a Solid Customer Base

One of the most important ways to establish a successful business is to build a solid base of customers who stick with you through thick and thin. This solid customer base becomes the foundation on which you grow your business.

Of course, building a solid customer base is much easier said than done. At the heart of the process is creating a home business that values its current customers and goes out of its way to ensure their satisfaction and happiness. Customers are smart – they can tell whether they're high or low on a company's priority list. If they sense that you don't care much about whether or not they do business with you, they'll likely jump ship as soon as another company that really does care about them comes along.

Always remember the feeling you get when you land your first customer and receive your first payment for your products; then treat all your customers as though they were your first. Value them every day and, in turn, they'll value you.

Ask for Referrals

The word-of-mouth referral is probably the least expensive and the most effective way of getting new business – for any business – which makes referrals the most important way for home-based businesses to market themselves. Here are some of the best ways to earn great referrals from customers:

- ✔ **Do great work.** When you do great work, your clients are happy to give you great referrals. When you do less-than-great work, your clients will spread the word that you weren't up to scratch.

- ✔ **Do your work on time and within budget.** The quickest way to your customer's heart is to do your work on time and within budget. If you consistently deliver on your promises, you'll soon have more business coming in. And you'll earn your clients' referrals at the same time.

- ✔ **Keep your clients well informed.** When clients spend their money on you, they want to be kept updated on your progress, not only to stay in touch with the project, but also to keep a watchful eye out for problems before they get out of hand. Do your clients a favour and keep them informed about your project's progress. Whether the news is good or bad, your clients and customers appreciate your openness and honesty.

- ✔ **Be dependable.** If anything, always keep your word – even when it hurts. If you promise to do something, do everything in your power to keep your promise, no matter what it takes to follow through on it.

- ✔ **Be flexible.** Customers and clients appreciate suppliers who are flexible and willing to meet their needs, no matter what those needs may be. Not only do they appreciate that flexibility, but they also pay more for it. Think about what you can do in your business to better meet your customers' needs, and then do it.

- ✔ **Thank your clients for their referrals.** Everyone likes to be appreciated for what they do. Your customers are no different. Be sure to thank them for their referrals with a card or small gift, if appropriate.

Many small businesses get the vast majority of their new business through referrals. They really are worth their weight in gold. Take a look at Chapter 4 for more on referrals.

Chapter 15

Ten Enduring Home Business Opportunities

Some home-business opportunities are here today, gone tomorrow. In this chapter, in alphabetical order, we present ten home business opportunities that are built to last. Get started with one of these, and you're likely to have a business you can grow old with.

Architectural Salvage

Whether you're motivated by the fact that you can make money from reusing what would otherwise be landfill, or saving something from the past, architectural salvage may be just the right business for you. Architectural salvage as a business field will continue to grow in the future as the economies of China, India and other nations continue to expand rapidly, gobbling up building supplies and materials in the process and pushing up prices.

When you pull down or renovate a home or other building, you can reuse (and thus sell) bathroom fixtures, bricks, ceramic tiles, fireplaces, piping and so on. Architectural salvage experts typically operate by arranging to collect salvage for free and then selling on the useful bits for a profit – how much you can charge depends on what you find!

Obtaining these materials requires carefully deconstructing a home or building brick by brick, which is a slower process than just tearing it down, which is where you as an entrepreneur come in. You do the deconstruction in exchange for what's salvaged. Before you can sell what you salvage, you may need to renovate or refurbish it. Then you can sell the salvage to one of the many architectural salvage sites around the UK, via an architectural salvage fair or online through the small ads of architectural salvage websites such as www.salvo.co.uk.

No training courses are available in the UK specifically for Architectural Salvage specialists, but many courses and qualifications in relevant subjects could be beneficial and set you apart from your competitors. Buildingconservation.com (www.buildingconservation.com) provides a list of specialist courses and training providers on its website, while City and Guilds (www.cityandguilds.com) provides a database of vocational qualification courses on its website.

Catering and Food Preparation

People are always going to get married, christened, hold engagement parties, birthday parties, annual sports club dinners and funerals – and that means that if you set up a home-based business providing outside catering for functions then you're likely to find demand in both good times and bad. You may also choose to make food such as cakes and pies that you can supply to local delicatessens and cafes. This not only provides a steady income stream in the quieter months when there are fewer big events to cater for, it's also a great way of building your brand and spreading the word about how good your food is. Depending on the type of event and the kind of food required, caterers can typically charge between £5 and £25 per guest – however, out of that you need to pay for the food, any staff you need on the night, and the cost of transport, so make sure you're charging enough to be able to make a profit for yourself.

If you want to ensure your cooking has that professional edge, take a course to find out how the experts do it. Check out the database on the Floodlight website (www.floodlight.co.uk), which lists cookery courses across the UK on everything from pasta to pies to pastries.

The secret to being a successful outside caterer is to be efficient, to be on time and to have the highest possible cleanliness standards. It's no good making wonderful canapés if they're sitting in a van stuck in traffic when the wedding guests are supposed to be tucking in to them. So when starting up your business, focus on the bits the clients don't see as much as on the bits they do.

Helen Colley started running her outside catering business from the kitchen of her parents' farmhouse in Lancashire. She had a thousand advertising leaflets printed, and her brother handed them out in the local neighbourhood. Initially she got work doing teas for a friend's parents who ran a funeral business. She also made pies and bread to sell in post offices and local shops. As word spread she started catering for weddings and parties in the north of England. Then one day she made some sticky toffee puddings for a charity coffee morning, and they were such a success she started supplying them to local delicatessens. Colley began to make other traditional puddings and her business, Farmhouse Fare, was such a success that in 2006 she sold it for £10 million.

Childcare Services

As increasing numbers of mothers go back to work, either through choice or necessity, there's a growing need for childcare services to look after babies, toddlers and young children in a safe and secure environment. A childminder is a self-employed carer who looks after up to six children in his or her own home for more than two hours a day. Duties include providing a safe, loving environment as well as helping with children's physical, intellectual, emotional and social development. A typical day might include visiting a park or library, reading, creative play and providing meals and snacks. Depending on the area in which you operate, as a childminder you can typically charge £3 to £4 per child per hour.

If you're going to be looking after children between 0 and 8 years old you need to be registered by the Office for Standards in Education, Children's Services and Skills (Ofsted: www.ofsted.gov.uk). To become a registered childminder you also have to:

1. Have an enhanced Criminal Records Bureau (CRB) check.

2. Attend a training course.

3. Hold a first aid qualification for babies and children.

Check your local council website for information and advice and to help you to access training.

The Professional Association for Childcare and Early Years (www.pacey. org.uk) has more information about becoming a childminder on its website.

Cleaning Services

Although many people regard having a cleaner a luxury – and something that may be cut when budgets are tight – this business won't go away until the supply of dust and mould runs out. In fact, new opportunities arise in a low-growth economy as office and shop owners decide to contract out cleaning services instead of paying salaries and benefits for full-time employees.

Cleaning services take many forms, ranging from home and office cleaning services that do routine cleaning, to more specialised services that require either specific equipment, such as pressure cleaning and rug cleaning, or the willingness to do particularly challenging or unpleasant work, such as window washing, crime scene and disaster clean-up, and rubbish removal. Depending on the area in which you operate, cleaners can charge £9 to £13 an hour; more for specialised work.

A growing number of people who associate allergies and respiratory illnesses with air pollutants seek environmentally friendly cleaning services for their homes and offices. Environmentally friendly cleaning services use special cleaning methods, non-toxic products, and equipment and supplies like special filter vacuum cleaners and microfibre cloths that clean surfaces without chemicals.

Another significant market for cleaning services is elderly people living independently who no longer have the physical ability to do their own cleaning.

Both City and Guilds (www.cityandguilds.com) and the British Institute of Cleaning Science (www.bics.org.uk) run courses on cleaning that provide qualifications for people wanting to enter the industry.

Debt Collection Work

Debt collectors keep busy because companies, service providers and government agencies have to collect money owed to them. Small businesses in particular can find it hard to find the time to chase unpaid bills, even though late payment is one of the key reasons why small firms fail. This reality and the fact that people fall behind in paying all kinds of bills translates into a home business for anyone who can help debtors organise their finances to repay what they owe. Most people want to pay their bills but are under economic pressure, and so need coaxing and coaching to do so.

Home-based debt collectors with low overhead expenses have an advantage over high-pressure, results-driven staffs of large debt collection companies because they can take the time to be more successful in working with debtors and establish a personal relationship with the people dealing with the accounts in the businesses that owe money. Having second-language skills can also give you an edge over your competition because you're able to chase money owned by companies based overseas. How much you earn depends on how good you are at collecting debts – debt collectors typically charge between 25 and 33 per cent of the amount they collect. Although no formal qualifications are needed to become a debt collector, you need a good understanding of business practices and good telephone and correspondence skills.

Before you can start your debt collection agency you need to obtain a Consumer Credit Licence from the Office of Fair Trading (www.oft.gov.uk).

You can find out more about this type of business from the Credit Services Association (CSA), the voice of the UK debt collection industry: www.csa-uk.com.

Driving Instructor

No matter what the state of the economic climate, people are always going to need to learn how to drive a car or van. If you qualify as an Approved Driving Instructor (ADI) you can start your own driving school or buy a franchise from an established driving school. You can typically charge £20 an hour for lessons, although from this you need to pay for the cost of the franchise – around £175 a week – plus the cost of maintaining your instructor car. To become an ADI you need to be over 21 and have held a full UK driving licence for at least three years. You must also:

1. Get a Criminal Records Bureau (CRB) check for driving instructors. You can apply for this via the Gov.uk website at www.gov.uk.

2. Apply to the Driving Standards Agency to start the application process, either online via the Gov.uk website or by post. Several driving schools offer ADI training.

3. Take and pass three qualifying tests.

4. Apply for your Approved Driving Instructor badge.

Your application to become an Approved Driving Instructor may be refused if you have ever been disqualified from driving, if you have six or more penalty points on your licence or if you've ever been convicted of any non-motoring offences.

Handyman Services

Handyman (or woman!) businesses do particularly well during economic downturns because people prefer to spend a little bit of money getting things around the house repaired rather than spending a lot of money to get them replaced. However, surveys also show that people plan to remain cost conscious even when the economy picks up. This attitude bodes well for handyman services because fixing or restoring something often costs less than throwing out the old and buying something new, particularly when what's new isn't affordable.

The kind of jobs done by a handyman range from replacing light bulbs, painting walls, fixing cupboards, putting up picture frames, repairing door handles – all the DIY tasks that homeowners put on their to-do lists but never quite get round to, because the jobs are too hard, too time consuming or because they lack the necessary tools or skills.

Handyman services typically charge by the hour – with a minimum call-out charge of, say, 30 minutes – so that clients can draw up a list of several small jobs that need to be done which wouldn't in themselves be worth calling a handyman out for. The amount you can charge depends on the area in which you operate but you can typically earn £20 to £30 an hour. Having a flat charge also makes it easier for you as it means you don't have to try to price small individual jobs.

You can brush up on all the DIY skills you need to operate a handyman business by attending a home maintenance course such as the two-day weekend course run by the Builder Trading Centre (www.thebtc.co.uk).

Getting listed on sites such as www.checkatrade.com, www.findatrade.com or www.safelocaltrades.com may help your business gain visibility.

Party Entertainer

Gone are the days when children's parties consisted of pass the parcel followed by jelly and ice cream. Nowadays no children's party is complete without an entertainer. Popular entertainers with names like Arty Party, Sharky and George, and Mr Boo Boo are often booked up months in advance with prices starting in some areas at £350 for an hour's entertainment. If you're good with children and enjoy making them laugh you could have a thriving business this way.

Think about what kind of entertainer you want to be and what sort of props you'll need – are you going to be a clown, a magician, a singer, a comedian, a daredevil stuntman? You need to create a character for yourself that can form the basis of your brand.

Remember that every time you do a party you're also effectively marketing yourself and your show to 20 or more potential customers (and their parents). This means that if you get it right, word-of-mouth can do much of your marketing for you. Make sure you take business cards or brochures to every party you're booked to do, and if you get a chance, make time to talk to the parents afterwards too.

Check out the online Alliance of Children's Entertainers at `www.allianceof childrensentertainers.com`.

Personal Tuition

As getting into the best schools and universities becomes increasingly competitive, a growing number of parents are hiring personal tutors to help their children through the process. Having been mostly hired to provide extra tuition for A levels in the past, personal tutors are now increasingly in demand for younger children, some as young as four years old, to help them pass the tests needed to get into over-subscribed private schools. Depending on your local area, private tutors can earn up to £40 an hour.

As a personal tutor you can choose to offer your services directly to families, or through one of several tutor agencies, some of which operate online. Search on Google for agencies in your area. As a general rule you need a university degree to give tuition in academic subjects.

Although as a self-employed tutor you can technically set your own hours, be aware that most demand for personal tuition is for the hours after school from 3 p.m. to 8 p.m., in the school holidays and at weekends.

Providing Services for Elderly People

It's no secret that people are living longer. Already more than 3 million people in the UK are over 80 years old and that figure is predicted to double by 2030 as advances in medical care enable people to live longer and longer. At the same time, the geographic scattering of families means that fewer children are able to look after their elderly parents themselves and provide all the care and comfort they need. Even when elderly people are able to remain independent and live on their own in their own homes, they often require support services of one kind of another. Which is where you come in. This need for support means potential customers for many home-based home-care businesses.

Support for elderly clients can include a range of daily activities such as doing their washing and grocery shopping, paying their bills and cleaning their homes. It might involve helping them with personal grooming and driving them to hospital appointments, or it might mean cooking for them and helping them get repairs done around the house. You can choose to provide elderly services as a care worker directly through your own business or by offering your services through an approved private agency. Depending on your qualifications you can earn between £10 and £30 an hour. Find out more from the UK Homecare Association (www.ukhca.org.uk), the professional association of homecare providers, which provides a code of practice.

When seniors can't afford to pay you, often their adult children – who may live far away or who just can't provide these services themselves – are willing to pick up the tab.

Age UK (www.ageuk.org.uk), the charity formed from Age Concern and Help the Aged, has a wealth of information about the elderly, what home-care services they need and how they're provided and paid for, on its website. Plenty of volunteering opportunities exist if you want to gain some experience.

Chapter 16

Ten Things to Do When Times Are Tough

Make no mistake about it: starting and operating a home-based business – and making a profit – isn't easy. In fact, it can be extremely hard work, and many people give up every year. Why? Because even the best plans sometimes go awry, if only for a short time. Because of your business's inherent smallness, you may not have enough clients to manage the financial roller coaster that can result due to a recession or when a customer goes bankrupt, pays you late or switches suppliers.

Good planning can help you see far enough out on the horizon to anticipate the most serious financial shortfalls – and then take steps to avoid them – but it's impossible to anticipate each and every bump in the road. Use the ten tips in this chapter to help you weather the unpredictable storms and emerge stronger than ever.

Save for a Rainy Day

Even if you find yourself making a lot of money for some period of time – for weeks, or even months – every business owner knows that there are no guarantees, and tough times can be right around the corner. One of the best things you can do is put aside money when times are good. Although it's tempting (and fun!) to run out and purchase the latest computer, the most recent software update or a new desk when the money's rolling in, first make sure that you set aside cash in your business savings account to help you through the rough patches.

Here's a financial goal to help you weather a storm when it arrives: build a cash reserve sufficient to run your business for a minimum of three months, and preferably six to twelve months. After you have your cash reserve established and funded, you can go out and buy all the fun stuff you've had your eye on!

Manage Your Cash Flow

Cash flow – more specifically, maintaining a *positive* cash flow – is by far the number-one financial issue facing every small business owner. And if you rely 100 per cent on the proceeds of your home-based business to support you and your family or significant other, without the kind of steady income that a regular job brings, a shortfall in cash can quickly bring financial disaster.

The solution is to manage your cash flow (see Chapter 6), which means making a habit of doing the following:

✔ **Keep an eye on your net cash flow.** List all the cash you expect to receive (cash inflows) during a specific period of time and compare that amount with the cash you expect to pay out (cash outflows) during the same period of time. Study this information religiously, at least once a week. You can put together a simple handwritten or computerised spreadsheet, or many popular business accounting programs have built-in functions for monitoring cash flow. Use them!

✔ **Be proactive in bringing cash into your business as quickly as possible.** Don't sit around waiting for customers to pay you when they get around to it; get your money as soon as you can. Try to get paid when you deliver your products or services, or even beforehand, instead of invoicing your customers after the event. You can do so by requiring customers to pay by credit card or by negotiating advance payments with them. Or simply require payment by cash or cheque upon delivery. If you sell over the Internet or through an online-shop host (such as Amazon.co.uk), most customers already expect to pay in advance by credit card, debit card or a payment service such as PayPal.

✔ **Pay your bills only when they're due, but do so in time to avoid interest and penalties.** There's no advantage for you to pay your bills before they're due. In fact, after you pay a bill, you lose any interest the cash may have made in your own bank account. If payment on a supplier invoice isn't due for 30 days from today, don't pay it tomorrow. Pay it when it's due. If you make your payment online, pay your bill a day or two before it's due to ensure your payment is credited electronically by the due date. If you post your payment, do so a week before the due date. The idea is to be paid by your clients before you have to turn around and make payments to your suppliers. By paying as late as you possibly can – while still paying on time – you can optimise your cash flow.

Keep in Touch with Your Customers

Business is all about relationships. Many businesses have found incredible success because of the close relationships their owners have established with their clients and customers. After all, given the option, wouldn't you rather work with someone you like and have a great rapport with than someone you don't?

When times get tough, your first priority should be to ensure that your current customer relationships are *solid.* Drop in for a visit, schedule a lunch, send an email message, send some flowers, do whatever you can to keep your relationship on the front burner. And while you're busy keeping your relationship active, let your customers know that you're actively seeking more work. This gentle reminder that you're out there can often lead customers to send more work your way – exactly what you need when times are tough.

Push Your Clients to Pay Their Bills

On the list of things that home-based businesspeople enjoy least about their jobs is having to call clients to encourage them to pay their bills. But no matter how great your customers are, at times you're going to have to do just that.

So how do you know when payments due to your business are running behind? You can find out by monitoring *receivables* – the money owed to your company by your clients and customers. Business accounting software programs make the task easy by showing you who owes you money, how much they owe, when it's due to be paid and how late the payment is if you haven't yet received it (see Chapter 6 for more about accounting programs). And when you discover that one of your client's payments is overdue, act immediately – especially when the amount owed is substantial.

Here are some tried-and-tested ways for collecting your money:

  ✔ **Call or visit your customer and ask for payment.** The direct approach is often the best when it comes to getting customers to pay overdue invoices. Don't simply rubber-stamp a copy of the invoice with a note that says 'We value your business – we hope you'll pay soon' or 'Second notice – we would really like to be paid now'. Chances are these half-hearted efforts will be disregarded. Make a personal appeal for payment that can't be ignored!

✔ **Offer to help.** More times than most companies like to admit, a payment gets held up because the accounting department loses an invoice, doesn't have proof of delivery or can't find the purchase order that authorised the item in the first place. Find out what's holding up payment and offer to assist in getting what the customer needs.

✔ **As a last resort – and only if you aren't concerned about getting any future business from your client – you can take court action.** Often just sending a formal letter on headed notepaper from a solicitor threatening court action is enough to persuade clients to pay up, but if not, for a small fee you can issue a claim through your local county court. If your client still refuses to pay up, a hearing is held at which each side presents their case to a judge. Find details of your local court at www.hmcourts-service.gov.uk or you can make a claim online at www.moneyclaim.gov.uk.

Whatever you do, when a payment is late, get on it immediately – don't wait for days or weeks (or months!), hoping it'll come in. Keeping the money coming in on time should be one of your key concerns, and this task needs your immediate attention. Check out Chapter 6 for more details.

Minimise Expenses

When times are tough, you essentially have two ways to hunker down: increase the amount of money that comes into your business or decrease the amount of money that goes out (or both). Minimising expenses is one of the quickest ways to help weather the storm, and you need to act immediately when you go into survival mode.

Before you buy *anything*, ask yourself if you can survive without it for a while. Can you defer the expense for a few days, a few weeks or even a few months? Can you borrow or rent equipment instead of purchasing it? Can you barter your services or products in exchange for the products and services of other businesses?

Be careful, however, about exactly what expenses you cut. Do *not* cut expenses that can bring significantly more money into your business; instead, you may actually need to increase them.

Offer a Special Promotion

By far the best way to turn things around when times are tough financially is to bring in more business. Cutting expenses certainly helps, but it isn't the best long-term solution. The best long-term solution is selling more of your products and services.

To generate more business quickly, offer your customers a special deal on your products or services – perhaps 10 per cent off all orders during July or a two-for-the-price-of-one offer. The exact form of your promotion will vary, depending on the nature of your business, but be clear to your customers that they need to act quickly to take advantage of the special offer.

Alternatively, offer your clients and customers a premium – a value-added product or service – for placing an order during a specific period of time. For example, every customer who places an order of at least £100 during February receives a gift certificate for £10 worth of products or a free video. You can also offer a special price to customers who are willing to commit to a contract. Perhaps if your client introduces someone new to you who makes a purchase, you can offer a discount to both of them. Be creative!

Subcontract for Others

Many home-based businesses – especially those with only one employee (you!) – are subject to extreme swings in business. One month, your business may be overwhelmed with orders; the next month, the phone may never ring.

To help offset these extreme business swings, develop a network of business contacts – perhaps other home-based businesses – to subcontract your work *to* in times of feast and to subcontract work *from* in times of famine. It may sound a bit strange to turn work over to a competitor, but it actually makes good business sense. The key is for you to remain the primary contact with the client and to ensure that the work from the contractor is of the same high quality that you would insist on if you did it yourself.

Volunteer

Every business has times when the workload is down. Down times are perfect for developing new contacts who may eventually turn into customers or who may refer you to future customers. If you still have time left after providing for your current customers, consider doing volunteer work in your local neighbourhood as a way of meeting new people.

Not only can volunteering be a terrific way to put your skills to work for your local neighbourhood, but it's also a good way to increase your network of potential clients. And as that network expands, so can your future business. Believe us, you never know whom you'll meet when you volunteer in your local area. That woman next to you doing volunteer work at a children's hospice may be the operations director of a big local firm or the purchasing manager of a large manufacturer.

Networking or getting into business-related events is also really effective. Search for business training and networking events at `www.gov.uk/events-finder`. You can set the price to '0' to show only free events.

Get a Part-time Job

When starting your business, it's a good idea to keep your day job – at least until your home-based business is generating enough income to enable you to pay all your bills. But even after your business is established, you may find that having a part-time job offers a number of benefits, including the following:

- ✔ Creating a steady source of income that you can rely on, independent of the ups and downs of your home-based business's income.

- ✔ Providing a range of benefits that your own business doesn't, such as sick pay, holiday pay, a pension plan and so on.

- ✔ Being a potential source of work for your home-based business (for example, if your part-time job is working in a delicatessen and your home-based business is making cakes, you may be able to arrange for the delicatessen to sell your cakes).

If you do decide to get a part-time job, make sure you're not taking too much time away from your own business – time that you could devote to building higher levels of sales or expanding your business.

Refuse to Give Up!

When times are tough, you may be tempted to throw in the towel and give up. But what's much more challenging – and ultimately much more rewarding – is to fight for your business and refuse to give up, *no matter what.* When interviewed, successful entrepreneurs most consistently attribute their good fortune to *persistence*.

You can fail only if you allow yourself to do so. By not considering giving up an option, you force yourself to focus on doing the things that help pull you through your tough times – things like the other nine items in this chapter.

Index

• I •

About the Authors

Rachel Bridge is a journalist, public speaker and author of five best-selling books about entrepreneurs, including *How to Make a Million Before Lunch and How to Start a Business without any Money.* She is the former Enterprise Editor of *The Sunday Times* and now writes an opinion column about entrepreneurs and small businesses for *The Sunday Telegraph.* She took a one-woman show about entrepreneurs to the Edinburgh comedy festival and has an MA Economics degree from Cambridge University.

Paul and Sarah Edwards are award-winning authors of 17 books with over two million books in print. Sarah, a licensed clinical social worker with a PhD in ecopsychology, and Paul, a licensed attorney, are recognised as pioneers in the working-from-home field. With the emergence of a global economy that challenges the environment and everyone's personal, family and community wellbeing, they are focusing their efforts on finding pathways to transition to a sustainable Elm Street economy in which home business plays a vital role. Paul and Sarah write a quarterly column for *The Costco Connection.* They hosted *The Working From Home Show* on HGTV in the US and have been regular commentators on CNBC.

Paul and Sarah provide a wealth of ongoing information, resources and support at www.pathwaystotransition.com.

Peter Economy, who lives in La Jolla, California, is a home-based business author, ghostwriter and publishing consultant, and the author or coauthor of more than 50 books, including *Why Aren't You Your Own Boss?* with Paul and Sarah Edwards (Three Rivers Press), *Managing For Dummies,* 2nd Edition, and *Consulting For Dummies,* 2nd Edition, with Bob Nelson (Wiley) and *Writing Children's Books For Dummies* with Lisa Rojany Buccieri (Wiley). Peter is also associate editor for the Apex Award-winning magazine *Leader to Leader.*

Peter combines his writing experience with more than 15 years of hands-on management experience. He received his bachelor's degree in economics from Stanford University and a postgraduate certificate in business administration from the Edinburgh Business School. Peter invites you to visit his website at www.petereconomy.com.

Dedications

To Harry and Jack

— RB

Authors' Acknowledgements

We would like thank all the entrepreneurs whose stories we've included in this book, and the team at Wiley for their help and assistance.

Publisher's Acknowledgements

Project Editor: Rachael Chilvers

Commissioning Editor: Claire Ruston

Associate Commissioning Editor: Ben Kemble

Copyeditor: Kelly Cattermole

Technical Editor: Colin Barrow

Proofreader: Emily Kearns

Production Manager: Daniel Mersey

Publisher: Miles Kendall

Cover Photos: ©iStockphoto.com/ Maartje van Caspel

Composition Services

Project Coordinator: Kristie Rees

Layout and Graphics: Carrie A. Cesavice, Andrea Hornberger, Kathie Rickard, Erin Zeltner

Proofreaders: Melissa Cossell, Jessica Kramer

Indexer: BIM Indexing & Proofreading Services

FOR DUMMIES

Making Everything Easier! ™

UK editions

BUSINESS

978-1-118-34689-1

978-1-118-44349-1

978-1-119-97527-4

MUSIC

978-1-119-94276-4

978-0-470-97799-6

978-0-470-66372-1

HOBBIES

978-1-118-41156-8

978-1-119-99417-6

978-1-119-97250-1

Asperger's Syndrome For Dummies
978-0-470-66087-4

Basic Maths For Dummies
978-1-119-97452-9

**Body Language For Dummies,
2nd Edition**
978-1-119-95351-7

Boosting Self-Esteem For Dummies
978-0-470-74193-1

Business Continuity For Dummies
978-1-118-32683-1

Cricket For Dummies
978-0-470-03454-5

Diabetes For Dummies, 3rd Edition
978-0-470-97711-8

eBay For Dummies, 3rd Edition
978-1-119-94122-4

English Grammar For Dummies
978-0-470-05752-0

Flirting For Dummies
978-0-470-74259-4

IBS For Dummies
978-0-470-51737-6

ITIL For Dummies
978-1-119-95013-4

**Management For Dummies,
2nd Edition**
978-0-470-97769-9

**Managing Anxiety with CBT
For Dummies**
978-1-118-36606-6

**Neuro-linguistic Programming
For Dummies, 2nd Edition**
978-0-470-66543-5

Nutrition For Dummies, 2nd Edition
978-0-470-97276-2

Organic Gardening For Dummies
978-1-119-97706-3

FOR DUMMIES®

Making Everything Easier! ™

UK editions

SELF-HELP

978-0-470-66541-1

978-1-119-99264-6

978-0-470-66086-7

LANGUAGES

978-0-470-68815-1

978-1-119-97959-3

978-0-470-69477-0

HISTORY

978-0-470-68792-5

978-0-470-74783-4

978-0-470-97819-1

Origami Kit For Dummies
978-0-470-75857-1

Overcoming Depression For Dummies
978-0-470-69430-5

Positive Psychology For Dummies
978-0-470-72136-0

PRINCE2 For Dummies, 2009 Edition
978-0-470-71025-8

Project Management For Dummies
978-0-470-71119-4

Psychology Statistics For Dummies
978-1-119-95287-9

Psychometric Tests For Dummies
978-0-470-75366-8

Renting Out Your Property For Dummies, 3rd Edition
978-1-119-97640-0

Rugby Union For Dummies, 3rd Edition
978-1-119-99092-5

Sage One For Dummies
978-1-119-95236-7

Self-Hypnosis For Dummies
978-0-470-66073-7

Storing and Preserving Garden Produce For Dummies
978-1-119-95156-8

Teaching English as a Foreign Language For Dummies
978-0-470-74576-2

Time Management For Dummies
978-0-470-77765-7

Training Your Brain For Dummies
978-0-470-97449-0

Voice and Speaking Skills For Dummies
978-1-119-94512-3

Work-Life Balance For Dummies
978-0-470-71380-8

FOR DUMMIES

Making Everything Easier! ™

COMPUTER BASICS

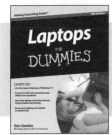

Laptops For Dummies
978-1-118-11533-6

PCs All-in-One For Dummies
978-0-470-61454-9

Windows 7 For Dummies
978-0-470-49743-2

DIGITAL PHOTOGRAPHY

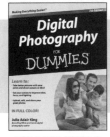

Digital Photography For Dummies
978-1-118-09203-3

Digital SLR Photography All-in-One For Dummies
978-0-470-76878-5

Nikon D3100 For Dummies
978-1-118-00472-2

SCIENCE AND MATHS

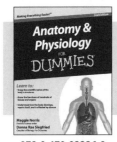

Anatomy & Physiology For Dummies
978-0-470-92326-9

Algebra I For Dummies
978-0-470-55964-2

Physics I For Dummies
978-0-470-90324-7

Art For Dummies
978-0-7645-5104-8

Computers For Seniors For Dummies, 3rd Edition
978-1-118-11553-4

Criminology For Dummies
978-0-470-39696-4

Currency Trading For Dummies, 2nd Edition
978-0-470-01851-4

Drawing For Dummies, 2nd Edition
978-0-470-61842-4

Forensics For Dummies
978-0-7645-5580-0

French For Dummies, 2nd Edition
978-1-118-00464-7

Guitar For Dummies, 2nd Edition
978-0-7645-9904-0

Hinduism For Dummies
978-0-470-87858-3

Index Investing For Dummies
978-0-470-29406-2

Islamic Finance For Dummies
978-0-470-43069-9

Knitting For Dummies, 2nd Edition
978-0-470-28747-7

Music Theory For Dummies, 2nd Edition
978-1-118-09550-8

Office 2010 For Dummies
978-0-470-48998-7

Piano For Dummies, 2nd Edition
978-0-470-49644-2

Photoshop CS6 For Dummies
978-1-118-17457-9

Schizophrenia For Dummies
978-0-470-25927-6

WordPress For Dummies, 5th Edition
978-1-118-38318-6